Intranet as Groupware

MELLANIE HILLS

Wiley Computer Publishing

John Wiley & Sons, Inc.

New York ◆ Chichester ◆ Brisbane ◆ Toronto ◆ Singapore ◆ Weinheim

*To my husband, Dave, and my son, Jason—thank
you for your endless patience and support through
these long months while I wrote both books*

Executive Publisher: Katherine Schowalter
Editor: Terri Hudson
Managing Editor: Brian Snapp
Text Design & Composition: North Market Street Graphics

Library of Congress Cataloging-in-Publication Data:
Hills, Mellanie.
    Intranet as Groupware / Mellanie Hills.
       p.   cm.
    Includes index.
    ISBN 0-471-16373-2 (pbk. : alk. paper)
     1. Intranets (Computer networks) 2. Groupware (Computer software)
    I. Title.
    HD30.385.H548 1997   96-35811
    651.7'9—dc20   CIP

Printed in the United States of America
10 9 8 7 6 5 4 3 2 1

About the Author

Mellanie Hills is the founder of Knowledgies, a consulting firm that focuses on helping Fortune 500 companies develop knowledge strategies with intranet and groupware technologies. She also consults with companies on using the Internet for competitive advantage and is a frequent speaker about the Internet and intranets.

Mellanie has more than twenty years of business experience. Prior to founding Knowledgies, she led JC Penney's cross-functional Internet/Intranet Team. Mellanie has always led organizational improvement and change, and is an experienced facilitator, trainer, and coach. She facilitated business process improvement teams at JC Penney, and also worked on the development of JC Penney's data warehouse. Her previous experience included managing end-user computing, financial accounting, and cost accounting, and she has a great depth of knowledge in the manufacturing, distribution, and retail industries.

She is also the author of *Intranet Business Strategies,* published by Wiley.

mhills@knowledgies.com

http://www.knowledgies.com/knowledgies/

Acknowledgments

So many people contributed to this book, and I wish to acknowledge and thank them all. My warmest thanks to the following people:

- My father, Howard True, for your assistance with this book, and my mother, Celesta True, for your faith and encouragement
- My second set of parents, Dave and Joyce Hills, for always being there when we need you
- Jim Sterne, for inspiring me to write this book, and pushing me forward with it
- Terri Hudson, my editor, for pushing and pulling me along through this process
- My colleagues on the Internet Team at JCPenney, for all you taught me and for your support
- The following people who shared and contributed so much to this book—I am especially indebted to you:

    - Amgen—Peter Armerding
    - AT&T—Ron Ponder and Andy Daudelin
    - Bell Atlantic—Ralph Szygenda, Susan Gayle, Richard Austin, Eric Vaughn, Brenda Mason, and Eric Robinson

- ◆ Booz Allen & Hamilton—Ed Vaccaro and Aron Dutta
- ◆ EDS—Todd Carlson, Greg Mitchell, Cathy Meister, Tim Lambert, and Bruce Bunn
- ◆ JCPenney—Cathy Mills, Steve Wolff, and Lloyd Grover
- ◆ International Data Corporation—Ian Campbell
- ◆ Rockwell International—Jim Sutter, Harry Meyer, and Dana Abrams
- ◆ SAS Institute—Lauren Bednarcyk
- ◆ Texas Instruments—Jodie Ray and Gene Phifer
- ◆ Turner Broadcasting—Jimi Stricklin, Susan Huffman, and Melissa Hoberg
- ◆ United Parcel Service—Marc Dodge
- ◆ Those who asked to remain anonymous and yet provided so much input

◆ The following organizations for allowing me to use screen shots of their products in this book:
- ◆ Action Technologies, Inc.
- ◆ DataBeam Corporation
- ◆ Digital Equipment Corporation
- ◆ NetManage, Inc.
- ◆ Open Text Corporation
- ◆ Proxima, Inc.
- ◆ Sandia National Laboratories
- ◆ WebFlow Corporation

◆ Gale Duff-Bloom, of JCPenney, for helping me recognize the ability to explain complicated things in a noncomplicated way

◆ Dave Evans, of JCPenney, for your guidance and support

◆ Dave Cahall, of JCPenney, for your technical assistance with this book

◆ Many friends and relatives, for passing along valuable information to me

Many thanks to all of you.

contents

Introduction   ix

Background   ix
Who Is This Book For?   x

Part 1   What Is an Intranet?   1

Chapter 1   What Is an Intranet?   3

History of Intranets   4
Growth of Intranets   6
What Are the Uses of Intranets?   7
What Are the Pieces of Intranets?   8
The Future of Intranets   15

Chapter 2   Why Have Organizations Created Intranets and What Are the Advantages and Disadvantages?   17

Why Have Organizations Created Intranets?   17
Advantages of Intranets   21
Advantages of Intranets over Client/Server   29
Disadvantages and Risks of Intranets   30
What Size Company Does It Take to Need an Intranet?   32

Chapter 3   How Will Intranets Change You and Your Organization?   33

What Changes Will Occur?   33
Other Ways Intranets Will Impact Organizations   39

Part 2 What Is Groupware and How Do You Use It?   43

Chapter 4   What Is Groupware and Why Do You Need It?   45

What Is Groupware?   45
What Does Groupware Do?   47
Why Do You Need Groupware?   52
Why Should You Consider Intranet Groupware?   55

Chapter 5   How Do You Use Groupware?   59

What Do Groupware Tools Do?   59
How Do You Use Groupware?   71

Chapter 6   Intranet Groupware and Workflow Products   95

Introduction   95
IBM/Lotus   97
Netscape/Collabra   101
Microsoft   109
Novell: GroupWise 5   114
Open Text: Livelink Intranet   114
Action Technologies: Metro 1.1   121
Allaire: Forums and Cold Fusion   126
Amicus Networks: Community Builder   127
Attachmate: Open Mind 3.0   128
Cap Gemini Innovation: WebFlow   129
Connectix: VideoPhone 1.1 for Windows   130
DataBeam: neT.120 Conference Server   131
Digital: AltaVista Forum 2.0   132
ForeFront: RoundTable   135
FTP/Campbell Services: OnTime Web Edition 4.0   135
Galacticomm: Worldgroup Internet Server   135
JetForm   135
Lundeen: Web Crossing   136
McCall, Szerdy & Associates: C.A. Facilitator for the Web   136
Motet   136

NetManage   136
Now Software: Now Up-to-Date   138
Oracle: InterOffice   138
O'Reilly: WebBoard   139
Paradigm Software: WorkWise-Enterprise   139
Proxima: Podium 2.01   139
Quarterdeck/Future Labs: TALKShow   140
RadNet: WebShare   141
Screen Porch: Caucus 3.0   141
Searchlight Software: Spinnaker   142
Spyglass/OS TECHnologies: WebNotes   142
Symantec/Delrina: FormFlow 2.0   142
Thuridion: CREW   142
UES: Track-It   143
Ultimus: WebFlow   143
Ulysses Telemedia Networks/Intraprise Technologies: Odyssey   144
WebCal   144
WebFlow: SamePage   144
White Pine: Enhanced CU-SeeMe   146
Miscellaneous   147

Chapter 7 How Do You Choose Intranet Groupware and What Are the Advantages and Disadvantages? 149

How Do You Choose Which Intranet Groupware Products to Use?   149
Advantages and Benefits of Intranet Groupware   164
Disadvantages of Intranet Groupware   166
Checklist: Choosing Intranet Groupware   168

Part 3 How Do You Implement Groupware and What Is the Impact of It? 181

Chapter 8 Building Your Intranet 183

Two Different Ways You Can Get Started   183
Traditional Model   183

Internet Model   194
The Traditional Model or the Internet Model: To Bureaucratize or Not?   229

Chapter 9   What's So Hard about Groupware?   231

The People Part Is Hard   231
Change Is Hard   233
Factors That Contribute to a Successful Groupware Implementation   239

Chapter 10   Two Approaches to Implementing Groupware   241

Introduction   241
The User-Focused Approach   241
Business Process Improvement Approach   261
How Can a Consultant Help You Implement Groupware and
    Workflow?   270
Groupware Dos and Don'ts   271
Checklist: Implementing Groupware   273

Chapter 11   The Impact of Groupware and Workflow   287

How Will Groupware Change Organizations?   287
How Will Groupware Change Business Processes?   288
The Future of Intranet Groupware and Workflow   289
Summary   290

Appendix   Groupware and Intranet Resources   291

Companies That Contributed to This Book—Introduction   291
Netiquette—Chapter 1   291
What Is Happening in Businesses Today—Chapter 2   292
Learning Organizations—Chapter 4   292
Uses of Intranets—Chapter 5   292
Intranet Groupware Products—Chapter 6   292
Building Your Intranet—Chapter 8   294
People Issues and Change Management—Chapter 9   299
Implementing Groupware—Chapter 10   299

Index   303

introduction

Background

Groupware has become very popular and has proven its worth in companies worldwide. The problem with groupware is that it's been very expensive and difficult to implement. With the introduction of cheap and easy-to-construct intranets, that's no longer the case. You can now get the benefits of groupware on your intranet. As I write this, we're just now seeing traditional groupware products move to the Web, and the pace of this transition continues to escalate.

Today, organizations must do things cheaper, faster, and better in order to remain competitive. Intranets and groupware facilitate this by helping employees to communicate more effectively, capture and share their knowledge, and learn and innovate. This makes it possible for organizations to get better products to market faster than their competitors and to meet or exceed their customers' expectations. These things give organizations a competitive edge.

I first became involved with intranets in 1994 when I was at JCPenney, a Fortune 50 retailer. I had just finished facilitating a business process improvement team and was working on implementing part of the new process on the Internet. I evangelized about the Internet and what we could do with it to anybody who would listen. At the same time, the advanced technology group was building the infrastructure for us to access the Internet and had created an internal web called jWeb. The CIO asked me to create and lead a team to develop both jWeb and an external Web site, and to market them to the entire company. We were very enthusiastic about the many things we could do with jWeb, including using it for collaboration and sharing knowledge.

The use of the term *intranet* has become common for describing *internal webs,* but there are distinctions between them. I use *internal web* to refer to the use of World Wide Web (WWW) technology, such as Web servers and browsers, inside the organization. I use *intranet* to describe the larger environment, which includes the network, internal web, e-mail, newsgroups, mail lists, and other Internet tools and technologies.

Throughout this book I'll often use the terms *groupware* and *collaborative computing* interchangeably. In addition, I'll generally include workflow under the umbrella of groupware. *Workgroup tools,* such as spreadsheets, word processors, and personal information managers, may or may not be classified as groupware tools. Since the direction of many vendors is blurring the distinction, I'll discuss workgroup tools under the umbrella of groupware when they enable collaboration.

This book also mentions *knowledge systems,* which is a term for groupware tools that capture and store corporate knowledge. They generally include discussion databases, newsgroups, and process rules embedded in workflow.

In this book, I'll often use the term *user.* I don't like the term, but it's much clearer than my preferred terms of *internal customer* and *internal client.* For the sake of clarity, I'll use the term user.

In researching this book and its companion, *Intranet Business Strategies,* I spoke with many companies. Some of them shared lots of information and others couldn't share anything. One company was able to share its experiences but wished to remain anonymous. In industries where intranets are rare and considered a competitive advantage, companies don't want to give away their trade secrets. In industries where many companies have intranets, they're not so confidential. The 13 companies that contributed their experiences and insights to this book are as follows:

1. Amgen Incorporated
2. AT&T Corp.
3. Bell Atlantic Corporation
4. Booz Allen & Hamilton Inc.
5. EDS
6. JCPenney Company, Inc.
7. Rockwell International Corporation
8. SAS Institute Inc.
9. Silicon Graphics, Inc. (SGI)
10. Texas Instruments Incorporated (TI)
11. Turner Broadcasting System, Inc.
12. United Parcel Service of America, Inc. (UPS)
13. One anonymous company

Who Is This Book For?

This book is for senior business managers with a technical background, IT managers, systems analysts, network administrators, webmasters, web developers, and others interested in implementing groupware in their organization. I won't get into technical details. The book is more concerned with how to select the appropriate intranet groupware and deploy it in your organization.

I'll discuss at length the people issues that affect implementation of intranet groupware. My goal is to give you a process for implementing intranet groupware as easily and painlessly as possible. Table I shows what's in this book and how it's organized.

TABLE I

Part 1: What Is an Intranet?
(Chapters 1 through 3 are background material for those who haven't read *Intranet Business Strategies*.)

Chapter 1: What Is an Intranet?	Discusses what intranets are, where they came from, how fast they're growing, and what components make them up.
Chapter 2: Why Have Organizations Created Intranets and What Are the Advantages and Disadvantages?	Explains why organizations are creating intranets, their advantages and disadvantages, and what size company it takes to need one.
Chapter 3: How Will Intranets Change You and Your Organization?	Considers what's happening to cause changes in your organization and what changes an intranet will cause.

Part 2: What Is Groupware and How Do You Use It?

Chapter 4: What Is Groupware and Why Do You Need It?	Explains what groupware is, what it does, why you need it, and why you should consider intranet groupware.
Chapter 5: How Do You Use Groupware?	Discusses different types of groupware tools, what they do, and how to use them in organizations.
Chapter 6: Intranet Groupware and Workflow Products	Lists and describes various intranet groupware products as well as web-enabled proprietary groupware.
Chapter 7: How Do You Choose Intranet Groupware and What Are the Advantages and Disadvantages?	Describes how to select the right intranet groupware products and discusses the advantages and disadvantages of intranet groupware.

Part 3: How Do You Implement Groupware and What Is the Impact of It?

Chapter 8: Building Your Intranet — Discusses two different approaches to use to create an intranet. (This chapter is background material for those who haven't read *Intranet Business Strategies*.)

Chapter 9: What's So Hard about Groupware? — Considers the people and change issues that make groupware so difficult to implement and suggests some factors that contribute to a successful groupware implementation.

Chapter 10: Two Approaches to Implementing Groupware — Describes two approaches you can use to implement groupware, how a consultant can help, and dos and don'ts in implementing groupware.

Chapter 11: The Impact of Groupware and Workflow — Explains how groupware will change organizations and business processes, and discusses the future of groupware and workflow.

Appendix: Intranet Resources

All Internet locations and URLs cited in this book were accurate at the time of this writing, though it's likely that by now some may have changed. The various search engines can help you find current locations for that information.

I hope you'll enjoy reading this book. I wish you the best in implementing groupware and workflow within, and beyond, your organization. I'd like to hear about your experiences and what you've learned. You can reach me at mhills@knowledgies.com. Also, you'll find electronic versions of the checklists in this book at the John Wiley Web site at http://www.wiley.com/compbooks/.

Finally, I'd like to thank all the many folks at Amgen, AT&T, Bell Atlantic, Booz Allen & Hamilton, EDS, JCPenney, Rockwell International, SAS Institute, Silicon Graphics, Texas Instruments, Turner Broadcasting, United Parcel Service, and one anonymous company—you know who you are—for sharing your stories. You made this book possible. Many thanks.

PART ONE
What Is an Intranet?

chapter one

What Is an Intranet?

This chapter and the next two chapters are a level-set for those who haven't read my Intranet Business Strategies *book.*

Let's imagine that you're the CIO of a global company. The director of communications needs your help to solve her problem. She must communicate all company policies and announcements to employees in 2,000 locations in 50 countries. She really doesn't have an effective way to do this.

1. Mail is too slow.
2. E-mail is too time-consuming because she must keep up with the constant personnel and address changes in these locations.
3. Telephone is very expensive and time-consuming, and suffers from the same problem of difficulty in keeping up with personnel and phone number changes.
4. Fax is also expensive and time-consuming for the same reasons as the telephone.
5. Overnight letters and packages just aren't practical or cost-effective for so many locations.
6. Videoconference is much too expensive.

You've already helped her to communicate with those outside the company by putting up an external Web site and publishing information for the media and analysts. Those same tools can help her to reach everyone inside the company. In fact, an internal internet, or *intranet,* is one of the best things to come along for communicating inside organizations.

So what is it? To make it simple, it's nothing more than a private internet inside your organization. A firewall keeps out intruders from the outside world. An intranet is an internal network that's based on the Internet's TCP/IP protocol. It uses World Wide Web (WWW or Web) tools such as Hypertext Markup Language (HTML) to give you all the features of the Internet on your own private network. With Web tools, almost any information is just a few mouse clicks away. When you click on a WWW link, you see information from a computer that may be on the other side of the world. It doesn't matter where the information resides. You merely point and click to bring the information to you. It is truly powerful in its simplicity.

Intranets are just as easy to build as they are to use, so this may be just the perfect solution to connect all parts of your organization and share information throughout. Intranets allow your employees to do a better job of making decisions and serving customers. If this sounds good to you, you're probably wondering if there's a catch. Interestingly, there isn't! Not only is the intranet easy to build and easy to use, it's also easy on the budget.

History of Intranets

Where did intranets come from? Let's first talk about the history of the Internet and the Web and then about intranets. If you already know all about the Internet, just skip the next two sections.

First, the Internet

The U.S. government created the Internet in the 1970s for national security reasons. Its purpose was to protect U.S. military communications in case of nuclear attack. The destruction of any computer on the network would not affect the rest of the network. In the 1980s, the National Science Foundation (NSF) expanded the network to include universities in order to provide researchers with access to expensive supercomputers that would facilitate their research.

In the early 1990s, the NSF allowed commercial interests to take over the Internet, and its growth rate exploded. Each year, more and more people join the Internet community, and commerce on the Web continues to flourish.

Enter the Web

The World Wide Web originated in 1989 as the creation of Tim Berners-Lee at the European Laboratory for Particle Physics (CERN). The Web provides easy access to information through hypertext, which is the linking of information. When you click on a word or phrase of hypertext, additional information comes to your computer. The beauty of hypertext is that the computer knows where to find the information so that you don't have to. The information can reside in your office or halfway around the world.

The Web consists of *home pages,* which are simply starting points for locating information. Hypertext links on home pages give you access to all kinds of information, which may be text, pictures, sound, and/or video.

To make it easier to access information on the Web, Marc Andreessen and some fellow students at the University of Illinois' National Center for Supercomputing Applications (NCSA) created a graphical user interface to the Web, which they named *Mosaic.* They made it available for free on the Internet, and as people found out about it and downloaded it, the Web took off.

The Intranet

With the introduction of Mosaic in 1993, some businesses became intrigued by the power of the Web and Mosaic. The media wrote about some of the first organizations to create internal webs, which included Lockheed, Hughes, and SAS Institute. Often, someone familiar with Internet tools came on board from an academic environment. Such individuals knew what these tools could do, and they often tried pilot programs to determine if the tools had any value in a commercial environment. They quickly found that the tools were very useful. As word got around, other companies became interested.

Many of these companies began to experiment with the Internet, often by creating an Internet gateway that hooked their e-mail systems to the rest of the world. Next they added Web servers and browsers for accessing the World Wide Web. In the process of doing this, they discovered how valuable these tools could be for providing access to internal information. They then started putting their policy manuals and documentation on the internal web server and secured it from the outside world. Later, as they brought in Internet newsgroups, they realized the value of providing internal newsgroups as well. This seems to be the normal evolutionary process that many companies follow.

Before we knew it, these internal internets took on many different names. They became known as *internal webs, internet clones, private webs,* and *corporate webs.* One story that I've heard with increasing frequency is that in 1994 someone at Amdahl referred to its internal internet as an *intranet.* The media picked up on the name and it stuck. I know of others who also used the term independently for their own internal internets. I guess it was one of those ideas that occurs simultaneously in several places. Now, everyone calls them intranets.

Growth of Intranets

The Internet, the Web, and intranets have had spectacular growth. Often, the media is a good indicator of what's hot and what's not. The only way to avoid hearing about the growth of the Internet and the Web is to move to another planet. Short of that, it's hard to avoid. The same is becoming true of intranets. The June 10, 1996, issue of *Computerworld* listed the number of press mentions of the word *intranet:*

- In 1994, there were 28 mentions of intranet.
- In 1995, there were 554 mentions of intranet.
- As of June, 1996, there were 5,737 mentions of intranet.

It's getting hard not to hear about intranets. That's a good indicator that people are getting on the intranet bandwagon.

We don't know how many intranets there are and how fast they're growing. Only a few of the organizations that have them are willing to talk about them. We do know that many of the Web server and browser vendors claim that a significant portion of their sales are for intranet use. One estimate, from Ian Campbell, who is Director of Collaborative Technologies for International Data Corporation (IDC), is that there were 100,000 *intranet* web servers in 1995, and by the year 2000 that number will grow to 4.7 million. Web browsers in 1995 numbered approximately 10 million. By 1996, Campbell expects that number to reach 40 million, and by 2000 it may be 180 million. Those numbers are pretty phenomenal.

What Are the Uses of Intranets?

The uses for intranets are almost unlimited. You can publish information, enhance communication, or even use them for groupware. Some uses require only pages created with HTML, a simple page-creation language, whereas others involve sophisticated programming and links to databases. You can make your intranet as simple or as fancy as you like. Some examples of uses include the following:

- E-mail
- Directories
- Organization charts
- Newsletters and publications
- News feeds
- Personnel manuals
- Benefits information
- Training
- Job postings
- Memos
- Newsgroups
- Sales reports

- Financial reports
- Customer information
- Marketing brochures, videos, and presentations
- Product information
- Product development information and drawings
- Vendor information
- Supply and component catalogs
- Inventory information
- Quality statistics
- System user documentation
- Network management
- Asset management
- Groupware and workflow

What Are the Pieces of Intranets?

Every intranet is different, but there are many pieces in common from one to the next. In some companies, the intranet consists only of an internal web. In other companies, the intranet consists of the entire network, which includes an internal web and lots of other tools. In this book, I will consider the intranet as the entire network, with the internal web being simply a component of the intranet. Here are common intranet components.

- Network
- E-mail
- Internal web
- Mail lists and Listservs
- Newsgroups
- Chat
- FTP
- Gopher
- Telnet

Network

First, we'll talk about the network, which is the most complex and most critical part of an intranet. It may consist of a single network or, in larger organizations, multiple networks. Networks can be as simple as a local area network (LAN), which covers a single building or part of a building. You can have the following types of LANs:

- *Ethernet.* These LANs consist of coaxial cables or twisted-pair (standard telephone) wire hooked to a hub, which is the traffic cop for the network.
- *Token Ring.* These LANs also consist of coaxial cables or twisted-pair wires. These wires attach to a Media Attachment Unit (MAU), which simulates a ring. Computers on the ring take turns transmitting as a token passes to each device on the ring, allowing it to transmit.
- *Fiber Distributed Data Interface (FDDI).* These networks use fiber-optic cable instead of twisted-pair wires, and they pass a token as in Token Ring networks.

Wireless LANs are an emerging technology. They are slow and expensive, and they work best for applications where you can't easily install a wired network.

Transmission Control Protocol/Internet Protocol (TCP/IP)

The Transmission Control Protocol/Internet Protocol (TCP/IP) is the basis for the Internet. Its role is to control transmission of data from place to place across the Internet. Though you can create an intranet without TCP/IP if you don't need to connect to the Internet, by doing so your organization misses out on a valuable resource. In most cases, you will have to use TCP/IP.

E-mail

Electronic mail has taken the business world by storm. It allows you to easily write a message and send it to people electronically.

It's equally easy for the recipient to compose a reply and send it back to you. E-mail goes just as easily to a person across the hall as to a person across the world. Now you can use e-mail for voice, video, and presentations along with ordinary text.

E-mail has been around in organizations long before the Internet and was likely their first Internet application. Their first Internet access was probably via an e-mail gateway. This required both an e-mail server and e-mail software, which could accommodate long Internet e-mail addresses. E-mail essentially became their first *intranet* application as well.

Internal Web

Once Internet e-mail is up and running, organizations start looking for ways to use the Internet and the Web. Although people generally think that internal webs and intranets are the same, they're really not. The internal web is only a part of the intranet, though it's a very important part.

An internal web uses Web tools inside your organization to make your corporate information easy to access. Users need only know how to point and click with a mouse to find the information they need. If you add search tools to your internal web, users who can type can find almost anything they need.

Let's examine a possible scenario that I'm sure occurs often in businesses. A potential customer calls in and wants to buy your product. He has some questions for you, and you know that he's ready to buy. If you can just locate the information to answer his questions, the sale will be yours. You start looking through the LAN, but you can't find the marketing information. You can't find it in your files, either. You try to call someone who would know, but no one answers. You know you've seen the information, and that it'll be in the product update that is currently out at the printer. The customer just can't wait. You promise to call back with the information, but you know that he'll hang up and call your competitor, and you've lost the sale. This has happened more than once to you and to others as well.

There's a solution—an intranet. It lets you bridge those islands of information and give employees easy access to the information they need to make better decisions and to serve your customers better.

If we change our story and create an intranet, let's see what happens. Your customer just called with lots of questions. All you have to do is point your mouse at the Search icon and click. You type in your customer's question and submit it. Instantly, you get a page of information from the latest marketing brochure. With it, you answer all his questions, and he's ready to order. You type in his order and submit it to shipping, who sends it to your customer. What a difference between these two scenarios!

An internal web provides your users with all kinds of information, including access to the Internet itself. An internal web consists of two major components:

1. Server
2. Browser or client

Server

A web server is the hub of an intranet because it contains the web pages. It involves the use of the hypertext transfer protocol (HTTP) to fetch pages from the server.

Browser or Client

The browser, or client, resides on *your* computer and is the graphical user interface between you and the web server. Its job is to request and display pages that contain text, graphics, sound, and video. With a mouse, you can point and click your way to the information you need.

Marc Andreessen, who developed Mosaic, the first Web browser, has gone on to create a commercial browser called *Netscape.* In addition to Mosaic and Netscape, there are numerous other browsers. They exist for nearly every computer platform. The browser is quickly becoming a universal user interface, and many companies feel that browsers will be the user interface for all their future systems.

Browser Enhancement Tools

There are many tools you can add to browsers. Netscape's latest browser incorporates built-in audio, video, 3D, phone, chat, whiteboarding, and caching of video. There are also lots of plug-ins you can add, such as remote-control software, collaborative software, engineering-drawing and chemical-structures viewers, viewers for word processing documents and spreadsheets, data-entry forms, news service, application development tools, and computer-based training (CBT) viewers.

Mail Lists or Listservs

A mail list is like sending an e-mail to lots of people with whom you have a common interest. You can ask questions or take part in a conversation. In contrast to normal e-mail, you don't have to maintain a list of all the members. The list owner does that for you. You simply send your message to the list and it goes to every-one on the list automatically. Certainly, the list owner has work to do in maintaining a changing list of members. Fortunately, he or she has help from the major mail list programs, Listserv and Majordomo, because they can automate subscription changes.

There are Internet mail lists on every imaginable subject, from business topics through personal topics. Most mail lists have members throughout the world. Your organization can have mail lists as well, and they can be on business topics, hobbies, and recreation. There can be members from all parts of the organization. All you need is e-mail in order to use a mail list. Those who have access to browsers may find that newsgroups better suit their needs.

Newsgroups

Newsgroups consist of threaded discussions, which do the same things as mail lists. Some browsers can read newsgroups; some need a separate newsreader to access them. You can use e-mail or your newsreader to post a message or reply to one. These mes-sages are then placed on a kind of bulletin board so everyone can access them. Newsgroups are a form of groupware.

An advantage of newsgroups when compared to mail lists is that you check newsgroups when you want to, and needn't worry about being bombarded with e-mail when you check for messages. Since only a single copy of newsgroups exists, newsgroups are more efficient with resources. With a mail list, every member gets every message. In addition, you don't have to subscribe or unsubscribe to newsgroups as you do with a mail list.

Newsgroups do the same things as mail lists. You ask questions or join discussions. There are thousands of Internet newsgroups, called *Usenet,* and they exist for every imaginable topic. Anyone interested in computers can find hundreds of them on computer topics alone. Anyone interested in groupware may want to check out some of the newsgroups on that subject:

comp.groupware	Discussion of groupware software and hardware in general
comp.groupware.groupwise	Discussion of Novell's Groupwise product
comp.groupware.lotus-notes.admin	Discussion of Lotus Notes system administration
comp.groupware.lotus-notes.apps	Discussion of application software for Lotus Notes
comp.groupware.lotus-notes.misc	Discussion of miscellaneous topics related to Lotus Notes
comp.groupware.lotus-notes.programmer	Discussion of programming for Lotus Notes

Your intranet can have as many newsgroups as you desire on any relevant topic. Here are some examples of groups that could benefit from having a newsgroup:

- *New-product developers.* These folks could discuss schedules, status, problems, and solutions.
- *Engineers.* If you have engineers spread across multiple projects or locations who might share an interest in a specific technology, you can bring them together to discuss ideas and share resources.

- *Computer techies.*   The techies with interest in certain technologies could share information, pose questions, or just discuss how to apply the technology.
- *Users.*   Any user needing help with a specific application could pose a question here. A moderator could answer user questions.
- *Everyone.*   Everyone with an interest in a specific hobby or sport can discuss it. Clubs could have their own newsgroups, such as the day-care parents or the volunteer group.

The Internet has certain rules of etiquette, called *netiquette.* People are expected to follow netiquette and observe certain manners and common courtesy in dealing with others on the Net. This is very important because there are so many cultures on the Net. To find the rules of netiquette, go to *The Net: User Guidelines and Netiquette* at http://www.fau.edu/rinaldi/net/index.htm.

It's important that employees follow these same rules on an intranet when dealing with other employees. Unfortunately, you may have to frequently remind some immature users that using bad language and flaming colleagues won't win friends and influence people—at least not influence them favorably! I recommend creating and publishing your own *intranetiquette guidelines.*

You can have either moderated or unmoderated newsgroups and mail lists. Moderators review postings for appropriateness before posting or distributing. In most cases, you won't need moderators if proper business etiquette prevails.

Chat

With Internet Relay Chat (IRC), people can converse with each other over the Internet. Chat approximates real-time communication and can take the place of expensive long-distance phone calls and conference calls among locations. Using this tool, you facilitate brainstorming sessions where participants are together at the same time but not in the same place. Chat works well for impromptu conversations about topics of common interest.

FTP

File transfer protocol (FTP) provides a library of readily accessible information that you can download to your own computer. It works especially well for large files that you wouldn't want to send by e-mail. Some browsers, such as Netscape, allow you to upload to and download from FTP sites. You can also acquire stand-alone FTP tools. You can use FTP on an intranet to do the following:

- Provide sophisticated users with the ability to download software and patches.
- Let your web publishers load their web pages to the server.
- Allow the transfer of large files such as technical drawings and specifications.

Gopher

Gopher provides text information that you access from a menu. It's easy to drill down through various levels of menus to access the information you need. Before the Web, gopher servers were the richest sources of information on the Internet. Today, you can use browsers such as Netscape to access gopher servers. Though the Web has mostly replaced them, you can still find vast resources available on government and university gopher servers.

Telnet

With Telnet, you can log in to remote computers, which are generally mainframe computers. Telnet (TN) 3270 lets you emulate a 3270 host–based terminal so you can access university library card catalogs and databases.

The Future of Intranets

As the browser becomes the universal user interface, employees will spend much of their time accessing information and communicating with others through their browsers. In companies that have intranets, we see users creating their own repositories of information to share with the rest of the organization. The web is quickly becoming the strategic computing platform for the future.

As all this unfolds, companies that produce proprietary client/server computing software and groupware are getting on the bandwagon and Web-enabling their applications. As a result, proprietary applications are becoming more open and will be accessible by anyone with a browser and the appropriate security. Intranets are starting to support all business processes and will therefore become woven throughout the fabric of the business.

Once everything is accessible from their browsers, most users won't pay much attention to the differences in operating systems. The operating system fervor and battles may subside as these differences become inconsequential.

Finally, training will change. Web browsers are easy to use and require almost no training. With browsers as the universal front end, user training will focus more on how to use specific applications to gain business benefits from them. Training can focus more on creating a competitive advantage than on how to work a specific program. Intranets will make it easier to deliver computer-based training (CBT) just in time. Users will have access to the most up-to-date version of the training.

These are just a few of the ways that I believe intranets will affect organizations. Next, let's look at why organizations are creating intranets.

chapter two

Why Have Organizations Created Intranets and What Are the Advantages and Disadvantages?

Why Have Organizations Created Intranets?

InfoWorld surveys subscribers in its *Corporate Intranets in the Enterprise* study and the latest survey found that 51 percent of subscribers' companies have an intranet. Considering that intranets have been around for only a few years, that's an extremely large percentage. We can be sure that the percentage will be much higher next time InfoWorld repeats its survey.

Why are we seeing an explosion of intranets? It seems to stem from a combination of the demands on businesses today and the capability of intranets to help companies meet those demands. We'll first look at those demands and then at how intranets can help meet those demands.

What Is Happening in Businesses Today

Competition in business today is fierce. You will have to change just about everything you do simply to survive. Change continues to occur faster and faster and today has become a fact of life in business. The five major drivers of business change today are as follows:

1. Customers want everything faster.
2. Customers want everything cheaper.
3. Customers want better-quality products and services.
4. Business has gone global.
5. All the rules have changed.

Customers Want Everything Faster

Since customers want everything faster, companies have reengineered and streamlined their processes to do things faster. Because of this, companies face increasing pressure not only to do things faster, but to speed things up more than their competition. It's like a treadmill that keeps getting faster and faster. Customers have started to expect to receive things instantly. These days, it seems that nobody's willing to wait longer than overnight for delivery of products. The Internet has further accelerated that because now you can get products, such as news and software, instantly.

With everything happening faster and faster, your products will have shorter and shorter lives. Your competitors can gain control of the market by making your products obsolete. If your product is first to market, you can gain control of the market and become the most profitable. This happens because cumulative experience at making a product allows you to improve the process and decrease the cost. Since your cost decreases faster than that of your competitors, you can price your product more competitively and pick up more sales. It becomes even harder for your competitors to compete on price. Therefore, it's always best to be the one to render your own products obsolete—don't let your competitors do it. Microsoft is a great example of this. Companies are using a variety of techniques, including the following:

- *Concurrent development.* This is where multiple areas work simultaneously on the product. They use computer-aided design tools and collaboration tools.
- *Shared development.* This involves having multiple shifts work on the same product, a technique frequently used in software development. A company could have

sites in the United States, Europe, and Asia. As one shift
finishes, it transfers the work for the next shift to continue.

Intranet tools help with both concurrent development and shared
development.

Thanks to Federal Express and other companies that provide
faster services, customers expect instant service as well as instant
products. Service companies have had to reengineer to provide
that faster service. One way to do that is to let customers provide
their own service. We see intranets allowing IT groups to do just
that with their internal customers, who can provide the level of
services they need by creating and maintaining their own information.

Customers Want Everything Cheaper

Customers want things cheaper as well as faster. This makes it
even harder on companies. Many have cut costs everywhere they
can, especially through downsizing. With reengineering, your
competitors have taken unnecessary steps out of their processes
and cut their costs. If they've downsized, there are fewer people
and they're probably trying to do the same amount of work. This
means that they can beat your prices on products and services.

Fortunately, intranets are cheap and can help companies leverage their employees and their skills. Intranets improve internal
communications and the productivity of knowledge workers.
They can also help by eliminating printing, decreasing communications costs, and speeding up product development cycles. This
has led to the increasing popularity of intranets.

Customers Want Better-Quality Products and Services

Customers also want better quality, and they won't settle for less.
If they can't get it from you, they'll go to your competitors. Companies have been improving their processes with the help of customer comments and quality statistics. Intranets make a great
feedback mechanism. For example, at AT&T, when a customer
calls in, customer-care representatives use their intranet-based
Knowledge-Management System to help solve that customer's

problem quickly. This allows AT&T to provide better-quality service to its customers and to learn what it needs to change.

Business Has Gone Global

Competition has really changed. Your competitors are now all over the world, not just down the street. Your customers may be global as well. This is all possible because of technology, and the Internet and intranets have facilitated this through ease of communication.

All the Rules Have Changed

A major change in business today is that the old rules no longer apply. These days, a significant part of your workforce may be telecommuters, or they may not even be your employees. You may be part of a virtual corporation. Technology has allowed you to develop partnerships with customers and suppliers, and even your competitors may be your business partners. That certainly changes things!

The way we market has also changed. Instead of blanketing everyone with your message, you may be tailoring your messages not only to a specific market niche, but maybe to individual customers.

How Do Intranets Help?

Technology helps meet the demands caused by these five drivers of business change. It improves communications inside the organization and with suppliers and customers. Here are some examples of the ways intranets help meet those demands:

- ◆ Provide easy access to up-to-date information
- ◆ Contribute to operational efficiency, which saves time and money
- ◆ Enable better coordination and communication
- ◆ Permit sharing of expertise
- ◆ Tap into employees' creativity and innovation

The benefits of an intranet greatly outweigh its risks. According to Gene Phifer, Senior IT Manager at Texas Instruments, the intranet is causing IT to completely rethink how they share information. Todd Carlson, CIO at EDS, says that the intranet has been a real competitive enabler for his company.

Your competition is building an intranet—or already has one. Can you afford not to?

Advantages of Intranets

What are the advantages of intranets? Because there are so many of them, I've separated them into two types: tangible and intangible. *Tangible benefits* are those that you can measure or quantify. *Intangible benefits* are those that you can't readily measure but that you know have a positive impact. Intangible benefits seem to have a greater impact on profitability since they often help the business grow.

1. Tangible benefits of intranets

   - Fast and easy to implement
   - Cheap to implement
   - Easy to use
   - Save time
   - Provide operational efficiency
   - Save cost
   - Based on open standards
   - Connect and communicate among disparate platforms
   - Put users in control of their data
   - Secure
   - Scalable
   - Flexible

- ◆ Provide the richness of multimedia
- ◆ Leverage your infrastructure and applications investment

2. Intangible benefits of intranets

- ◆ Provide better communication
- ◆ Provide access to accurate information
- ◆ Capture and share knowledge and expertise
- ◆ Provide better coordination and collaboration
- ◆ Provide for creativity and innovation
- ◆ Provide new business opportunities
- ◆ Provide new business partnerships through access by suppliers and customers

Tangible Benefits of Intranets

As we said, you can measure or quantify tangible benefits, such as saving so much money or so much time.

Fast and Easy to Implement

You can set up intranets quickly and easily. You might start with a simple pilot to understand the technology and develop the skills. That's how many companies started. As you start setting up an intranet, you'll need to address these three areas:

1. *Server.*   A web server is fast and easy to configure and manage.
2. *Client or browser.*   Browsers are also easy to install. If you have technical users, they can probably do the installation themselves.
3. *Publishing and development.*   HTML is the language used for developing web content. It's a simple language based on tags that you add to a document to tell the browser how to display it. It's very easy to learn. More sophisticated web tools are coming and seem fairly easy

to use. You can develop things quickly so that you can pilot applications and make refinements as you go along. Your users can get value from your application while you continue to work on it.

You can create an installation kit for each of these areas to make installation easy for users. Making an intranet easy to set up will help it take off. If you make these kits easily accessible by users, you will increase the likelihood of their use. EDS put its installation kits on its FTP servers and on its desktop computing product catalog.

Cheap to Implement

Not only is an intranet fast and easy to implement, it's also fairly cheap to set up and run.

- *Servers.*   You can start with a spare computer and download free server software directly from the Internet. You could also consider commercial software, which is relatively inexpensive. It's also inexpensive to run a server, as most companies haven't added additional employees to run them.
- *Client or browser.*   Browsers are also cheap, ranging from free to maybe as much as $40 per user.
- *Publishing and development.*   It's cheap to get started publishing in HTML. You need very little training to start, and most early HTML publishers were self-taught from the information available on the World Wide Web. That's pretty cheap!

Easy to Use

They're also easy for people to use. All they have to know is how to point and click with a mouse, and they generally don't need training. Web browsers provide a consistent user interface, which you can even use to access legacy applications and databases. You don't have to provide training for each new application that comes along. Search tools make it even easier to locate information.

Save Time

Intranets provide quick access to information, which saves employees time. They have information at their fingertips rather than having to chase it down in files or by phone. They can also work from any location, which saves downtime. There's more time to do the important things.

Provide Operational Efficiency

Client/server systems have created a heavy load for IT groups, and intranets provide welcome relief. Users take responsibility for setting up and maintaining content. The web browser provides the user interface so IT doesn't have to build and deploy graphical user interfaces (GUIs) on user computers. Since applications reside on the server, there is no need to deploy that to user computers, either. Many administrative tasks have disappeared with the advent of intranets, so you need fewer people. In addition, operational resources may also decrease, since only a single copy of each page or message exists. As you can see, intranets can stretch your IT budget.

Save Cost

Most companies created intranets to save the costs of printing and distributing paper documents. With the speed of change, most of these documents were already obsolete before they distributed them. Therefore, employees couldn't trust that the information was up-to-date, and spent time chasing around to validate the information. As fast as things move today, no one has time for that! With an internal web, it's easy to keep information up-to-date, so employees can trust the information. That boosts productivity and saves money.

You can also save money by using e-mail rather than faxes and memos. Extending this to suppliers and customers, you can further save by using the Internet and your intranet for electronic data interchange (EDI) with business partners.

As I mentioned before, you don't have to develop GUI screens and rollout applications, which also saves money. You can make new versions of software available by clicking on an icon to download and install them rather than having someone go around to each computer to install them.

There are also savings from training and support. Intranet tools require so little training and support that you can save lots of money here.

Based on Open Standards

Intranets are built on open standards such as TCP/IP, HTTP, HTML, CGI, and MIME, which gives you greater flexibility.

Connect and Communicate among Disparate Platforms

This may be the first technology to bridge all the different operating systems and types of computers on the network. It doesn't matter whether you use a PC, Macintosh, or workstation. They can all use the same version of a file without converting it or knowing which kind of computer created it. We've struggled with this problem for years. It's hard to believe we can solve this problem so cheaply. There are browsers for all the major platforms, which means that applications developers don't have to create special versions for each platform. We finally have a way to do IT faster, cheaper, and better.

Put Users in Control of Their Data

We've wrestled with this for years, so this is a major advantage of intranets. Your users can now control their own destiny, and you can focus on bringing value to your organization.

As we moved away from centralized IT, we created islands of information. Product development areas put crocodiles around their islands and marketing departments put hammerhead sharks around theirs. If you needed access to their information, you might find its location, but you still couldn't get to it. Now, various departments are realizing the value of sharing information and are more willing to do so. They can make their information easily available to other departments and can access information belonging to other departments as well.

You can start by creating a corporate web server and providing security for individual departments to create, update, and delete their own information on the server. As departments get more comfortable, each can create and maintain its own web server. Users may be afraid that they will have to hire programmers to do this, but any department with sophisticated end users shouldn't have trouble. Tools are getting easier and easier to use, and conversion tools are starting to make it relatively painless to convert existing documents.

Secure

Since intranets usually employ firewalls and/or proxy servers to separate them from the Internet, they are generally fairly secure from outsiders. You can use security within your intranet to allow access to certain types of information. For example, perhaps only executives can access highly confidential information, and maybe only human resources (HR) folks can access payroll information. You can also use security to permit suppliers or customers to access your intranet from across the Internet.

Scalable

Intranet applications can scale up, just like those on the Internet. This is an advantage over client/server applications, which may *hit the wall* or bog down when you try to add more users.

Flexible

The flexibility of intranets allows you to do enterprise-wide pilots where everyone can benefit from the application while you're still working on it. There's only a single copy, which resides on the server. You simply replace that copy with the most up-to-date version until you get what you want.

Provide the Richness of Multimedia

Internal webs provide organizations with the richness of multimedia for training and communication. The real value of multimedia is in its effectiveness in meeting the needs of all three kinds of learners:

- ◆ *Visual learners.* About 35 percent of us are visual learners. We learn by seeing. Multimedia shows you how something works.

- *Auditory learners.*   Approximately 25 percent of us are auditory learners. We learn by hearing. Multimedia lets you hear a description of how something works.
- *Kinesthetic learners.*   Roughly 40 percent of us are kinesthetic learners. We learn by doing. Multimedia lets you actually practice doing something.

With a multisensory approach, multimedia can enable you to learn something in about half as much time, and you'll retain it two or three times longer than with conventional methods of learning. This makes it possible to do things faster, better, and cheaper.

The multimedia application resides on the server, and you can update it as necessary. It's available when you need it and should always be up-to-date. The major issue regarding multimedia on the web is the need for more bandwidth, but that will become a nonissue.

Some companies now use video and streaming audio on their intranets to communicate messages from executives. This way, everyone gets the same message.

Leverage Your Infrastructure and Applications Investment

Web solutions can leverage your investment in your existing hardware, software, and even legacy applications and databases. You use a web front end to make access easy and friendly so you don't have to throw away what you already have.

Intangible Benefits of Intranets

It's very hard to put a value on intangible benefits. However, they may be more valuable than the tangible ones. How can you put a value on making your organization more competitive or on having more knowledgeable and self-reliant employees? If your employees are more productive, make better decisions, and do a better job of serving customers, you can see the results in the bottom line, but you can't know for sure that the intranet was the cause.

Provide Better Communication

While some companies created intranets to improve their internal communications, others discovered that this was a by-product of their intranets. Even though companies want to save costs, most know that internal communication is more vital than ever. There are several forms that internal communications can take:

- ◆ *Communications from executives, corporate communications departments, and other departments.* Companies can publish announcements, bulletins, and newsletters on the internal web, and all locations can have simultaneous access.
- ◆ *Communications among colleagues.* Intranet e-mails and newsgroups allow employees in any location to communicate with all others.

Provide Access to Accurate Information

Access to accurate information seems to be the common reason that companies build intranets. To find information, you don't even have to know where it's located. For years, we've had vast reserves of data hidden away on departmental servers. Those outside the department had to know where information resided, and even then they still might not be able to tap into it.

With intranets, everyone can access the most up-to-date information. It's much easier to point and click than to plow through files or manuals. This access to information also makes employees more knowledgeable and self-reliant.

Capture and Share Knowledge and Expertise

An intranet enables you to capture and save information by publishing content on the internal web and by capturing knowledge from newsgroup discussions. By doing so, the information is available when needed. You can avoid the proverbial reinventing of the wheel.

Provide Better Coordination and Collaboration

Intranets also enable better coordination and collaboration of workgroups and teams and can be used to support workgroup conferencing.

Provide for Creativity and Innovation

Intranets promote creativity, exploration, and innovation. For example, through an internal engineering newsgroup, a product development engineer can ask for ideas and suggestions to help solve a problem. By trying, and combining, some potential solutions, the engineer finds out exactly what will work, and then posts the results back to the newsgroup to share with others. This same engineer might also get ideas for new product features by interacting with customers on the company's customer newsgroup.

Provide New Business Partnerships through Access by Suppliers and Customers

Through intranets, companies can develop valuable business relationships with suppliers and customers, as Federal Express did by allowing customers to access its internal package-tracking application on the Internet. One day, EDI will take place with your trading partners by using the Internet or by accessing your intranet.

Provide New Business Opportunities

Some companies have reaped new business opportunities from their intranets. What new products and services could you provide because of your intranet?

Advantages of Intranets over Client/Server

Client/server was a less expensive solution to replace expensive mainframe computers and dumb terminals. I've already mentioned many of the advantages of intranets over client/server, but to recap, here are the primary advantages of internal webs and intranets over client/server:

- Web browser software is much less expensive.
- Intranets are easier to set up, use, and manage.
- The web already has the three-tier architecture that client/server is moving toward.
- The web is far more scalable.
- Web browsers provide a single user interface for all applications.
- Web browsers exist for all operating systems, so you don't have to build and roll out different applications for each platform.
- Client/server development requires lots of programming expertise, whereas end users can publish on the internal web.
- Web applications are more flexible and don't require the user to follow a specific sequence of steps.

Disadvantages and Risks of Intranets

We must, of course, look at the disadvantages and risks as well, which include the following:

- Potential for chaos
- Security risks
- Management fears
- Information overload
- Waste of productivity
- Not an integrated solution
- Hidden or unknown complexity and cost

Potential for Chaos

This technology is so easy to install that we have the same potential for chaos we saw with PCs and with client/server. This frightens some IT managers, while others consider this to be an opportunity for users to take control of their destiny. My own view, and that of some IT managers I spoke with, is that allowing the intranet to be a grassroots effort is the best way for it to reach critical mass. If you involve your entire organization in building the intranet, you will find that it takes off quickly. If you put IT into a leadership role early, you can introduce the technology to your organization. You can then help all areas do things cost-effectively and in a way that meets the needs of your business.

Security Risks

Intranet security is a major concern in most organizations. If you're cautious in how you set up your security, then outsiders shouldn't be able to wander through your company information. Remote access to an intranet can be a challenge, but you can use dial-back modems and challenge security/password systems to make sure that only those you have authorized can enter your intranet.

E-mail should be a concern because careless or malicious employees can easily mail sensitive information outside your organization. You should educate employees about what information should and shouldn't be e-mailed, posted on your external Web site, or placed on your FTP server.

For most companies that create intranets, the actual security may be easier than dispelling people's fears over it.

Management Fears: Fear of Sharing Information and the Loss of Control

Middle managers who have always hoarded information find that intranets are scary. When people are no longer in the dark, the balance of power changes. Intranets empower employees so that you no longer have to manage them.

Information Overload

All the information available from intranets, combined with access to the Internet and news feeds, has the potential to overwhelm employees. This is an issue we're just starting to deal with. Use of intelligent agents is one answer, and we can expect to see others.

Waste of Productivity

Managers become frightened by what will happen when you open up the company and let people surf the Net. They visualize people spending all their time surfing and not working. As with any new toy, people play until the novelty wears off, and then they settle into using it more appropriately. Ironically, surfing is mighty cheap Internet training.

Not an Integrated Solution

Until recently, you couldn't get an off-the-shelf intranet solution. You had to put the pieces together yourself, and maybe they didn't fit. However, vendors have started to address this problem, and alliances between hardware and software companies are also filling this niche. This problem is quickly going away.

Hidden or Unknown Complexity and Cost

Intranets are just in their infancy and, at this stage, are relatively inexpensive in comparison to other solutions. However, as we start tackling access to legacy applications and databases, the cost will certainly increase. Even so, this should still be cheaper than proprietary client/server solutions. It may be some time before we know the extent of the complexity and cost involved.

What Size Company Does It Take to Need an Intranet?

You may be wondering how big your company needs to be for an intranet to make sense. I've seen this asked on intranet discussion groups, and the frequent answer is 50 to 100 users. I believe that companies much smaller than that can benefit from an intranet. I believe the real question is *Do you need one?* If so, why not create it?

I fully expect to see them appearing in homes as families start networking their computers. Why not put up the family address and phone list, complete with birthdays, anniversaries, and other occasions? What other ways might you use one at home?

chapter three

How Will Intranets Change You and Your Organization?

What Changes Will Occur?

In researching this book and its companion, *Intranet Business Strategies,* I worked with 13 major corporations. These corporation's names appear in the introduction to this book. In Chapter 2, I talked about the *reasons* companies create intranets. In this chapter, I'll talk about the *results* these 13 companies received from implementing intranets. I will briefly repeat some of the reasons I gave in Chapter 2, because these companies achieved the results for which they created their intranets. The results are of two major types, with lots of variations within each:

1. Improved competitiveness through operational efficiency and productivity

    ◆ Improves access to up-to-date information
    ◆ Cost savings
    ◆ Time savings
    ◆ Improves productivity
    ◆ Improves operational efficiency and effectiveness
    ◆ Improves decision making
    ◆ Improves ability to respond to customers and to be proactive

- ◆ Empowers users
- ◆ Leverages intellectual capital
- ◆ Provides new business and revenue-generating opportunities
- ◆ Improves service to customers

2. Breaking down walls: Building a culture of sharing and collaboration

- ◆ Improves communication
- ◆ Enables sharing of knowledge and collaboration
- ◆ Empowers people
- ◆ Facilitates organizational learning
- ◆ Facilitated organizational change: Breaking down bureaucracy
- ◆ Facilitates organizational bonding
- ◆ Improves the quality of life at work

Improved Competitiveness through Operational Efficiency and Productivity

When everyone has an intranet, how can you gain competitive advantage from having one? You do that by incorporating your unique applications and databases into it. Your employees can then leverage that information to improve their decision making, productivity, and service to your customers. This improved productivity and customer service becomes your competitive advantage.

Improves Access to Up-to-Date Information

At almost every company, improved access to up-to-date information was one of the major results from its intranet. At SAS, the intranet is now the de facto standard for publishing. People can find information and documentation without searching blindly through the file system or asking others for access locations. Amgen's most effective use so far is in providing access to their corporate library materials. AT&T believes its information is more accurate now since employees do their own updates. At Turner Broadcasting, even employees without computers have access to HR information through freestanding kiosks.

Intranets will become the primary distribution and communications vehicles in many companies. For example, EDS is adding the PointCast I-Server to its intranet so employees can have customized news reports, with both company announcements and external news, delivered directly to their employees' computers.

The web browser is becoming the universal user interface for corporate information. Most companies are adding web front ends to their legacy and client/server applications, and they are also developing many new applications for the internal web.

Cost Savings

One of the results you hear most about is that intranets save costs. Certainly, free or cheap servers and browsers save you costs when compared with proprietary solutions. In addition, printed manuals and documents are giving way to the web, which saves untold amounts of money over printing and distributing information. Also, you can reap savings in network and communications costs. AT&T has estimated that consolidating its individual networks into a single global intranet has saved about $30 million per year. Bell Atlantic reported saving several hundred thousand dollars through consolidation and reduced printing, and the company is now experimenting with moving EDI to the intranet for additional cost savings.

Time Savings

With intranets, users have saved time. With information only a mouse click away, people don't waste time hunting things or verifying their accuracy, which yields greater productivity.

Improves Productivity

Intranets increase productivity because users have the information they need and receive new information more quickly. EDS also mentioned that the web browser's more intuitive user interface improves people's comprehension.

Silicon Graphics (SGI) has moved on into workflow on its intranet, and this has increased organizational productivity. For example, its Electronic Requisition System manages the purchase order process and has reduced the amount of time involved in processing requisitions.

Improves Operational Efficiency and Effectiveness

Several companies reported that their intranets allow users to do things more efficiently and more effectively. This applies to the IT group as well, since intranets are easy to maintain and require fewer people. In addition, the internal web has become the platform of choice for new development projects, which allows the IT budget to go further.

Improves Decision Making

Since intranets provide timely access to people and information, you can stop playing telephone tag. The information you need to make decisions is right at your fingertips, so you can quickly make those decisions. Decisions based on facts are better than those made without the facts.

Improves Ability to Respond to Competitors and to Be Proactive

The Net can really help you deal with competitive situations. For example, if Sun brings out a new product, SGI can have a video on Silicon Junction, its intranet, by the next day to help salespeople respond.

Empowers Users

Intranets put users in control of their own destiny, which is good news for IT. At Texas Instruments (IT), intranets make end users less dependent on the IT department. Users can put up their own servers, and by registering them in the server registry, they can make their information available to anyone in the organization.

Leverages Intellectual Capital

Both Booz Allen and EDS said the same thing—their intranets allowed them to leverage their intellectual capital. They put customer profiles and project information on the internal web to capitalize on the organization's intellectual capital.

Provides New Business and Revenue-Generating Opportunities

Several companies capitalized on new business development opportunities presented by their intranets. One of the most interesting twists is that several companies generate significant revenue from vendors who pay to advertise to employees on the internal web.

Improves Service to Customers

The best news is that all of this translates into better service for your customers. Isn't that what we're after? Making customers happy translates into more sales and profits.

Breaking Down Walls: Building a Culture of Sharing and Collaboration

Operational results are important, but your best results may come from the cultural changes the intranet causes. Intranets promote communication and collaboration among employees, flatten the hierarchy and facilitate organizational bonding.

Improves Communication

Improved communication was one of the most often cited results among the companies I worked with. For example, Cathy Mills, Vice President and Director of Company Communications at JCPenney, believes that JCPenney's intranet is a critical tool for communicating with employees in 37 countries. Without it, communication requires phone calls, e-mails, and faxes, which are far more expensive than using the web. Intranets impact communications in the following ways:

- *Speed.*   Communications are immediate.
- *Comprehension.*   The user interface helps the message to be understood.
- *Consistency.*   The message is the same to everyone. It doesn't become distorted with each subsequent delivery.
- *Availability.*   Intranets make communications available when and where you need them.

- *Universality.* Intranets make communications available to everyone, everywhere, at the same time.
- *Flow.* Intranets encourage freely flowing conversation and break down the walls between organizations.

Companies have even started communicating with suppliers and customers over their intranets to promote partnership and coordination.

Enables Sharing of Knowledge and Collaboration

Many of the companies I worked with felt that improved sharing of information across the enterprise resulted from their intranets. They felt this was critical to their operations. AT&T and TI said that their intranets facilitated collaboration among widely dispersed teams. For example, geographically dispersed teams at AT&T use the intranet for a virtual meeting place.

Empowers People

Since intranets make it easy for leaders to share their vision with everyone, the entire organization can move in the same direction together. This is a powerful force for change or for empowering the organization to meet the needs of customers.

Facilitates Organizational Learning

Intranets facilitate organizational learning in the following ways:

- *Career development.* Intranets hold career development information so employees can be proactive in their own development.
- *Training.* Web-based multimedia combines the richness of sound, pictures, animation, and videos, which increases learning and retention.
- *Scheduling training classes.* Training schedules and registration on the intranet make it easy to schedule classes.
- *Documentation.* Systems user documentation on the intranet supports learning.

- *Newsgroups.* Internal and external newsgroups provide access to knowledge and information.

Facilitates Organizational Change: Breaking Down Bureaucracy

Intranets facilitate communication from the leader to all employees, so the organization develops the shared vision and commitment necessary to propel the organization forward.

Facilitates Organizational Bonding

An unexpected result was the feeling of belonging that the intranet developed. When everyone gets the same information at the same time, and everyone can communicate with everyone else, people start to feel more a part of the team. When the organization uses the intranet to share its vision, goals, and strategies, it helps employees understand what happens and why so they can become part of making it happen.

Improves the Quality of Life at Work

Intranets even made the workplace more open and the work more fun in the companies I studied.

Other Ways Intranets Will Impact Organizations

So far, we've seen only the early results. We can expect intranets to cause profound changes in organizations. Let's look at some of those changes:

- How will the role of information technology change?
- How will business processes change?
- How will the culture change?

How Will the Role of Information Technology Change?

The role of the information technology organization will definitely change, because users can now take responsibility for creating and maintaining their own data and even applications. The IT group will focus on providing the infrastructure and services to the rest of the organization. We'll also see a change in the kind of skills IT people need:

◆ *Technical support people.* We may not need as many technical support folks, other than to support the network and the servers. This is because the browser will become the universal user interface, and all that's required is to download it directly to the user's machine.

◆ *Applications developers.* With the browser as the universal user interface, there won't be much need for creating GUI screens. With the move toward web-enabled databases for future applications development, organizations will value web and database skills.

◆ *Systems trainers.* Browser-based applications are easy to learn, so we won't need as many computer applications trainers, but we will need trainers who can teach users to get the most business value from applications.

◆ *Business liaisons.* Those employees with the skills to help business users structure and present their information on the intranet will find themselves in demand. To take on this new role, IT folks will need to develop good communications skills and the ability to work effectively on cross-functional teams. IT people will become more business-focused and will become valued business partners.

How Will Business Processes Change?

Intranets will streamline business processes and eliminate layers of bureaucracy by using workflow tools. Groupware tools will allow cross-functional teams to share knowledge and ideas and to be more innovative. We'll talk more about these in Chapter 4.

Intranets will also support virtual offices so salespeople can spend more time with customers, which should increase sales. More people will also be able to telecommute because they can still have access to the information they need. You can even move to 24-hour workdays by moving work around the globe with each shift. These are ways to cut costs and improve productivity.

If you incorporate reengineering best practices and process-management tools into the intranet you can share information about your processes.

How Will the Culture Change?

Intranets will bring about a new information community that will change corporate cultures. Some of the ways intranets may change cultures are as follows:

- ◆ People will cooperate and share information.
- ◆ Managers will manage results, not people. The new manager will coach and empower his or her team. This role may include the following:

  - ◆ Help the team develop its vision.
  - ◆ Get resources for the team, including training.
  - ◆ Eliminate obstacles and roadblocks.
  - ◆ Encourage, guide, and support the team.
  - ◆ Listen and advise.
  - ◆ Stay out of the team's way so it can achieve results.
  - ◆ Reward the team for its accomplishments.

- ◆ Empowered people will be self-sufficient and will not be afraid to try new things.
- ◆ Cross-functional teams will become the way to do projects in the future. These cross-functional teams develop communication between areas and break down functional walls.
- ◆ Access to information, coupled with a shared vision throughout the organization, will move the whole organization purposefully in a single direction.

In Part 1, we've discussed the nature of intranets.

1. Chapter 1 discussed what an intranet is, the history and growth of intranets, uses of intranets, pieces of intranets, and the future of intranets.
2. Chapter 2 discussed why organizations have created intranets, the advantages and disadvantages, and what size company it takes to need an intranet.
3. Chapter 3 discussed how intranets will change you and your organization, what is causing the changes, what changes will occur, and other ways intranets will impact your organization.

In Part 2, we'll discuss the nature of groupware and how to use it.

1. Chapter 4 will define groupware and explain why you need it.
2. Chapter 5 will examine what groupware does and how we use it.
3. Chapter 6 will look at selected intranet groupware and workflow products.
4. Chapter 7 will discuss how to choose intranet groupware and the advantages and disadvantages of it.

PART TWO

What Is Groupware and How Do You Use It?

chapter four

What Is Groupware and Why Do You Need It?

What Is Groupware?

Groupware is simply a tool that helps people work together more easily or more effectively. It typically allows them to communicate, coordinate, and collaborate. Other names sometimes used for groupware include *collaborative computing* or *group support systems* (GSS). Groupware encourages the free flow of information, which enhances innovation and supports and facilitates collective leadership. The use of groupware should result in an organization better prepared to meet today's marketplace challenges.

One of the simplest tools that helps people work together is the telephone, though we don't usually think of it as a groupware tool. For instance, if you and I are in the same office building, rather than spending 10 or 15 minutes walking to your office I can simply call you on the telephone. That saves time and makes it easier for us to work together. We don't always have to be face-to-face.

In the past, there's been a distinction between groupware tools and workgroup tools. Workgroup tools are generally personal productivity tools, such as spreadsheets and word processors, plus personal calendaring and scheduling tools that people use to coordinate their activities. Many vendors of these workgroup tools are turning them into collaborative tools, so the distinctions are starting to blur. Therefore, I'll incorporate workgroup tools into this book insofar as they enable collaboration.

Groupware supports people working together in groups and teams. These tools let people work together more easily *if* they want to work together. That's a big *if*—it presumes that they *want* to work together. If they don't, no amount of groupware will help.

What about Workflow?

Workflow is somewhat different from groupware, but is generally categorized as part of groupware since many groupware tools include workflow capabilities. Like groupware, workflow makes it easier for people to work together. The major difference is that groupware tools are generally somewhat ad hoc and free-form, whereas workflow tools are usually more rigid. Workflow performs specific transactions and routes those transactions among workgroup members. Workflow follows specific routes based on rules that support business processes.

How Big Is Groupware?

Just like the Internet, the groupware market is also heating up. Some of this growth is due to all the changing demands on businesses today and the reengineering projects spun off, and some is due to the growth in intranets. According to Ian Campbell, Director of Collaborative Technologies at International Data Corporation,

> *The groupware market is one of the strongest growth areas in high tech as corporations recognize the value of groupware as the framework for messaging and the entire industry is being carried by the Internet wave which promises to eliminate the barriers to deployment of groupware. The evolution of networking bodes well for the collaborative applications software market, which will grow largely as a result of users taking advantage of increasingly pervasive networking opportunities. Within organizations, the number of networked business PCs worldwide will double from 90 million in 1995 to 180 million in the year 2000. With over 80 percent of all business PC users connected to private networks, almost every user will have the capability of collaborating with almost any other user within their organizations.*

Campbell says that IDC's Collaborative Computing Market Review and Forecast shows that worldwide collaborative software revenues exceeded $2 billion in 1995. They should reach $2.5 billion in 1996, $3.3 billion in 1997, and $6.6 billion by the year 2000. This represents a compound annual growth rate of 27 percent. The installed base of collaborative software users grew 33 percent for 1995, reaching almost 54 million users. That number will increase 39 percent each year in 1996 and 1997, to almost 75 million users and 104 million users, respectively. By the year 2000, they expect the number of users to reach 241 million, representing a compound annual growth rate of 35 percent.

What Does Groupware Do?

Groupware consists of hardware and software on a network. It does many of the following things:

- Helps two or more people work together
- Lets them share knowledge and expertise
- Automates their activities
- Helps create an organizational memory
- Bridges geography and time

Groupware generally serves three purposes:

1. *Communication.*   Helps people share information.
2. *Coordination.*   Helps people coordinate their individual roles with each other.
3. *Collaboration.*   Helps people work together.

Those of us who are techies tend to want to talk about the tools right away, but that's really the least important part. Let's look first at the people part and what people do before we discuss the technology.

What kinds of things do people do when they work by themselves?

- Think
- Learn
- Brainstorm
- Write
- Design
- Create
- Analyze
- Decide

People do the same kinds of things in groups, with the addition of three more things they do in meetings.

- Share
- Discuss
- Present

As you can see, we do many of the same things individually and in groups. Our productivity tools, such as word processors and spreadsheets, help us do those things individually but not in groups. That's why we call them *personal productivity tools.* Thus we end up doing these things in groups, but we do them by hand because we lack the appropriate tools. Then someone enters them into a computer and brings them back to the group for review and revision. It would be so much easier if we had the collaborative tools to let us work together in groups and do the same kinds of things that we would normally do individually. The tools could record what we had accomplished and print out our final version. That way, meetings could actually accomplish work rather than simply communicate and review work.

That's just one example of the kinds of things we can do with groupware. What are some other things we can do with groupware? The list is somewhat long, so we need a way to group them in order to talk about one category at a time. The way that works best for me is to categorize groupware according to how people use each tool: Are they working together when they use it or are they working by themselves? They don't have to physically be in the same place to be working together.

1. *Working together.*   For this, people can work together at
   the same place or from different places, but they must be
   working together at the same time. The purpose of these
   tools is to make meetings more effective and enhance
   collaboration.
2. *Working individually.*   For this, it doesn't matter when
   or where a person is working. The purpose of these tools
   is to replace meetings and make them unnecessary while
   still providing ways to collaborate.

Let's look at these individually.

Working Together

Groupware tools in this category allow people to work together at
the same time and be in the same place or a different place. The
purpose of these tools is to improve meetings, make them more
effective, and improve the resulting work products. It really
doesn't matter whether the meeting is two people or a larger
group, whether it's a formal meeting or an informal one. You may
be more familiar with these kinds of tools, as many of them are
already in use throughout organizations. What's different is that
the newest tools work over the Web. Some of the tools that help
people work together include the following:

◆ *Calendaring and scheduling tools.*   Calendaring and
  scheduling tools ease the burden of scheduling meetings. You may even use them in meetings. They allow
  you to set up meetings, alert participants, and request
  confirmation. Their role in collaboration is to allow people to schedule the time to work together.
◆ *Voice conferencing.*   Voice conferencing tools consist of
  telephones and speakerphones. They allow people in
  two or more locations to meet by telephone and discuss
  things.
◆ *Videoconferencing.*   Videoconferencing allows people
  in two or more locations to each use a telephone and
  video camera to see and hear the other participants and

share documents and whiteboards. We can use video-conferencing in conference rooms or from individual desktops.

- *Electronic meeting systems (EMS).* An EMS uses computers to connect all participants in a meeting so they can simultaneously share ideas. The meeting focuses around the computer screen in the front of the room, where all participants can contribute ideas simultaneously. These systems work especially well for brainstorming sessions. One of their most widely hailed features is that they allow people to contribute or vote anonymously. In certain cultures, this can be invaluable. A variation of EMS is to use keypads to vote on specific questions.

- *Whiteboards or data conferencing.* Whiteboards allow two or more people or locations to view and mark up the same document simultaneously. Some tools in this category simply let you mark up the document, but someone still has to enter the changes to the file. Other tools save the changes to the file and allow you to print a copy for everyone.

- *Chat tools.* Chat tools allow you to converse and share ideas simply by typing on a keyboard and seeing responses on your computer screen. These conversations take place simultaneously at very close to real-time speeds.

Working Individually

Groupware tools in this category allow people to collaborate and share information, but generally not at the same time. They may work on a project or contribute ideas whenever they wish and from wherever they happen to be. They just aren't working together at the same time. People in different time zones can collaborate just as easily as people across the hall from each other. Since these tools capture knowledge and information, and sometimes even transactions, they make this information available to others any time they need it. These tools are the foundation of knowledge systems, and include the following:

- *Discussion and knowledge-repository tools.* Discussion tools let you have conversations and share ideas in close to real time or at vastly different times. Knowledge-repository tools let you insert documents or publish information so it's available for all who need to read it or use it at some time in the future. These tools take several forms:

  - *E-mail.* E-mail lets you share ideas and converse with one person or many people. E-mail tools use a variety of e-mail protocols. They may include Internet protocols such as Simple Mail Transfer Protocol (SMTP), Post Office Protocol 3 (POP3), and Internet Mail Access Protocol 4 (IMAP4). They may include proprietary protocols such as Microsoft's Mail Application Programming Interface (MAPI) and Lotus' Vendor Independent Messaging (VIM). The trend is to adopt a variety of protocols to enhance compatibility with other e-mail systems.

  - *Conferencing and discussions.* Newsgroups, forums, threaded discussions, and discussion databases all provide ways for users to post information that others can access and reply to. These usually involve the use of e-mail tools for posting and the use of the Internet's Network News Transfer Protocol (NNTP) or a proprietary protocol for providing access.

  - *Knowledge repositories.* Public folders, document management systems, and internal webs all allow you to place documents such as memos and reports in a location where others can access them when they wish. Knowledge repositories provide information for reference and future use. You can share thoughts and discoveries as well as your work products.

◆ *Group writing or shared document editing tools.* These tools allow two or more contributors to collaborate by individually working on a document whenever it's convenient for them. They may even help resolve discrepancies where there are simultaneous changes to the same passages. These tools enhance personal productivity tools by turning them into interpersonal productivity tools.

◆ *Workflow tools.* Workflow tools let you work with a form or application, do your part of the process, and forward it to the next person who should work with it. Workflow applications use either e-mail messaging or document management databases.

Why Do You Need Groupware?

You may be thinking that things are working just fine, so why change them? These tools sound interesting, but why not just keep doing things the way you're already doing them? After all, it's working. If it's not broken, why fix it? Here's why you need groupware.

Collaboration Yields a Product That's Greater than the Sum of Its Parts

Collaboration is about working together to produce a product that's much greater than the sum of its parts. Through the process the collaborators develop a shared understanding that's much deeper than they could have developed working on their own or contributing pieces to the product. That's why some of the greatest breakthroughs in science, medicine, and other fields have resulted from the efforts of two or more collaborators. The power is so great that unless you've experienced it, it's really hard to understand. The process taps into the collective wisdom, knowledge, and even subconscious minds of the collaborators. This powerful phenomenon is becoming a requirement to effectively compete in today's marketplace. However, most companies just don't get it! They soon will!

Over the years I've participated in numerous collaborative efforts, but one stands out as the key to my breakthrough in understanding the power of this phenomenon. A few years ago, a colleague and I collaborated to create a presentation for top management. Our entire team had worked at a whiteboard to sketch out our ideas, and one of the team members had taken the sketches and turned them into presentation slides. It was now time for someone to sit down and write the speech that went with the slides. Because of the very short time frame, my colleague and I decided to sit down together and create the speech. She and I took a laptop computer into a conference room and started working. We sat side by side at the computer, looking at the slides, discussing our ideas, and writing. We took turns *driving* the computer, and we discussed our thoughts and revised the speech as we went along. The ideas just seemed to pour forth and it all seemed to come together with incredible ease. At the time, we had only a simple word processor and a single keyboard to work with. With the collaborative tools available today the process would have been much easier. When we finished, we were both amazed at how well we worked together as a team. We seemed to be on the same wavelength and could even finish each other's thoughts. It was almost spooky. We both felt an intense sense of accomplishment and pride because we knew the result was something better than either of us could have done separately. We realized that we had developed a shared understanding that was much greater than the sum of our two inputs. Since then, I've experienced the same phenomenon many times with a variety of collaborators. I now know to expect the product of a collaboration to be much more than the sum of its parts. I truly believe that the key to surpassing your competition is to develop this kind of shared understanding—one that engages the hearts and minds of everyone in your organization. If you can do this, your competition doesn't stand a chance.

Groupware Lets You Capture and Share Knowledge

What is knowledge and how do you capture and share it? We've found over the years that we can take data and put it in reports, but to make it truly useful, someone must interpret the data and do something with it. In the past few years, we've added tools to turn data into information by identifying trends. With knowledge, we move forward another step. We capture more than just the numbers and trends: We capture what people do with those numbers and their potential impact. We capture the organization's expertise to share with everyone. Knowledge can be any or all of the following:

◆ What people have learned while developing your products

◆ What you know about your competition and their products

◆ What you know about who your customers are, what they want, and what they think about your products and your competitor's products

◆ The expertise of your most knowledgeable employees

Once you capture knowledge, it's what you do with it that gives you a competitive edge. Since your employees are your greatest asset, capturing and sharing their ideas, inventions, and innovations will be the key to your future competitiveness.

Collecting and maintaining that knowledge is one of the many roles of groupware. Companies have invested millions of dollars in building knowledge systems using groupware tools such as Lotus Notes. They wouldn't do that if they didn't believe they would gain a significant competitive advantage from doing so. These systems make it easy to tap into the collective knowledge of your organization. You can use search tools to easily find the people and information you need. These knowledge bases can even extend beyond the boundaries of your organization and out to your business partners.

Knowledge systems can be very expensive, although that's changing with the arrival of intranet-based groupware. Companies see that they can get many of the benefits of these knowledge systems by creating intranets for very little cost. This is one of the reasons intranets took off so quickly. Organizations realize that intranets provide a quick and easy way to capture and store knowledge. You can capture knowledge through threads of discussion groups and through publishing documents on the internal web. Though intranet groupware isn't yet as sophisticated as proprietary groupware, that's changing quickly as groupware vendors bring their wares to the Internet.

Groupware Promotes Learning and Empowers Employees

According to Peter Senge in *The Fifth Discipline: The Art and Practice of the Learning Organization,* the only sustainable competitive advantage comes from an organization's ability to learn. Senge created the concept of a Learning Organization, which encourages learning, creativity, and innovation, and empowers its employees to solve problems. Learning Organizations learn quickly, and they incorporate that learning into the organization's culture. They empower their employees and allow them the flexibility to make good judgments. Organizations that have embraced the Learning Organization are moving ahead of their competitors.

Intranets and groupware are valuable tools in creating a Learning Organization and empowering your employees. Why should this matter to you? It matters because your future is at stake. What will happen to you if your competitor does it before you do? You may be history! Many companies have had their strategic advantage evaporate overnight.

Why Should You Consider Intranet Groupware?

You may be thinking that if it's so important, why don't more organizations have groupware? There are a variety of reasons for this.

- ◆ Groupware has been so expensive that many companies stopped at the cost-justification stage. They couldn't justify an expensive solution such as Notes, or they had trouble trying to measure the potential results. How can you put a monetary value on improved productivity? It came down to the fact that the cost was too high and the measurable benefits were too low. That stopped many companies from going any further.

- ◆ Then there were the companies that undertook to install groupware for their organizations and found themselves unsuccessful for a variety of reasons—most of them people-related. Many implementations have failed because techies aren't generally comfortable addressing and solving people issues. Most estimates put the people issues in implementing groupware at 95 percent and the technology issues at only 5 percent.

As a result, groupware hasn't been on the *must-have* list in most technology organizations. The groupware name just hasn't had the cachet of many other technology tools. The situation has been so bad that Lotus hired a firm to determine how to position Notes as something other than groupware—and found that they couldn't. So what's changed and why am I touting groupware? The intranet seems to have changed the groupware paradigm in the following ways:

- ◆ The cost of proprietary groupware is coming down rapidly to compete with intranet solutions.
- ◆ Most proprietary groupware vendors have been hopping onto the intranet bandwagon, and if they don't yet have a product shipping that is Web-enabled, they soon will.
- ◆ Once an intranet is in place, it's easy and cheap to add groupware solutions to it.
- ◆ Since many organizations built intranets without going through ROI and cost justification, it's easy to add group-ware to it without going through those cost-justification exercises.
- ◆ Intranets were *pulled* through many organizations because everyone wanted them. I expect that intranet groupware will be that way as well. People won't even know that this is groupware, and they really won't care. Once they see what the tools can do for them, they'll want them.

Therefore, enough has changed that if you already have an intranet, it may be time for you to start seriously looking into groupware. If you don't yet have an intranet, it may be time for you to start working on it.

Intranets, as we currently use them, are just a form of groupware because they provide conferencing and knowledge repositories for storing and sharing information. We've already talked at length about the benefits of intranets. An intranet is a great way to save money and improve productivity, but the real payoffs come through groupware when everyone works in unison. That's when you'll see better decisions, better products, and better customer service.

chapter five

How Do You Use Groupware?

What Do Groupware Tools Do?

In Chapter 4 we categorized groupware tools by how people use them: working together or working individually. Now we'll take a look at each of these tools.

As we look at these tools, let's use a common business scenario to illustrate the use of groupware. Let's imagine that a large product development team is working on a new, radically different product. The team has design engineers from two of the company's design centers, chemists from the R&D lab, manufacturing engineers from two of the company's manufacturing plants, and representatives from marketing, sales, and customer support. The team members represent six locations in various parts of the world, so their groupware tools make it possible for them to work together easily.

Working Together

Tools that allow people to collaborate while working together could also be considered meeting-enhancement tools. Some, such as electronic meeting systems, work when all participants are together in a single meeting room. Others, such as voice conferencing and videoconferencing, bring participants in different physical locations together so they can meet. These tools work for meetings of any size, but generally work best with small groups.

Calendaring and Scheduling Tools

Calendaring and scheduling tools are really an outgrowth of the category of personal information managers, which are tools that allow you to keep your calendar, phone book, and to-do list on the computer. These products have grown up into group scheduling tools for use on a network, allowing you to see other people's calendars and schedule them for meetings. The purpose of group calendaring and scheduling is to make it easy to get people together for meetings. Though calendaring and scheduling usually fall into the category of workgroup computing tools, they're being incorporated into so many groupware products that they're now being considered groupware tools. Even the next release of Lotus Notes will incorporate calendaring and scheduling. These tools fit into the category of groupware because they make it easier to collaborate.

These tools contain a calendar that lets you denote meetings and appointments. When you need to schedule a meeting, you check everyone's calendar. Some tools even let you select attendees and specify a time frame, and then they check all calendars and propose potential times to meet. You can accept a time, schedule the meeting, send meeting notices by e-mail, and ask for confirmation from attendees. Some calendars even let you reserve the meeting room and audiovisual equipment through them.

The difference in productivity with group calendaring can be incredible. The norm without it is to call all participants to see when they're available. As soon as they all call back and you schedule a meeting, one of the participants has had to schedule another meeting in that time slot, so you start all over. These tools really ease the burden of scheduling meetings. With group calendars, the time saving is dramatic. You can also use these calendars in meetings to schedule the next meeting and place it on everyone's calendar. Calendaring allows people to schedule the time to work together.

Unfortunately, when you first introduce calendaring, some people feel as though they've lost some of their freedom and autonomy. They soon learn that they still have control and can block out and reserve times on their calendars to work undisturbed.

Another downside is that sometimes two meetings simultaneously grab an unscheduled spot on your calendar. That's something that more sophisticated tools overcome.

The product development team we talked about uses calendaring to schedule its meetings. Meeting notices contain a detailed agenda with a list of what each team member should do to prepare for the meeting. Team members then add the items requiring individual preparation to their calendar's to-do list.

Some of the tools and companies that have, or soon will have, intranet calendaring and scheduling are Lotus Notes Release 4.5, Netscape Navigator, Microsoft Exchange and Outlook, Novell GroupWise, Digital AltaVista Forum, FTP/Campbell Services OnTime Web Edition, NetManage Chameleon, Now Software Now Up-to-Date, Oracle InterOffice, RadNet WebShare, Thuridion CREW, Ulysses Telemedia Networks/Intraprise Technologies Odyssey, and WebCal.

Voice Conferencing

Both telephones and speakerphones are tools for voice conferencing. We don't typically think of telephones as collaboration tools, but with the emergence of Internet telephone, that's changing. Internet telephone is a tool for providing phone conversations over the Internet and intranets. Some of the newest Internet phone tools include both chat and whiteboarding and can link multiple locations.

Voice conference calls can be a bit disorienting due to time lags and pauses, but that's something the participants quickly get used to. When you have three or more locations on a conference call, you sometimes resort to identifying yourself each time you speak, and that can be bothersome. I've been on conference calls with up to 12 people in different locations, some of whom were first-time participants. In that kind of situation, it's important to take the time to have people introduce themselves and talk a little, just as you would in a face-to-face meeting, before starting the business of the meeting. That way, people can get oriented and start putting voices together with names. That's much more productive than just plunging right into the meeting.

Our product development team will get together face-to-face for its first meeting, but will use voice conference calls for some of its subsequent meetings. The design engineering subteam will use voice conferencing for its daily meetings to update each other and discuss issues, problems, and status.

Intranet voice conferencing tools include Netscape CoolTalk, Microsoft NetMeeting, Connectix VideoPhone for Windows, Net-Manage Chameleon/InPerson, and White Pine Enhanced CU-SeeMe.

Videoconferencing

Videoconferencing involves using telephone lines to carry both audio and video. A video camera provides pictures of participants as well as pictures of documents. Many of the current videoconferencing setups even include computerized sharing of documents. Videoconferencing can connect more than just two locations, and you can use it in conference rooms or from individual desktops.

A problem for now is the amount of bandwidth required to carry videoconferencing. As organizations see the value that high-bandwidth applications provide, bandwidth will be less and less of an issue. For now, the quality of videoconferencing is somewhat inconsistent. Even with sufficient bandwidth, motions can seem jerky. It sometimes seems like a meeting of "talking heads" since you lose much of the nonverbal communication that comprises about 80 to 90 percent of the message. I've done a few Internet demos to remote locations by videoconference and found it to be much harder to connect with an audience whom I'd never met.

The product development team we've talked about will use videoconferencing for its weekly status meetings, and individual subteams may also use it for meetings where they review drawings and specifications. Fortunately, they're already familiar with each other, so the disadvantages of videoconferencing have very little impact, and it's certainly much easier than traveling.

Videoconferencing tools for the Internet and intranet are still in their infancy, but one, White Pine's CU-SeeMe, has been around for a while. It was originally available only in black and white, but is now available in color. Color desktop video cameras are under

$200, so this technology is within the reach of most organizations. Other tools that provide or support intranet videoconferencing include Connectix VideoPhone for Windows, Galacticomm World-group Internet Server, and NetManage Chameleon/InPerson.

Electronic Meeting Systems (EMS)

Most meetings are very poorly run, and the purpose of electronic meeting systems is to overcome the barriers to effective meetings. Some have said that with a good facilitator, you may not need an EMS. Good facilitators aren't always easy to come by, so an EMS can help make meetings more effective.

An EMS makes it possible for all participants to share brainstorming ideas simultaneously. Attendees can contribute their ideas anonymously when they don't feel comfortable expressing their true opinions. All participants use computers hooked into a large computer screen at the front of the room. This screen becomes the focal point of the meeting. You can use different kinds of software depending upon the expected output from the session.

The purpose of these systems is to overcome many of the problems that make most meetings such a tremendous waste of time. Part of that is due to the sequential order of input of ideas. The EMS gets around this and allows everyone to contribute ideas simultaneously. You can even contribute new ideas while other ideas are being discussed. This tends to lead to less participant frustration. Electronic meetings are highly productive. In order to get the maximum benefit you should have a trained EMS facilitator run the meeting.

Keypads are a variation on the EMS. They're small boxes that look similar to the numeric keypad on a computer. Keypads hook into a central computer, which tallies votes. Since they allow only limited input, participants can't contribute ideas as they can with a conventional EMS. Keypads allow a meeting leader to ask questions or to program questions into the system in advance so they show up on the screen. Participants anonymously vote yes or no, or they can rank something on a scale of 1 to 9. Keypads work particularly well in meetings that contain a wide range of participants at different levels of the organization. Anonymous voting gives intimidated participants an opportunity to express their true beliefs and opinions without the fear of retribution.

A disadvantage of electronic meetings is that they take some getting used to. This technology is very disorienting and intimidating to those unfamiliar with computers. They may find it hard or uncomfortable to contribute to the meeting. You certainly don't want to use a tool that's counterproductive, so it's best to use this with those who are already comfortable with computers. In my work with business process improvement teams, we found that you could gradually introduce more and more new technology as long as each new tool made things easier for the team. Just make sure it's gradual and that the technology is just a nonintrusive tool.

Our product development team will have its kickoff meeting face-to-face, as it's important for all team members to get to know each other and build relationships before getting down to work. All team members are computer-savvy, so the facilitator has booked the kickoff meeting for one of the electronic meeting rooms. The team will use the EMS to brainstorm and prioritize features and requirements for the new product. They'll also use it to develop a detailed project plan. Later in the project, they'll again use the EMS for problem-solving sessions.

For now, we're not seeing many commercial electronic meeting systems for intranets. A meeting room on the LAN with computers equipped with a chat tool would make a good start for an EMS. One commercial EMS, C.A. Facilitator for the Web, is available from McCall, Szerdy & Associates.

Whiteboards and Data Conferencing

Whiteboarding is the current Internet name for tools more commonly known as *data conferencing.* I'll use whiteboarding and data conferencing interchangeably.

There are several varieties of whiteboards. One variety is for use in a conference room. The attached computer captures everything you write on the whiteboard and saves it in a file. You can also project documents or drawing files on the whiteboard so meeting participants can make changes and save them to the file. Another variety is a personal whiteboard that connects two or more computers by telephone. All participants can share documents and files on both computers and mark them up with revisions. The whiteboard may or may not automatically capture those changes to the file. If so, each location can print a copy to record the results of the meeting. These tools work well for creating and reviewing reports, presentations, project plans, budgets, and product designs, but they still have many limitations.

The product development team will make extensive use of whiteboarding and data conferencing tools. Since members of the design engineering subteam are in two locations, they'll use this from their desktops to share and discuss drawings and specifications. The manufacturing subteam will do the same for their manufacturing plans and issues. The whole team may use this for milestone reviews where they want to share drawings and specification files.

Whiteboarding tools for intranets are just emerging as of this writing and are really in their infancy. For now, you can mostly work with drawings but can't really do much to change files. Coming tools will allow you to work with and change word processing documents, spreadsheets, presentations, and other types of files. We can expect to see lots of experimenting with these tools in geographically dispersed organizations.

Intranet whiteboarding and data conferencing tools include Netscape CoolTalk, Microsoft NetMeeting, Connectix VideoPhone for Windows, DataBeam neT.120 Conference Server, ForeFront RoundTable, Galacticomm Worldgroup Internet Server, NetManage Chameleon/InPerson, Quarterdeck/Future Labs TALKShow, and White Pine Enhanced CU-SeeMe.

Chat Tools

Chat tools are primarily an Internet technology and provide a way to connect multiple locations through computer keyboards. Collaboration takes place by typing on a keyboard to send messages and discuss topics. You can consider this working together since all parties are physically present at the same time. Chat tools are one of the more common intranet collaborative tools, and their use will probably increase for a time until Internet phone use across the intranet becomes widespread.

A major advantage of chat is that it records the dialogue so you can store it for others to see later. You can have large numbers of users, even hundreds, involved in a chat dialogue. One downside is that long and deliberate comments sometimes fall by the wayside as the dialogue moves on to other topics.

The product development team and subteams will use chat to brainstorm and discuss issues when they're able to get participants together at the same time. The design subteam will use chat when sudden problems arise so that they can get their heads together to solve the problem. Transcripts from these sessions may be very valuable later for the manufacturing subteam, as members work through issues to put the product into production, and for future product development teams, as they come across similar problems.

Internet Relay Chat has been the predominant intranet chat tool. Other intranet chat tools include Netscape CoolTalk, Microsoft Comic Chat and NetMeeting, Amicus CommunityACT, ForeFront RoundTable, Galacticomm Worldgroup Internet Server, NetManage Chameleon, and White Pine Enhanced CU-SeeMe.

Working Individually

Now let's look at tools that allow individuals to collaborate with others at their convenience, not at some preappointed time. These tools allow for collaborators to work from wherever they happen to be and whenever it fits their schedule, thus decreasing the need for meetings. You should still have face-to-face meetings to start a collaboration or project, but after that you can dramatically decrease the number of meetings required.

These groupware tools work particularly well across time zones when collaborators don't work the same schedules. These tools not only support collaboration, but also capture information to build a base of knowledge.

The goal is to have fewer meetings, because it's so hard to get busy people together, and busy people can't get any work done because they're always in meetings. That's why these tools have grown so quickly. They let you work alone when you want to and collaborate when you need to. You have more control over your schedule and your colleagues have more control over theirs, and you can still work together.

E-mail

E-mail is the first tool in this category and really provides the foundation for some of the other tools. E-mail has become pervasive in many organizations and provides the underlying messaging infrastructure that's a key piece of many collaborative tools. The purpose of e-mail is to communicate with one or more people. It lets you communicate information rather than calling a meeting to share that information. E-mail was probably the first true collaborative tool that most organizations implemented. It communicates at the convenience of the sender, and can be read at the convenience of the receiver. E-mail has largely replaced memos in many organizations and, with its flexibility, may soon largely replace faxes as well.

There are a variety of e-mail protocols to support, which include the Internet SMTP, POP3, and IMAP4 protocols. Also, e-mail that supports the Multipurpose Internet Mail Exchange (MIME) protocol allows users to send rich e-mail messages that include documents, spreadsheets, presentations, graphics, sound, and even video across the Internet. Some e-mail supports proprietary protocols, such as Microsoft's MAPI and Lotus' VIM. E-mail packages are supporting more and more protocols these days to make it easy to exchange mail with other e-mail systems across the Internet.

Our product development team will use e-mail for delivering time-critical information, such as status changes or items that need prompt attention. They may also use e-mail to send the address of a document or drawing that the team should review.

There are lots of products that provide and support intranet e-mail, or soon will, including Lotus Notes and Domino, Netscape Navigator, Microsoft Exchange and Internet Explorer, Novell GroupWise, Amicus CommunityACT, Galacticomm Worldgroup Internet Server, NetManage Chameleon, and Oracle InterOffice.

Conferencing and Discussions

Conferencing is the name generally given to a group of tools consisting of newsgroups, forums, threaded discussions, and discussion databases. Newsgroups are currently commonplace on the Internet and are becoming so on intranets as well. Anyone who has something to contribute can post it. Thus one person can communicate to a large audience. With conferencing, you can ask for input, brainstorm, make decisions, and review documents. To create and post messages, you can either use e-mail or tools specifically provided for that purpose. Many proprietary tools are starting to adopt the Internet's NNTP protocol. For now, this may be one of the most widely used intranet tools for collaboration and sharing.

Conferencing allows you to get input from everyone, whether they're in the office or on the road. It can be valuable when you don't really need to get a group together for a meeting, but do need everyone involved. Some tools even allow for anonymous contributions and voting, which can be used for sensitive issues. A disadvantage is that it can take longer to get everyone's input and agreement.

The product development team will use conferencing for the same types of discussions as chat, but which aren't as time-critical and don't need everyone together at the same time. Again, these threads will provide valuable documentation for future use.

Intranet-accessible conferencing and discussion tools include Lotus Notes and Domino, Netscape Navigator, Microsoft Exchange and Internet Explorer Mail and News, Open Text Livelink Intranet, Allaire Forums, Amicus CommunityACT, Attachmate Open Mind, Digital AltaVista Forum, Galacticomm Worldgroup Internet Server, Lundeen Web Crossing, Motet, NetManage IntraNet Forum Server and Chameleon, O'Reilly WebBoard, Proxima Podium, RadNet WebShare, Screen Porch Caucus, Searchlight Spinnaker, Spyglass/OS TECHnologies WebNotes, and WebFlow SamePage.

Knowledge Repositories

With these tools you can store documents and memos, publish reports and presentations, and catalog other relevant files to provide the organization with the wealth of knowledge that has been languishing on individual computers and networks. There's also a way to search that makes it easy to locate what you need. Knowledge repositories are a key piece of the infrastructure that supports collaboration.

The intranet uses internal web publishing to allow you to share information. Proprietary groupware tools use public folders and document management systems, and some have made progress in letting you access their knowledge repositories from browsers.

Our product development team will make extensive use of knowledge repositories. A team home page lists information about the project and its members. Team members will publish and store their team notes, decisions, documents, and drawings, and will provide links to all these resources from the home page. They'll also use the search engine to locate information from other projects that are relevant for their project. As they near completion of the development process, they'll use the home page for publishing and storing product information and marketing materials.

Intranet knowledge-repository tools are quite numerous. Lotus, Netscape, Microsoft, Open Text, Attachmate, Digital, Galacticomm, NetManage, Oracle, RadNet, Thuridion, WebFlow, and many other vendors provide a vast array of these tools. We'll talk in great detail about them in Chapter 6.

Group Writing and Shared Document Editing Tools

Recent research revealed that in most organizations several people work together to create, review, and revise most reports and presentations. In spite of this, we don't really have adequate tools to allow us to do this, so in the past we've just improvised. The need for such tools will generate lots of activity in the area of creating group writing tools. Many of these tools will modify our current workgroup or personal productivity applications to handle multiple simultaneous revisions. With these tools, two or more contributors can work separately on the same document at the same time. These tools will accept all changes except those where two or more contributors alter the same information. In those cases the document owner will determine which changes to save. It looks as though we may finally get shared productivity tools.

These tools can be wonderful for generating products that are greater than the sum of the individual contributions. The only problem is that sometimes it's hard to merge the ideas and various sections into a cohesive whole. As time goes on, we'll learn to do that more easily.

The product development team will be using group writing for jointly developing and revising design documents and specifications. Later in the development cycle, they'll use it for product descriptions, marketing materials, and white papers.

Attachmate Open Mind, Lotus Notes, Microsoft NetMeeting and Office 97, and WebFlow SamePage currently provide, or will soon provide, intranet group writing and shared document editing tools.

Workflow and Applications Development Tools

Workflow tools perform structured activities based on sets of rules that govern the flow of documents or forms. Workflow simply automates business processes. These tools rely on either e-mail or document databases to route the information to where it needs to go.

Workflow consists of forms designers to create forms and workflow engines to process sets of rules and route forms. By enforcing due dates, these tools make sure that a form or activity doesn't stay too long at one person's desk. Workflow is complicated to set up because it's based on complicated business processes and on business rules. However, it also tends to yield more measurable results than other forms of groupware.

With HTML 3.0 the Web can now support forms, which means that we'll see a proliferation of Web-based workflow applications. Over time, we can even expect intranet workflow to become sophisticated enough to integrate with design tools. There are already some tools for product data management, which integrates product information with the engineering design tools that create the products, though we're not yet seeing them for intranets.

The product development team is using workflow for its project and task management, and they'll keep watching for workflow tools that they can integrate with their design tools.

Current and future intranet workflow tools include Microsoft Exchange and Office 97, Open Text Livelink Intranet, Action Technologies Metro, Cap Gemini Innovation WebFlow, JetForm, Oracle InterOffice, Paradigm Software WorkWise-Enterprise, Symantec/Delrina FormFlow, UES Track-It, Ultimus WebFlow, and WebFlow SamePage. In addition, you can use Allaire Cold Fusion, Lotus Notes, RadNet WebShare, or a combination of tools from Netscape to build intranet workflow.

How Do You Use Groupware?

Intranet groupware is still in its infancy. Since many of the tools aren't yet available at the time of this writing, we can't discuss them in depth. Where I can, I'll use cases from actual companies; where the tools aren't generally available, I'll discuss them in general terms. By the time this book is published, some of these tools should be emerging, so the guidance provided here should help you get started.

The most important message I can give you is that the tools and how you use them matter very little in the greater scheme of things. They matter only in cost justification and the details of implementation. What's important, however, is the process you go through to prepare your organization to use these tools. That's the hardest part, whether you're using intranet groupware or any other groupware tools, and will be the subject of later chapters in this book.

Now let's look at some of the ways you can use groupware tools from a business process perspective. Business processes focus on adding value for the ultimate customer. They start with a specific customer need, and all steps work toward fulfilling that customer need. If a process doesn't specifically impact the ultimate customer, we'll define it as being a *support process.* Some examples of support processes are human resources (HR), information systems or information technology (IS or IT), finance, and legal. These processes support the other processes, such as product development and customer support, which *do* produce results for customers. The processes we'll look at include the following:

- Communications processes
- Support processes
- Product development processes
- Operational processes

- Marketing and sales processes
- Customer support processes

Communications Processes

We'll look at the two major communications processes: organizational communications and interpersonal and group communications.

Organizational Communications

Organizational communications consist of official corporate, departmental, or business unit communications. This communication typically goes to all of the organization or to selected parts of it. When organizations use groupware, they generally place this information in the knowledge repository to provide historical context for new employees and reference information for all employees. Here are some examples of the use of groupware in the organizational communications process.

Let's start with the official organization that handles all corporate communications. Communications can use groupware to build the publications they disseminate throughout the organization, such as bulletins, newsletters, and announcements. To involve them, you must first alert them that there is a message to disseminate. You can do this by e-mail or by requesting a meeting with someone who can handle your communication. Since calendaring and scheduling are universal throughout all processes, I generally won't discuss them again.

If there is a meeting, it may be in person or by phone, or it may be by voice or videoconferencing from a conference room or desktop equipment. At the meeting, they can use whiteboarding to outline what to communicate, or perhaps even use group writing or shared editing tools to draft and revise the communications piece. If they need artists or graphics designers for illustrations, they can join the meeting through the same communications mechanisms. With whiteboard tools they can share sketches and artwork. There can be just one meeting, or multiple meetings for especially large or sensitive communications.

Once it's complete, the communication goes to the traditional bulletin boards or is distributed as a memo or newsletter. It may go to the internal web or be distributed to newsgroups, forums, and public folders if the focus is on a specific target audience. Copies go to the document management system, discussion database, or other knowledge repository for future reference. In just this one process alone, most of the groupware tools can enhance the process by making it faster and more efficient. In addition, the information becomes part of the permanent knowledge base of the organization.

Departmental and business unit communications go through the same processes and are eventually placed in the knowledge repository. These days, the fastest-growing organizational knowledge repository is the internal web. Departments and business units use the internal web to publish their mission, responsibilities, organization charts, and newsletters. They may also provide links to the home pages of their subdivisions and projects, and perhaps even provide updates on the status of those projects. All of these processes vastly increase the corporate knowledge repository.

Besides the usual newsletters, bulletins, and announcements, most organizations have a wealth of other information that should be available in these knowledge repositories. This includes executive speeches, presentations from company and industry forums, company historical information, biographies of executives, press releases, and news clippings about the company and its competitors. For example, in *How Sun saves money, improves service using Internet technologies* (http://www.Sun.com:80/960101/ feature1/index.html/), Sun Microsystems says that it uses its intranet to capture and present this kind of information to its employees. Sun has a quarterly Leadership Conference in which employees see a variety of new technologies. Sun posts pictures and transcripts of the conference on its internal web for all employees to see.

This kind of information tells employees where the company has come from and where it's heading. It helps put business issues and concerns in context. Today, these items aren't just limited to text. They can include audio and video recordings of presentations and events.

Interpersonal and Group Communications

Interpersonal and group communications tools are used by individuals or workgroups to share information and ask questions. E-mail is currently the most widely used communication tool, and it's also the basis for communicating on newsgroups and forums. In addition to e-mail, the following are intranet groupware tools.

Newsgroups   Access to newsgroups seems to be a common feature at companies that have implemented intranets. The external Internet newsgroups provide ways for employees to collaborate beyond your organization. For instance, in IT groups, it's quite common for those working with new technologies to request or share information with others working with those same technologies. This kind of collaboration has definite benefits for companies.

In addition to external newsgroups, many organizations have created their own internal newsgroups as well. Once you have access to external newsgroups, it's an easy step to implement internal ones. Internal newsgroups generally focus on the Internet, technology, HR, sales and marketing, R&D, and engineering product development topics. Some companies have secure newsgroups, with highly restricted access, for confidential or classified projects. You might see more of this related to government and defense projects.

Since internal newsgroups are most active in proprietary areas, and companies are reluctant to share that kind of information, I can't show you anything proprietary. TI was able to share some screen shots of one of its internal Internet-focused newsgroups. Figure 5.1 shows threads posted to the *ti.internet.general* newsgroup, and Figure 5.2 shows a message posted to that newsgroup. Also, notice the help desk newsgroup, *ti.helpdesk.general.* As you can see, internal newsgroups look just like Usenet newsgroups except for their names.

Chat   Chats are like a scheduled conference call where people get together to converse at a specific time about a specific topic. You *call in* from your computer and use your keyboard to converse with others. Chats are somewhat like newsgroups, except

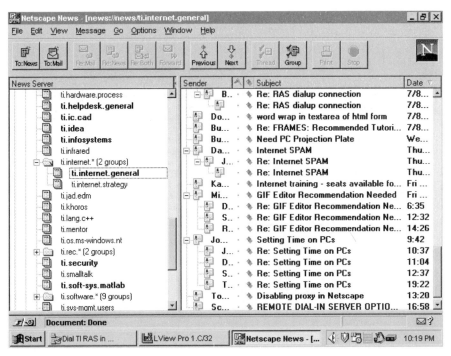

Figure 5.1 Texas Instruments internal newsgroup threads. (Used with permission Texas Instruments Incorporated, Copyright 1996.)

that the conversations take place in real time rather than being delayed. I suspect that chat is more widespread in technical parts of a company than in nontechnical areas. For instance, engineers and designers spread around the world could have real-time discussions about an emerging technology and its implications for a company's product development processes.

Chat isn't very common inside companies right now, but since it's a very useful tool for collaborating, its use may grow over time. The advantage is that once the network is in place, the cost of communication is negligible, unlike the cost of conference calls.

EDS uses chat as part of its Global Communicators Network, as pictured in Figure 5.3. Employees use this network to share information and coordinate activities.

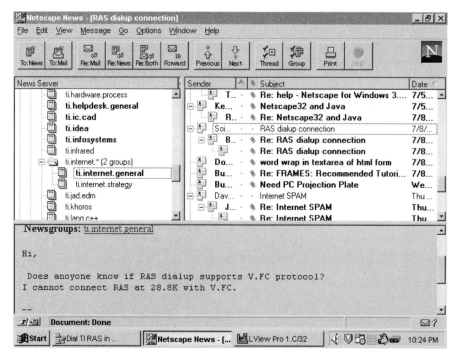

Figure 5.2 Texas Instruments internal newsgroup message. (Used with permission Texas Instruments Incorporated, Copyright 1996.)

Videoconferencing Videoconferencing is just emerging as an intranet groupware technology. Because of its high-bandwidth requirements, it's most suitable for corporate intranets. Because it is so advantageous for meetings and collaborations, it's inevitable that videoconferencing will be a widely used tool in corporations. As it becomes more valuable, the need for more bandwidth will become a nonissue, and videoconferencing may replace chat on corporate intranets.

Support Processes

Support processes are those processes that don't contribute directly to fulfilling a customer need. We'll discuss four support processes:

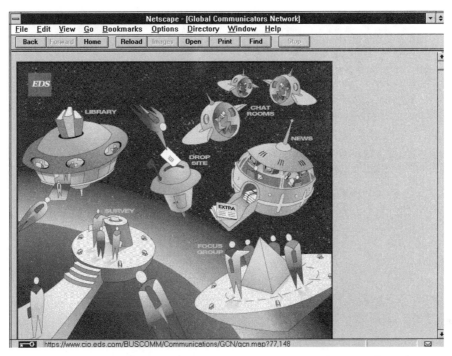

Figure 5.3   EDS Global Communicators Network. (Used with permission EDS, Copyright 1996.)

1. Human resources processes
2. Accounting and financial processes
3. Information systems, or technology provisioning and support processes
4. Process management processes

Human Resources Processes

One use of knowledge repositories related to HR processes would be the universal intranet application: the phone directory and organization chart. Figure 5.4 shows the EDS organization chart application, which includes a search for names, e-mail addresses, work locations, phone numbers, and organization charts. EDS is in the process of linking its messaging systems and this organization chart to an X.500 directory fed by the HR systems. This will

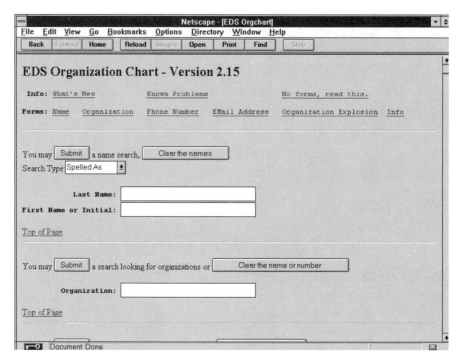

Figure 5.4 EDS Organization Chart. (Used with permission EDS, Copyright 1996.)

allow users on the intranet to locate and communicate with specific groups. This should enhance collaboration by making it easier to find specific groups or categories that you need.

Organization charts can also show reporting relationships or pictures. There might even be links to the individual's home page or to the projects on which that individual works. When a person begins work with a new group of people, he or she can easily go to the organization charts and the personal home pages and projects for more information. Knowing others' interests makes it easier to establish common interests upon which to build working relationships. When people build their own personal home pages, they learn skills that will make it easier for them to publish and share information with others in the future.

Another HR intranet groupware application could be to establish newsgroups or forums for discussing items of common interest, such as benefit plan options. You could even use them as focus groups to gain input for benefit plan changes.

Of course, HR has a wealth of possible workflow applications. For example, you can put forms for updating benefits plans on the intranet so that employees could simply fill them out and forward them to Benefits. These forms can even update benefits databases automatically. You can use the intranet as the repository for all benefits information and to provide employees with access to up-to-date status information. This can dramatically streamline the HR workflow and business processes and free HR staffers from answering routine questions and handling forms. They can then work on things that are far more important.

Intranet groupware tools can facilitate extending HR processes beyond the organization. For instance, you can use Internet video-conferencing in the recruiting process. Where universities have desktop videoconferencing software, you can do screening inter-views across the Internet, or potential recruits can come into company offices for screening interviews at other company locations.

Though not strictly a groupware use, you can use this videocon-ferencing tool for training sessions by facilitating distance learn-ing sessions over the intranet. When trainees are going through a continual training program that extends over a series of weeks, you can create a collaborative environment for each class by creat-ing its own newsgroup. Universities do this extensively. Trainees can use the newsgroup to work on cooperative projects and assignments, and can use voice conferencing and chat as auxiliary techniques to enhance the learning experience. The most impor-tant aspect of this is that you totally immerse your trainees in the new technology and in collaborating, which they can use to expand collaboration to others with whom they work after they complete their training.

Accounting and Financial Processes

Accounting processes are big users of workflow to transmit forms from all areas of the organization. For example, you can put expense reports and travel advances on the intranet. They can first be routed to appropriate managers for approval and then routed to accounting for processing. With links to transaction-based systems, you can process these forms automatically if you desire. You can set up other transactions that need to be processed by accounting as forms and workflow applications. Sun Microsystems discusses their Asset Managers Workbench in *How Sun saves money, improves service using Internet technologies* (http://www.Sun.com:80/960101/feature1/index.html). Sun created forms that managers use to query the corporate fixed-asset accounting system to find out what fixed assets they have. To request that an asset be transferred requires only that the manager fill out and submit an update form.

As a knowledge repository, intranets enhance the accounting and financial processes by providing access to vast stores of financial reports. Secured access can provide executives and others access to confidential financial information.

Information Systems, or Technology Provisioning and Support Processes

Since many IT groups must do more things with fewer resources, help desks and technical support groups can use all the help they can get. The help desk is an area that uses many of the intranet groupware and workflow solutions. These tools allow internal customers to provide some of their own solutions.

Before users open trouble tickets, they can have lots of resources at their disposal to try to solve problems themselves. The first step can be a Frequently Asked Questions (FAQ) list on the intranet to provide a list of things to check before calling for help. If that doesn't resolve the problem, they can access internal newsgroups to see if there's already a solution. Some products let you perform searches, and others will soon provide that capability, so you can find answers easily. Some tools search across all resources simultaneously, so with one search a user knows if the answer exists. If not, a quick post to a newsgroup may provide the answer. Finally, the user can always submit a trouble ticket form and follow its status using a workflow application. Users can also submit forms to request equipment moves and to get software installed.

One day, data conferencing will let help desks follow what's happening on a user's machine and solve the problem. We may see the help desk use intranet videoconferencing as bandwidth becomes more plentiful.

The IT organization at EDS uses Internet Relay Chat for the CIO's weekly chat with the troops, his organization of hundreds of people. The chats started in mid-1995 and will continue because they're so successful. Employees submit questions and topic suggestions in advance. Each week's chat session focuses on a specific topic. They can discuss anything from technical topics to organizational and employee-related topics. Tim Lambert, Communications Account Manager at EDS, talked about the pros and cons of these sessions. The advantages are that this works well for large and/or dispersed audiences and you have a written transcript of the entire conversation which can be valuable for participants and others. The disadvantage is that the flow of conversation can be somewhat fragmented when multiple users are asking, and responding to, questions simultaneously. If someone types a long comment, he or she may find that the discussion has moved on.

In the future, Internet phone and videoconferencing may replace chat sessions, but with chat you can have more people involved and you have a transcript. Currently, it wouldn't take too many people on a videoconference to bring the intranet to its knees.

Many IT groups are providing their organizations with access to document management systems and knowledge repositories. For example, TI is creating an enterprise-wide repository based on bringing together Saros Mezzanine document repositories, internal web servers, and Lotus Notes servers. With a browser, users will search and retrieve information from any of those servers. EDS is turning its intranet into a huge document repository for capturing information about its business processes. By tying their forms to the intranet, they're making it possible to conduct workflow directly from the intranet. These document repositories will hold all kinds of IT information, such as white papers, standards, product evaluations, documentation, and even utilities and software code. They can provide information about projects, such as team members, schedules, status, and accomplishments.

A major breakthrough for intranets is using browsers as front ends to access existing transaction systems and workflow. Applications are the next major intranet frontier, and we'll see much more of this as companies use their intranets to add value for their organizations and customers. EDS has created web front ends for some of its applications and databases, such as the employee locator, job postings, purchasing applications, and global customer contracts database.

Some companies are tying their electronic forms into their intranets. For example, EDS plans to have all of its businesses processes on its internal web, and to tie its electronic forms to those business processes. EDS uses the Microsoft Exchange Forms Designer to create its forms. The company then ties those forms to the intranet and will use the Exchange messaging infrastructure to route the forms through the organization. EDS has some electronic forms in other formats that it's in the process of converting to the Exchange format. Figure 5.5 shows an example of one of many forms EDS is converting to intranet-based workflow. This set of forms, which allows employees to arrange for attending technical training classes, will be workflow-enabled on its intranet.

Keep in mind that external Usenet newsgroups can expand collaboration beyond your organization. For instance, when a new technology comes out, Internet newsgroups can provide access to some great resources, such as gurus in the new technology and, often, even the vendor's people. Newsgroups can also provide IT with internal discussion forums for groups working on a specific technology or application, especially for geographically dispersed groups. Project team newsgroups can include project objectives, status, problems, accomplishments, decisions, and notes from meetings.

Our Internet team at JCPenney had a newsgroup for continuing the communication and camaraderie the team built during its meetings. The newsgroup let us continue our work between meetings. For those who couldn't attend a meeting, a quick check of the newsgroup brought them up-to-date. The newsgroup had the team's vision, mission, and objectives, the team roster and contact information, lists of subteams and their members, minutes from the meetings, an agenda for the coming meeting, and decisions the team had made. In addition, the subteams also posted their minutes and decisions. Team members posted bios, tips for working

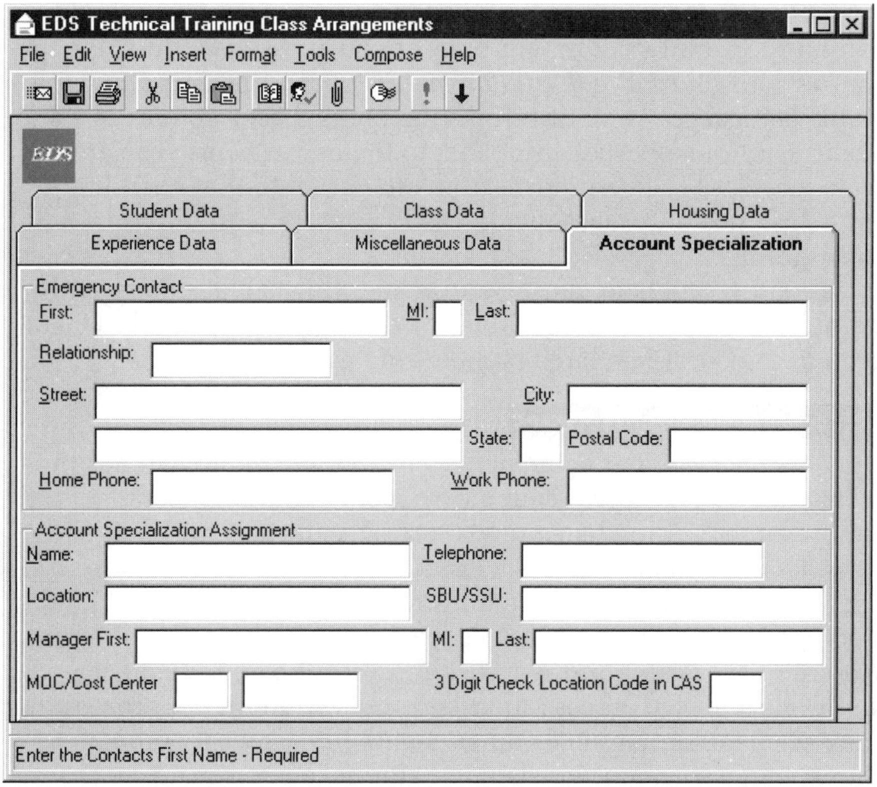

Figure 5.5 EDS Technical Training Class Arrangements form. (Used with permission EDS, Copyright 1996.)

on Web pages, interesting new sites, and neat new tools. The newsgroup also contained a vast array of tips, questions and answers, technical updates, and information gleaned from Internet conferences. Sometimes team members posted links to their work and asked for comments and suggestions. This newsgroup supported a large community of collaborators. To capture all this wealth of information and make it available for others, each subteam created internal web pages from its newsgroup information. That way, it was available for anyone interested in web publishing, and the team roster provided a list of experts who could provide additional help.

EDS provides access to both internal and external newsgroups. Though most internal newsgroups are business-specific, there's a newsgroup called *Break Room* where you can find just about anything being discussed. EDS links the Lotus discussion forums and their mainframe-based GroupTalk to the newsgroups. They replicate messages back and forth from one forum to the other. Lotus users can post messages just as easily as users with browsers and newsgroups.

Workflow and calendaring and scheduling can also help with applications development project management, especially where you must coordinate large numbers of developers.

Process Management Processes

Process management is the management of an organization's processes and can involve reengineering or business process improvement. Knowledge repositories can be an important part of process management and can hold information about best practices, benchmarks, and tools for improving processes. This kind of tool can be instrumental in helping organizations define their processes so they can build workflow applications into them.

EDS is a highly process-focused company and has a process management tool on its intranet. Figure 5.6 shows its Process Sourcerer, which assists users in defining, customizing, and improving their business processes.

Product Development Processes

Product development processes are core business processes that exist to fulfill customer requirements. This is an area that provides significant competitive advantage, so I'm unable to provide specifics from companies who use intranet groupware and workflow in these processes. However, we can talk about how to use intranet groupware in these processes.

Research and Development

R&D can share information with the rest of the organization by publishing it on the internal web, posting it in newsgroups, or placing it in the document or discussion databases. This can

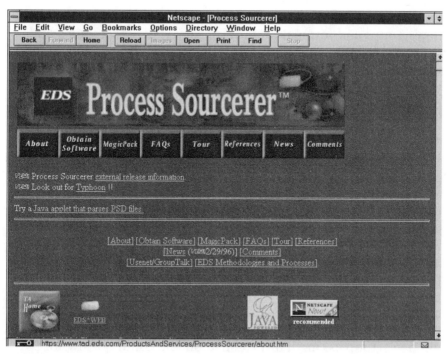

Figure 5.6   EDS Process Sourcerer. (Used with permission EDS, Copyright 1996.)

include market and product research, customer research, and other information. For example, EDS has acquired the right to place the U.S. Patent Information Services database on its intranet to provide full-text patentability and infringement searches. These kinds of knowledge repositories can also provide basic research information to users in various parts of the product development process.

Some organizations have large geographically dispersed research staffs that use newsgroups and forums to discuss projects and technologies. By publishing their findings, they can prevent others from the proverbial reinventing of the wheel. Collaboration is part of the discipline of scientists. They're very comfortable collaborating and keeping fellow researchers informed. In fact, the Web grew out of the desire by university researchers to share their work with colleagues around the world. Groupware tools, such as newsgroups and forums, provide an easy way for scientists and researchers to do what they naturally do so well. As an aside, when you're looking for groups that collaborate easily, consider your scientific community as a good candidate for a groupware pilot site.

If R&D has to prepare documentation for regulatory agencies, group writing and shared editing tools can allow them to work together to prepare this documentation more rapidly.

Design Engineering

Engineers may not be as open to groupware and collaboration as scientists, but they do tend to be comfortable with technology and tools, and may be among the first to adopt a new technology. TI shared an interesting story with me that may have occurred on a product development project. An engineer at TI needed to use a piece of test equipment for two weeks, but found that he couldn't rent it. It appeared that his project would have to spend $100,000 to buy the equipment. The engineer posted a message on an Internet newsgroup asking if anyone had one he could borrow for two weeks. A university researcher had one sitting unused in his lab and offered to lend it. The engineer borrowed the equipment, ran the tests, and saved TI $100,000. What does this have to do with an intranet? In a company as large as TI, with groups spread out all over the world, it could just as easily happen inside the company. With internal newsgroups, someone needing a specialized piece of equipment could see if anyone else had one to lend. In a vast, worldwide company, intranet newsgroups provide a way to locate resources you need for a specific project, whether that's equipment, software, people, or expertise. This is just another dimension of collaboration.

There are other ways to use groupware in the engineering part of the product development process. Internal newsgroups and forums provide engineers with access to expertise so they can discuss ideas and ask questions related to a specific technology. Through these newsgroups, they can facilitate brainstorming about features for new products and get valuable feedback on designs and plans. They can also use them to discuss certain topics with other areas of the business, such as discussing customer needs and feedback, finding out what the competition is doing, and learning about the kinds of problems incurred by field repair personnel. They can also share information about their projects, such as team members, plans, schedules, and progress, with other parts of the business. This information forms a knowledge base from which others can learn.

Through various knowledge repositories, they can have access to shared reference information and engineering design guides. They can capture expertise gained through the product development process and record information about how they solved various problems. They can publish product specifications, drawings, and computer-aided design models. They can even expand the collaboration beyond the organization to supplier partners by giving them selective access to drawings and designs in the knowledge repository. This cooperation and collaboration can dramatically reduce total product development time.

The new whiteboard tools allow you to share graphics files over the intranet and Internet so you can share designs and drawings. We may soon be able to annotate and change drawing files on the whiteboard and save those changes in the file.

You can also use groupware tools to collaborate with your customers in developing new or customized products. You can use newsgroups, Internet phone, or videoconferencing for focus groups, or you can provide individual customers with access to you intranet.

You can use workflow and calendaring and scheduling tools for managing product development projects. This can span organizations as well, using the Internet for sharing these tools between you and a business partner for joint development.

Operational Processes

Operational processes are core processes that produce results for customers. They include purchasing, electronic data interchange, manufacturing, and professional services development.

Purchasing

Several times I've mentioned collaborating with suppliers. Business partnerships are popping up all over, which seems to be an increasing trend for companies to gain the speed to market and cost reductions that make them more competitive. Therefore, using collaborative tools with those business partners is a necessary step to improve coordination with them. This will become increasingly important.

One common area of partnership is in the design and development of new products, which I discussed in the preceding section on engineering. Purchasing often coordinates this, so you have several areas of the organization collaborating with your business partners, which requires a lot of coordination. Once you have calendaring and scheduling tools that work across the Internet, you'll be able to use your intranet groupware to schedule meetings with people outside your organization.

Some of the obvious tools for meetings with suppliers are Internet phone, videoconferencing, and whiteboarding. These meetings may start with an initial discussion of specifications and defining who will do what, for which you can use whiteboarding to take notes and work out details. As you go through design and prototyping, whiteboarding can help you share design drawings and markup changes. When the product is complete, videoconferencing lets both parties see and discuss the product and make small changes if necessary.

Intranet-based purchasing workflow applications seem to have become the universal intranet workflow applications, similar to phone directories for internal web publishing. According to Michael Graves, CIO at SGI, his company has a purchase requisition and approval workflow application on its intranet. EDS is also working on intranet-based purchasing workflow by putting an intranet front end on its purchasing application. This kind of front end allows users to find information about what to order and then to place the order. Even vendors such as Dun and Bradstreet Software are developing these kinds of applications to run on intranets.

Another purchasing-related form of collaboration is to let suppliers take responsibility for maintaining the information about their products on your purchasing database. You can let them have intranet access to specific parts of databases and to use forms to change and add information related to their supplier number. You might even provide them with messaging-based workflow forms that send e-mail messages to input and update your databases. There are lots of different ways you can do this, which depend on how comfortable you feel having suppliers updating your databases. Workflow-based reports could alert purchasing employees to updated information that suppliers submit.

Electronic Data Interchange (EDI)

EDI is another example of workflow, as information moves in a standardized form from the computer system at one business to the computer system at another. These forms then update application systems. Many companies are experimenting with intranet-based EDI or are planning to soon.

Manufacturing

In manufacturing, you can use intranet newsgroups in the same ways as in the product development process. You can discuss schedules, procedures, and quality issues. You can share drawings and information about production processes. This is particularly valuable in companies where you make the same or similar parts in many different locations in different time zones and with different languages. Newsgroups can help solve production problems and allow for collaboration so that one location can help another. These are ways to help you get your products to market faster.

Professional Services Development

Consulting companies use knowledge repositories as part of their operational processes. They capture expertise and make it available to all consultants. For example, Booz Allen uses Knowledge On Line, its intranet, to record its expertise through reports, proposals, best practices, and collaboration conferences. If a consultant needs to collaborate with other consultants, the company's intranet makes it easy to find the appropriate people.

Marketing and Sales Processes

The marketing and sales processes benefit customers and are therefore core business processes. This is generally very sensitive information, so I don't have specifics to share with you in this area.

Marketing

Marketing also uses knowledge repositories to share information with others, and internal web publishing seems to be catching fire as a repository for this kind of information. Some of the things typically published on the internal web include product strategies, sales and marketing strategies, market research, product press releases, and product reviews. In addition, you can find catalogs, brochures, price lists, promotional pricing and schedules, technical specifications, presentation materials, advertisements, and trade show information. You may sometimes find newsletters, testimonials, question-and-answer sheets, proposal templates, and order forms.

Sales

At EDS, users with a browser can access the Global Customer Contracts database, which is a knowledge repository with information about its huge customer base. It contains information about what EDS provides for each customer and identifies the internal contact for that customer. In the future, systems such as this will have electronic forms built in so you can initiate specific actions based on the information you locate.

EDS has an application, shown in Figure 5.7, called infoAlert. It's part of the EDS Global Sales and Marketing Toolkit. As of this writing, the application uses proprietary software, but users will soon be able to access it from a browser. Users who subscribe receive customized news delivered from wire services, newspapers, industry publications, and various international sources. This information provides insight into EDS customers' businesses to make it easier to collaborate with them.

In the future, your salespeople will use more and more collaborative tools as an integral part of the sales process. When they

Figure 5.7   EDS infoAlert. (Used with permission EDS, Copyright 1996.)

work with customers, salespeople will connect their laptop computers into your intranet so together they can tailor your products to meet that customer's needs.

Knowledge repositories can provide access to sales information, such as sales forecasts and plans, promotion calendars, and customer information. The sales process can also utilize newsgroups for discussions about various accounts, competitors, and sales techniques. Salespeople can collaborate with customers and gather information and feedback through customer support newsgroups. They can also use newsgroups to funnel customer needs and feedback to product developers who can do something about them. Like SGI, you can sponsor reseller and distributor newsgroups. You can provide them with sales and marketing information, product availability, and workflow applications.

In addition, when customers have an urgent need and salespeople just can't get there fast enough, you can use Internet videoconferencing to be more face-to-face than you can with a telephone call. If you add data conferencing, you can make it easier to solve customer problems promptly.

Customer Support Processes

Finally, we get to the customer support processes, which are probably the most critical processes in your business. If you don't keep your customers happy, you won't be in business for very long.

Part of customer support is providing ways for customers to solve their problems with your products and for you to get feedback about your products and the problems customers experience. Collaborating with customers through newsgroups is becoming a standard way of doing this in many industries. You can have sales and product development personnel monitor these groups and offer assistance to customers. You can also use e-mail *mailto* addresses on your external Web site and in your ads so customers who don't have Internet newsgroups can access your company.

You might put survey forms on your external Web site that feed directly into your knowledge base. You can feed the daily output from these forms into intranet newsgroups for all to access. Using collaborative tools to track what's happening among your customers and turn that into product improvements is a great way to use these tools. You might also consider letting your customers have access to your technical support databases to help them solve their problems. You might capture customer testimonials and share them with everyone, and maybe even put them on your external Web site, with permission of course. If possible, you can make customer support more personalized by taking the time to follow up with every customer who posts something on the newsgroup. Personal customer service is what it's all about today.

chapter six

Intranet Groupware and Workflow Products

Introduction

Now it's time to talk about intranet groupware tools. When I started this book, I intended to compare and contrast proprietary groupware with intranet-based groupware. It's safe to say that in the meantime, the Web has turned the groupware market upside down. Now, almost every major groupware vendor has gotten on the Web bandwagon. They've announced that they've Web-enabled their products, or soon will, so the distinction is going away. Therefore, the purpose of this chapter is to give you a view of various intranet groupware options. I'll talk about what each product does and how it fits with the intranet. Many of these products aren't even shipping yet—they're still only a gleam in a CEO's eye. Therefore, it won't be possible to talk much about the advantages and disadvantages except in reference to company-supplied information.

Some tools we'll talk about aren't actually collaborative tools, but they do enable some aspects of people working together. In those cases, we'll talk about where they fit in and what they bring to collaboration. Since browsers are at the center of intranet groupware, I'll discuss some browsers and talk about features that relate to collaboration or workflow. Where servers provide necessary functionality, I'll talk about them as well. We'll look at products in a somewhat chronological order, as follows:

1. *IBM/Lotus.*   We'll start with Lotus Notes because it was one of the earliest groupware tools and was primarily responsible for putting groupware on the map. It seems to be the standard by which we judge all other groupware. Notes has quickly moved to incorporate the Web and intranets, and companies now use it for Web publishing.

2. *Netscape/Collabra.*   We'll look next at the Netscape and Collabra marriage, which started much of the debate about proprietary groupware versus intranet groupware. You frequently hear the forthcoming combined Netscape/Collabra product described as a *Notes killer.*

3. *Microsoft.*   Microsoft has recently entered the fray, so we'll look at the products it's bringing out for the groupware market.

4. *Novell.*   Novell has been in the proprietary groupware market for a while and is moving its product to take better advantage of the Web.

5. *Open Text.*   Then we'll look at the Open Text Livelink Intranet product, which Open Text bills as the first integrated groupware application suite for intranets.

6. From there, we'll look at other companies (in alphabetical order) and products that address the intranet groupware market. Many of these companies are small start-ups founded strictly to create Web-based groupware products.

This chapter will take a broad-brush look at intranet groupware tools. As much as I would like this to be a totally all-inclusive look at intranet collaboration tools, any attempt to do so would be foolish and almost impossible. The intranet groupware market is heating up with new announcements daily. It's very likely that there will be many new products announced just after I finish writing this book but before it reaches the stores. That's just the nature of this rapidly evolving intranet groupware market. If I've missed some products, I'm truly sorry.

IBM/Lotus

Lotus Notes is the most widely known of all groupware products and seems to be the defining product for the groupware category. Lotus Notes provides, or soon will provide, calendaring and scheduling, e-mail, conferencing, knowledge repositories, group writing and editing, and workflow, with both electronic forms and applications development.

IBM purchased Lotus in June of 1995. By the time this book reaches the stores, you'll be able to get Release 4.5, so that's where I'll begin my discussion of specific pieces of the Notes line. You can find information about the Lotus products on the Web at http://www.lotus.com.

Notes Release 4.5

Lotus Notes first came out in late 1989. Some people consider it a 1980s technology, but it was certainly ahead of its time and has stayed on a steady course of improvement. When most people think of groupware, they think of Lotus Notes. Now, Notes is moving onto the Internet and intranet by adopting Internet standards, but it's still a proprietary technology.

Notes runs on most platforms and provides a variety of tools. Since Notes is groupware, let's look at what it provides users and teams, especially as it interfaces to the intranet.

- *Notes databases* store documents and information.
- *Simple word processor* allows group editing of database documents.
- *Discussion forums* take place through Notes documents.
- *Document libraries* for Microsoft Office and Lotus SmartSuite let users create and share spreadsheets or presentations.
- *Notes e-mail* consists of mailed documents. The in box is simply another Notes database. Notes uses the Lotus Vendor Independent Mail (VIM) protocol, supports the

Microsoft Messaging Application Programming Interface (MAPI) protocol, and supports the Internet's Simple Mail Transfer Protocol (SMTP) and Post Office Protocol 3 (POP3) e-mail protocols. Notes users can use any POP3 mail client, such as Netscape Navigator, Microsoft Windows 95 Inbox, or Qualcomm's Eudora, to get their Notes e-mail.

- *Notes workspace* organizes Notes databases for you.
- *Integrated group calendaring and scheduling*
- *InterNotes Web Navigator browser* provides access to the Web from within Notes and includes the following:

    - Web Tours, which allows you to share a list of Web sites you visited with others for collaborative Web surfing
    - Site Minder, which notifies users of changes to specified Web pages
    - WebAhead, which brings Web pages into the background

- *InterNotes News 2.0* provides Notes users with access to both Internet newsgroups and internal newsgroups.
- *Remote access and replication* lets your computer call up Notes servers and download, or replicate, databases. With Server Passthru, you can access multiple servers in multiple locations by calling a single server.
- *Application development tools,* such as the following, let users create custom workflow applications.

    - Agent builders let users create agents to automate tasks.
    - Notes script language provides built-in functions like those in Lotus 1-2-3 spreadsheets and menu commands.
    - LotusScript is like Basic programming.
    - NotesFlow provides workflow tools.

- ◆ Java applets and Internet plug-ins, such as Macro-media's Shockwave.
- ◆ Lotus' Notes F/X 2.0 and Microsoft's OLE 2.0 for data transfer.
- ◆ Notes Reusable Subforms are forms you use alone or combined. They can contain rules for routing workflow or agents for automating tasks. By embedding LotusScripts or fields in them, they can perform operations.

◆ *Tools to connect to relational databases and legacy transaction systems* through the IBM MQSeries Link, Notes ODBC Driver, LotusScript:Data Object, and Lotus NotesPump.

InterNotes Web Publisher 4.0

Lotus jumped on the Web bandwagon in March of 1996 when it announced InterNotes Web Publisher 4.0. It turns Notes into an intranet tool. It lets you use Notes to create and manage your Web site and your intranet. You can translate any Notes document or form into HTML pages for use on the Web. You can use all Notes features for creating and managing Web content. The Notes full-text search engine lets you search for documents. Anyone with a Web browser can use any Notes workflow application by inputting information into forms. InterNotes Web Publisher then passes that information to a Notes database for use in the business process.

Domino

Lotus Release 4.5 will include the Domino server technology, which includes both an integrated full-fledged Web server and a Notes server. Many Notes customers use Domino for publishing their Web content. Domino features include the following:

- ◆ Content store for storing and managing Web content
- ◆ Threaded discussion
- ◆ Directory services to make it easy to manage and locate users and resources

- Replication and conflict resolution, even down to the field level
- E-mail and messaging support for POP3, MAPI, and eventually IMAP4
- Security through Secure Sockets Layer (SSL) for data encryption and server authentication
- Graphical form design tool
- Integrated messaging for applications and workflow

InterNotes Web Publisher converts Notes documents in batch to HTML and stores them as HTML for static document publishing, whereas Domino converts them to HTML on the fly and stores them as Notes documents for publishing dynamic data.

Lotus is bringing out three interactive Notes applications using Domino, called Net.App solutions. They serve as templates for custom applications:

1. Net.Prescence helps automate the creation of an intranet or an Internet presence.
2. Net.Marketing supports Web marketing and sales.
3. Net.Service supports customer service through knowledge bases and problem reporting.

The newly announced Domino II server is a Web server based entirely on Internet-only standards, such as TCP/IP, HTTP, SMTP, POP3, IMAP4, SSL, and Lightweight Directory Access Protocol (LDAP) for directories. It includes a Notes object store for storing and retrieving objects. Lotus will add specialized servers for mail and directory services, an Interactive Application Designer package for building mission-critical applications, and the Mobile Web Information Manager, a Web client for mobile users that supports messaging and collaboration.

Other Lotus

There are also many third-party vendors who supply software to extend Notes groupware capabilities. For example, Intel's

ProShare provides videoconferencing and data conferencing for Notes, and Action Technologies workflow tools generate code to build heavy-duty workflow applications in Notes.

Lotus Institute created Team Room, a software package to help address organizational issues. This product requires a facilitator to help a team set rules, create norms of behavior, and set up the package to help meet the team's goals. Lotus has also announced a series of training programs focused on the organizational impact of implementing Notes.

Other IBM: Internet Connection for FlowMark

IBM's Internet Connection for FlowMark links the FlowMark workflow product to the Web. It's components include the following:

- *WWW/FlowMark Process Initiation,* which allows a user to fill out a standard HTML form and submit it to the server for processing through FlowMark
- *WWW/FlowMark Worklist Integration,* which lets a workflow user see his or her worklist in a Web browser

You can get more information at http://www.software.ibm.com/ad/flowmark/exmn0b21.htm.

Netscape/Collabra

Through various products, Netscape provides voice conferencing, whiteboards, chat, e-mail, conferencing, knowledge repositories, and tools for building workflow applications.

In the fall of 1995, Netscape bought Collabra, one of the leaders in discussion tools. The upcoming Galileo release of Netscape Navigator will contain the Collabra Share product. Since Netscape Navigator 3.0 should be released by the time this book reaches the stores, that's where we'll begin our exploration of Netscape's groupware features. We'll discuss Netscape's products by the browser or server version to which they relate. You can find more information about Netscape products on their Web site at http://www.netscape.com/.

Netscape Navigator 3.0

Netscape Navigator 3.0 supports a wide variety of platforms, including Wintel, UNIX, and Apple, and comes in 11 languages. Its groupware functionality includes the following:

◆ *Newsgroups.*   Navigator has built-in support for newsgroups. By using the browser in conjunction with an NNTP server, you can access both the external Usenet newsgroups and your own internal ones. In addition, you can view and post multimedia messages. You saw examples of TI internal newsgroups in Netscape Navigator in Figures 5.1 and 5.2.

◆ *Mail.*   Navigator also has mail capabilities built into the browser. It supports the SMTP and POP3 protocols as well as MIME. Embedded URL hyperlinks let you access Web sites from your e-mail. Netscape Navigator's mail looks very similar to its newsgroups.

◆ *LiveMedia.*   With LiveAudio and LiveVideo, you can hear audio and view video directly from Web pages without launching a viewer. This provides an excellent medium for sharing presentations. With Live3D, users can travel through interactive 3D worlds, which enables engineers, architects, and product designers to navigate together through complex objects and data.

◆ *Plug-ins.*   Plug-ins are fairly recent additions to Navigator's capabilities, and are also being supported by other browsers such as Microsoft's Internet Explorer. Plug-ins allow you to do specialized and niche applications that aren't native to the browser. They're available from a wide array of vendors, and include capabilities such as collaboration and viewing of documents and multimedia.

For now, we still have to locate, download, and configure plug-ins. Netscape is working on automatically downloading and configuring plug-ins, which may be available by the time you're reading this book and will open up huge possibilities of things you can do on your intranet with minimal effort. Currently, the most popular plug-ins are the Adobe Acrobat Reader and Macromedia Shockwave. Here are just a few of the currently available groupware-related plug-ins.

- AboutPeople and AboutTime, from Now Software: Address book and calendar plug-ins. They integrate seamlessly with Now Up-to-Date Web Publisher, which we'll talk about later in this chapter.
- Acrobat Reader 3.0 beta, from Adobe: For viewing and printing Portable Document Format (PDF) files.
- Carbon Copy/Net, from Microcom: Lets you remotely control another PC over the Internet or intranet so you can remotely run applications and view or edit documents.
- Concerto, from Alpha Software: Allows data entry to forms with all data validation at the browser. This could be used for workflow.
- Ichat, from Ichat: Provides chat capability within Navigator. With Ichat's Web-tours, you can lead colleagues on a tour of the internal or external Web.
- Look@Me, from Farallon: Lets you look at another user's screen and watch what's happening on it. It lets you present information or training, review or change documents, and provide support.
- OpenScape, from Onewave: Lets you build interactive applications through a drag-and-drop environment and Visual Basic scripting.
- Quick View Plus, from Inso: Lets you view, copy, and print word processing documents, spreadsheets, databases, graphics, and presentation files from more than 200 file formats.
- Shockwave, from Macromedia: For interactive multimedia presentations.

Netscape has purchased Paper Software, the maker of the WebFX VRML plug-in, and will probably incorporate it and the Moving Worlds VRML standard into their products. The Moving Worlds standard adds animation and user interactions to Web experiences. From a business-user perspective, one day we may use VRML to examine huge quantities of data to determine relationships. This may have some applications in workflow or in customer analysis.

◆ *LiveConnect.* With LiveConnect, you can connect Java applications, JavaScript, and plug-ins so they interact together seamlessly.

CoolTalk

CoolTalk has been added to Navigator 3.0 to provide Internet phone, shared whiteboard, and chat. According to Eric Hahn, Senior Vice President of Enterprise Technology at Netscape, "CoolTalk is built on the Realtime Transport Protocol (RTP) rather than being released as a proprietary offering because you'd like to be able to call somebody else that doesn't have that product. This is a case of where Netscape's commitment to the standards process may actually hurt our ability to deliver products."

CoolTalk features include the following:

◆ *Internet phone.* You can talk with others over the Internet or intranet as though you were talking on the telephone. With dedicated Internet access, the call is practically free. CoolTalk includes a speed dialer, caller ID, call screening, mute, answering machine, and an integrated phone book.

◆ *Shared whiteboard.* The shared whiteboard allows for collaboration during phone calls. It lets you and the person you're calling view the same graphic image and mark it up in real time with a range of painting, drawing, and highlighting tools. You can print, save, or import graphics files in TIFF, GIF, JPEG, BMP, and other standard graphics formats. There's no mention yet of using CoolTalk for sharing applications such as word processing and spreadsheets.

◆ *Chat tool.* The chat tool lets you send and receive typed messages or text files.

Navigator Gold

Navigator Gold is a tool that lets users create their own documents for the intranet so they can share them with others. It combines the Netscape Navigator browser with a publishing tool to make it easy for anyone to create and publish content, regardless of whether they know HTML.

Using a browser window, you create HTML files in a what-you-see-is-what-you-get (WYSIWYG) environment that includes drag-and-drop capabilities. With proper security, you can even click a single button to publish pages directly to the Web. Anyone who can use a word processor can use this tool. It's my ten-year-old son's favorite Web publishing software. It comes with built-in templates, background color schemes, graphical images, and wizards to walk you through creating pages. In addition, you can also use Java applets and JavaScripts.

Galileo

Galileo is the name Netscape is using for their next major Navigator version, which will likely be Navigator 4.0. The expected release is by the end of 1996. Netscape's goal is to match and surpass the functionality of proprietary groupware such as Lotus Notes by late 1996 to mid-1997. It's reasonable to presume that the Collabra Share product will be in Galileo. The following are major enhancements through mid-1997 to both the Galileo browser and the Orion server, which is the next generation of the SuiteSpot server:

◆ *E-mail and discussion groups.* Both will have WYSIWYG editing, drag-and-drop capabilities, and search capabilities. The IMAP4 protocol will allow the processing and synchronizing of on-line and off-line e-mail and discussion groups. E-mail will include Secure MIME (S/MIME) for encrypting and authenticating e-mail messages, which will provide greater security for teams working on confidential projects.

♦ *Directory services.* LDAP directory services will make it easier to find others' addresses and security keys.

♦ *Agent services.* Agents will alert users to changes to documents for specific teams or projects.

Collabra Share

The Collabra Share conferencing and discussion product should be incorporated in Galileo and will provide enhanced features beyond Navigator's current newsgroup capabilities. Collabra billed the current Share product as "the group conferencing product that makes teams more effective, collaboration more affordable, and organizational learning automatic." It has won numerous awards because it offers 80 percent of Notes' functionality for 20 percent of the price. When incorporated in Navigator, it becomes even more of a bargain. Netscape's Hahn says:

> *Newsgroups can be like drinking from a firehose, and Collabra adds lots of tools to combat information overload—things like being able to search newsgroups in full text, organize newsgroups in different views, and move through newsgroups in almost a fast-forward, VCR-like metaphor. All have been in the Collabra product for many years and universally loved by users. You can be sure we are preserving them in the combined product. Our goal was to implement 100 percent of Collabra functionality and I think we're going to deliver on that goal.*

The combined Navigator/Collabra product will use the SMTP, IMAP4, and POP3 Internet mail protocols, and will work with e-mail clients, such as Microsoft Exchange, which use MAPI. Some of the expected features of the new product include the following:

♦ Support for rich text, graphics, images, audio, embedded objects, Java, JavaScript, and plug-ins in discussion groups

♦ Full-text search

♦ Enhanced security

♦ User initiation of new discussion groups

- Support for off-line use through replication
- Ability to post a summary message to wrap up the thread and discontinue discussion
- Ease of migration from the proprietary Collabra Share product through a Migration Agent

Server Capabilities

Some of the groupware capabilities will come about as a result of new or improved features in servers, such as the following:

- *Catalog Server.*   The Catalog Server will allow users to create personal views organized by specific topics.
- *Mail Server.*   The version of Mail Server incorporated in Orion in early 1997 will include the following:

  - *Calendaring and scheduling.*   This will include off-line access, plus the ability to send Internet e-mail to schedule meetings with those outside the company. Hahn said that currently a "huge impediment in calendaring is that there are no credible standards for multivendor interoperable calendaring, so for Netscape to enter that market tomorrow would require a proprietary product and that wouldn't meet our business objectives. Standards have to come before the products can come. Calendaring is a clear case of where we've had to evangelize standards before product."
  - *Catalog views.*   In conjunction with the Catalog Server, users will have personalized views of mail and discussion groups and can use the Catalog Server to search or browse that information simultaneously with enterprise-wide information sources.

- *News Server.*   The News Server provides external and internal newsgroups. Future capabilities include the following:

- Secured newsgroups
- Off-line processing and automatic resynchronization
- Instant user-created discussion groups that can easily migrate to and from e-mail
- Agents that sort and filter postings and provide users only what they need
- Newsgroups replicated by e-mail through the firewall to business partners
- Newsgroups as custom applications through the use of Java, JavaScript, and APIs
- Tools for migrating to News Server from Lotus Notes and Microsoft Exchange

Workflow Applications Tools

Netscape talks about building workflow applications by using HTML forms and JavaScript. In addition, Netscape LiveWire and LiveWire Database Connectivity Library let you create programs for querying and updating intranet relational databases in order to create workflow applications.

Hahn said that he sees workflow as being of two different types. First is the production-oriented, high-transaction-volume type of workflow, and Netscape has no plans to go into that market. The other type is ad hoc workflow, which is at the departmental or divisional process level and uses an office automation metaphor. It's this second type, allowing people to create and run ad hoc workflows, about which Netscape is excited. Hahn says:

> By the end of the year, we believe we will have most, but not all, of the components necessary to do that. The components that we will have are scriptable products, with Java and JavaScript; a directory strategy, which is needed for the routing function; a good certificate and authentication function with our Certificate Server; and secure transmission of workflows in the form of SSL at the link layer and Secure MIME at the store-and-forward layer. Many of the pieces needed for world-class workflow will be in place by year-end in a combination of Galileo at the client

and the various servers that I mentioned. The one piece that will not be there is a graphical workflow designer. I'm hoping that people who understand the mechanisms of these systems will separate that one issue out and will see that the hardest technical problems and the most important architectural problems are well implemented in the Netscape product line, but what is missing is the screen painter for painting out the flow. It's a matter of building a graphical design function for designing these flows and authoring the JavaScript to route the messages and check fields. That visual authoring environment is something you could expect from us next year.

Microsoft

Some consider Microsoft to be the major threat to the dominance of Lotus Notes. Microsoft offers voice conferencing, whiteboards, and chat through its NetMeeting product, and e-mail and newsgroups through Internet Explorer 3.0. It also provides tools for creating and supporting knowledge repositories through its Internet Information Server (IIS) Web server and Front Page for Web publishing. By the end of 1996, Microsoft will have tools that integrate with the Web to provide calendaring and scheduling, through Outlook, and shared writing and editing tools, through Office 97. Exchange can be linked to the intranet to provide workflow. You can find more information about Microsoft's products on its Web site at http://www.microsoft.com/.

Exchange

The original expectation was that Exchange would overthrow Notes. Microsoft eventually scaled back Exchange to the point where Notes and Exchange aren't mutually exclusive, and can even coexist in organizations. Exchange primarily focuses on messaging and forms.

Exchange is a component of the BackOffice family of products. These products work only in Microsoft environments. What are the features of Exchange that relate to the intranet?

- *E-mail and newsgroups.*   Exchange provides a universal in box for e-mail, faxes, meeting requests, and electronic forms. Exchange Server currently supports the Internet SMTP standard for e-mail, and by the end of 1996, will support the POP3 and IMAP4 protocols for e-mail, NNTP for newsgroups, and LDAP for directory access. Users will then be able to use standard Web browsers to access Exchange to send and receive mail, to view information, and to access personal and group calendars. Exchange users will also be able to use Exchange to access Internet newsgroups.

- *Discussions and knowledge repositories.*   Exchange has built-in bulletin boards and document libraries, which will be accessible from Web browsers.

- *Electronic forms and workflow.*   Exchange includes customer-tracking applications for workflow. It also includes Exchange Forms Designer, which supports Visual Basic and Visual C++, for further customizing of applications. In time, Exchange forms will integrate seamlessly with intranets.

- *Messaging-based replication*

Internet Explorer 3.0

Microsoft's Internet Explorer 3.0 is the equivalent version to Netscape's Navigator 3.0. It will be available in 27 languages. Its groupware functionality includes the following:

- *E-mail and news.*   Microsoft's Internet Mail and News integrates with Internet Explorer 3.0 and supports SMTP and POP3 protocols. It allows you to work off-line, and you can also create rules for managing your messages. The news client lets you subscribe to Internet newsgroups.

- *Multimedia.*   It supports numerous standard video and audio formats so you don't need helper applications. These tools are useful for group presentations.

- *Chat.*   It features Comic Chat, a comic-strip style chat client.
- *ActiveX Controls.*   ActiveX Controls automatically load and install themselves when needed to allow viewing and sharing of Excel and Word documents on an intranet.

NetMeeting

NetMeeting is an Internet Explorer 3.0 tool that provides functionality similar to CoolTalk. You can make telephone calls while sharing data and applications, recording things on a shared whiteboard, and chatting with others. NetMeeting lets you share a Word document with others, even if they don't have Word installed on their computers. Together, you can review the document and take turns editing it. The NetMeeting whiteboard has tools for drawing and making notes. You can transfer files during the conversation and use chat to share ideas or record minutes. You can use NetMeeting for presentations or for collaborating in group meetings. Even though you can share documents, this isn't truly shared editing because all participants can't be simultaneously revising the actual file.

You can use NetMeeting over the Internet, a corporate LAN, or a public telephone network. Currently, only two locations can use voice conferencing, but up to five locations can participate in a data conference. If you're using LAN-based conferencing, you can add more users, and could also use the office phone system for voice connections and use the LAN for your data connections.

Microsoft says that NetMeeting is the first Internet communications client based on the international T.120 data conferencing standard for real-time multiuser collaboration and file transfer over the Internet, intranet, or telephone network. It also supports the Internet Engineering Task Force (IETF) Realtime Protocol (RTP) for transmitting and synchronizing real-time streams over the Internet.

Since it's standards-based, NetMeeting works with other conferencing products. A number of established videoconferencing and collaborative tools' companies have announced support for Net-Meeting and plan to produce products that are compatible with it. Some of these include Intel, PictureTel, Xerox LiveWorks, and White Pine.

Unlike CoolTalk, NetMeeting provides sharing of actual applications, and can connect multiple locations rather than only two. Unfortunately, it will work only with Microsoft operating systems and Macintoshes.

Office 97

Office 97 is expected before the end of 1996. Office consists of personal productivity tools, such as Excel, Word, and Power Point, which are the tools we've made work for group writing and shared editing. Office 97 will transform these personal productivity tools into shared productivity and collaboration tools.

Microsoft's view of the world has changed. In the past, they viewed applications, such as Word or Excel, as the center of activity in the user's world, but the Internet has changed that. Now, they see that the user's universe revolves around a web of documents, with the user not knowing or caring which application generated those documents. Microsoft envisions that the environment should be aware of the type of document and should give the user the appropriate tools for manipulating it, so the user need not be concerned about that.

Collaboration and workflow features in Office 97 include the following:

- ◆ *Shared editing.* Office 97 will let multiple users simultaneously share and work on the same Word and Excel documents. When multiple users change the same data, Office 97 will let the document owner decide which changes to use. For documents distributed by e-mail for revisions, the merge capability will bring disparate versions together and merge them into a single file. The history of revisions by different users will appear in different colors or formatting. Microsoft says that Office applications will work seamlessly inside Web browsers so you can edit from within your browser.

- ◆ *Search.* Web Find Fast will do searches across any kind of network and bring back a variety of different types of documents.

- *Knowledge repository.*   Microsoft says that it will be as easy to publish an Excel or Word document on the Web as it is to print it, so everyone will create Web content. A new dialog box will make it easy to link documents. Microsoft Access will have a Publish to the Web Wizard which lets users put their Access databases on the intranet for publishing live data. They can convert database forms to HTML and link them to the Access database. Users can query, input, and update data from any browser, and replicate databases over the Internet or intranet.
- *Workflow.*   The addition of Visual Basic for Applications and ActiveX Controls in Office 97 applications will enable workflow solutions.

Outlook

Outlook is a new desktop information manager in Office 97. It will help users organize these items:

- *E-mail.*   Outlook works with Exchange and Internet e-mail to let users share information, and will support POP3 to let users communicate over the Internet. Office 97 contains message flags, such as follow-up or forward, and even lets you create your own flags. If you denote a date, it puts it in your task manager with a due date.
- *Calendars.*   Outlook will help users keep track of their personal schedules and schedule group meetings, even over the Internet.
- *Contact lists*
- *Task lists*
- *Documents and files.*   You can put information, such as company calendars, task lists, contact lists, or lists of URLs, in a public folder for everyone to access.
- *Workflow forms.*   Outlook has a built-in workflow-forms package. By incorporating ActiveX Document technology, you can embed Office documents or templates in Outlook forms. You could use this for budgets

or expense reports that are automatically e-mailed to the appropriate person for processing.

◆ *Journal.*   Outlook can create a journal of the work you do on your computer, which could be useful in tracking group progress.

Novell: GroupWise 5

Novell GroupWise 5 and GroupWise WebAccess let users who spend most of their day working from within their Web browsers access Groupwise functions from within their browsers. They can send e-mail and faxes, schedule meetings, retrieve and listen to voice mail, and receive documents. While GroupWise 5 provides only intranet accessible e-mail and calendaring and scheduling, we should expect Novell to make most features available from an intranet. It's still a proprietary groupware solution. You can find more information at the Novell GroupWise Web site at http://groupwise.novell.com. Features and functions of GroupWise 5, some of which aren't yet available from an intranet, include the following:

◆ E-mail, including support for SMTP/MIME, GroupWise PhoneAccess, pager, and fax

◆ Personal and group calendaring and task management

◆ Conferencing

◆ Shared folders

◆ Document management

◆ Development tools and forms creation, processing, and routing through GroupWise WorkFlow, InForms Designer, and InForms Filler

Open Text: Livelink Intranet

We've talked about a lot of promised products. Now let's look at some delivered ones.

Open Text's Livelink Intranet was one of the first workflow applications truly integrated into an intranet. It provides a knowledge repository, workflow, and conferencing and discussions. Livelink Intranet works entirely within your Web browser and dynamically generates intranet pages. It also utilizes conventional word processing tools. You can find more information about Open Text products at http://www.opentext.com. The Livelink Intranet suite is project-focused and includes the following four engines:

1. *Livelink Search.*   Search and indexing tools that support more than 40 different file formats.

2. *Livelink Library for Document Management.*   Provides checkout and check-in of documents, plus automatic version control, all of which can be intimidating to users. By doing this in an intranet environment, the user doesn't need to know that he or she is working with a document management database. Search and document management together provide and support a knowledge repository.

3. *Livelink Workflow.*   Provides management and tracking of project workflows by managing an in box and generating project-status maps. Developers can add Java applets or ActiveX objects to extend the workflow capabilities.

4. *Livelink Project Collaboration.*   Provides newsgroup-like discussion databases.

Livelink Intranet lets teams easily work together on projects from any location and helps them keep track of the many steps and tasks involved. This tool would be quite useful in those areas that depend upon project management tools, such as for product development.

The Livelink Intranet product is more workflow-oriented than most intranet products. Open Text has a very good and descriptive demo on their Web site. Since this is very different from the other products we've talked about, let's follow their demo to show how the product works. This demo includes searching, document management, workflow and project collaboration capabilities, all accessed from within your favorite Web browser. Livelink runs on top of standard, SQL databases.

The scenario of the demo (http://www.opentext.com/livelink/ ll_cavea.html) is about a fictitious product development project for the WristIO 2000, which we'll soon see has a problem since it shorts out in the shower!

We start from the corporate intranet home page, as shown in Figure 6.1. From the tools shown on the graphic at the top of the screen, you click on the In Box icon. The first thing you see is a log-in screen. After you log in, you see your in box, which contains your current tasks as pictured in Figure 6.2. One of your tasks is late and shows up with a red due date and a red alert comment. You click on that project to see the workflow details of the task.

In Figure 6.3, you can now see a picture of the workflow of this task as well as the detailed process steps. The workflow picture, drawn with Java, allows everyone related to, or interested in, the project to see where it stands. The arrows drawn through each figure indicate a completed step. The box around a step indicates the next waiting step—that's yours, and you can see that the project is on hold waiting for you. To solve the problem, you need to find any information related to the specific topic so you can finish your task. In Figure 6.4, you can search on that topic, polymer bonding, across all servers or even across the Internet.

In Figure 6.5, you can see a list of the available documents that meet your search criteria. This provides information for solving your problem.

In Figure 6.6, you can see your project workspace, which is a shared space that your team uses for collaborating and sharing information. From the home page, you can access a list of members, the task list, discussions, and documents. You clicked on Discussions to take you into the product safety project group discussions as shown in Figure 6.7.

Once you have all the information you need to solve the problem, it's time to update everything. In Figure 6.8, the workflow engine has placed the materials you need right there for you. Now it's time for you to update the final research report with your findings.

When you click on a report or document, Livelink Intranet launches your favorite editor and checks the document out of the document database for you as shown in Figure 6.9. You can work

Figure 6.1 Livelink Intranet Guided Tour—home page (http://www.opentext.com/livelink/tour/Rstart.html). (Used with permission Open Text Corporation, Copyright 1996.)

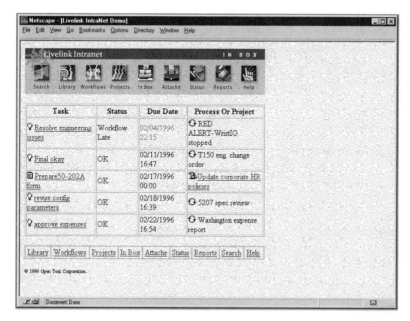

Figure 6.2 Livelink Intranet Guided Tour—in box (http://www.opentext.com/livelink/tour/Rstart.html). (Used with permission Open Text Corporation, Copyright 1996.)

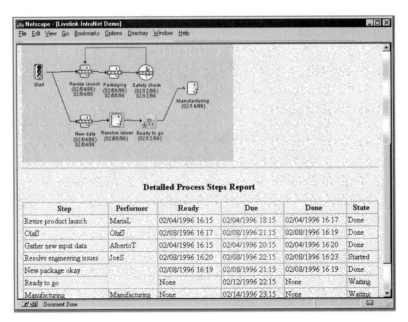

Figure 6.3 Livelink Intranet Guided Tour—workflow map and process steps (http://www.opentext.com/livelink/tour/Rstart.html). (Used with permission Open Text Corporation, Copyright 1996.)

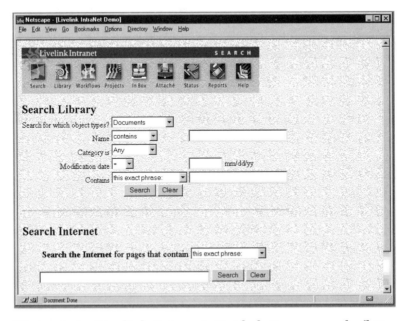

Figure 6.4 Livelink Intranet Guided Tour—search (http://www.opentext.com/livelink/tour/Rstart.html). (Used with permission Open Text Corporation, Copyright 1996.)

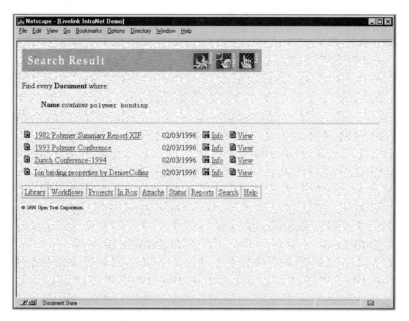

Figure 6.5 Livelink Intranet Guided Tour—search result (http://www.opentext.com/livelink/tour/Rstart.html). (Used with permission Open Text Corporation, Copyright 1996.)

Figure 6.6 Livelink Intranet Guided Tour—project workspace (http://www.opentext.com/livelink/tour/Rstart.html). (Used with permission Open Text Corporation, Copyright 1996.)

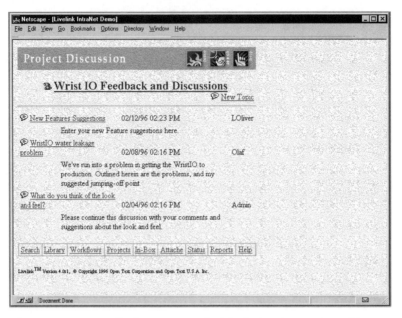

Figure 6.7 Livelink Intranet Guided Tour—project discussion (http://www.opentext.com/livelink/tour/Rstart.html). (Used with permission Open Text Corporation, Copyright 1996.)

Figure 6.8 Livelink Intranet Guided Tour—step assignment (http://www.opentext.com/livelink/tour/Rstart.html). (Used with permission Open Text Corporation, Copyright 1996.)

in any application, and you have the option of viewing over 40 different document formats all within your Web browser.

Once you've finished the report, you click the Update button shown in Figure 6.10, and Livelink Intranet transparently moves the document off your desk and checks it into the document database, handling all the version control for you automatically. This makes it possible to do workflow and document editing directly from your Web browser. As you go back to your In Box, as shown in Figure 6.11, you can see that the task no longer shows up there. You can also see, in Figure 6.12, the updated workflow drawing and that you've completed your portion.

Action Technologies: Metro 1.1

Action Technologies, a well-established workflow vendor, offers Metro, the first Web-enabled workflow application. To work, it requires the rest of the Action Workflow System, and is available only for Windows NT. You can find more information about these products at the Action Technologies Web site at http://www. actiontech.com.

Metro turns Web browsers, such as Netscape Navigator and Microsoft Internet Explorer, into workflow clients. It uses the Action Workflow System to process and route workflow, and requires the module that translates data and commands back and forth between the browser and the Action Workflow System.

Workflow depends upon forms. In Metro, users work in their browsers and see only forms—Metro hides everything else from them. Metro 1.1 has three pieces:

1. *ActionItem,* a basic application, which we'll look at below.
2. *Application Center,* a collection of more than 20 prebuilt application templates for use as is, or for turning into custom applications.
3. *Developer Starter Kit,* a set of tools for customizing these prebuilt applications.

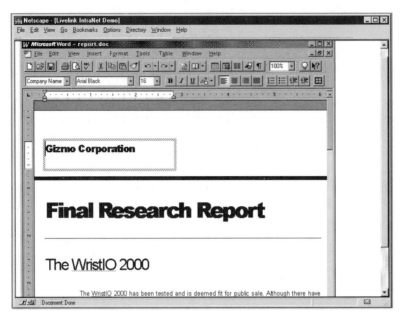

Figure 6.9 Livelink Intranet Guided Tour—document checkout (http://www.opentext.com/livelink/tour/Rstart. html). (Used with permission Open Text Corporation, Copyright 1996.)

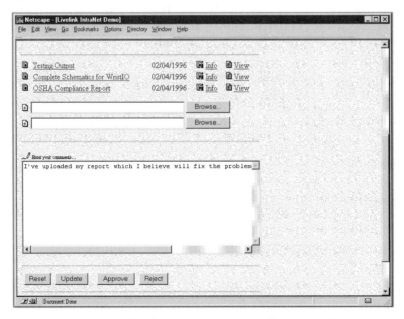

Figure 6.10 Livelink Intranet Guided Tour—document check-in (http://www.opentext.com/livelink/tour/Rstart. html). (Used with permission Open Text Corporation, Copyright 1996.)

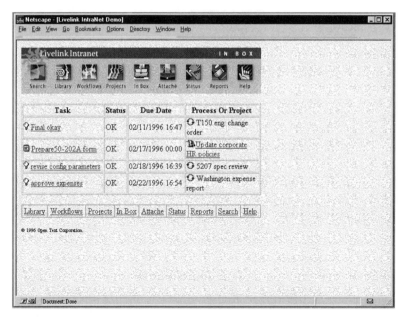

Figure 6.11 Livelink Intranet Guided Tour—in box (http://www.opentext.com/livelink/tour/Rstart.html). (Used with permission Open Text Corporation, Copyright 1996.)

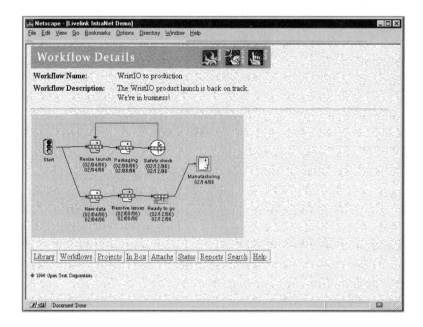

Figure 6.12 Livelink Intranet Guided Tour—workflow map (http://www.opentext.com/livelink/tour/Rstart.html). (Used with permission Open Text Corporation, Copyright 1996.)

There are three types of forms in Metro's applications. I'll use examples from the Metro Web site to illustrate these forms.

1. *Initiation forms.* These forms initiate action of some kind to start a workflow process. Figure 6.13 shows the ActionItem form on which a user makes some type of request. Figure 6.14 shows the Product Order form, which a customer can use to place an order. You can customize these forms to meet your needs. Figure 6.15 shows an example of a customized application, a New Hire Badge Request, from Sandia National Laboratories.

2. *Status and interaction forms.* These forms show the requester the status of the request and allow the recipient to reply or initiate some action. Figure 6.16 shows a Status and Review form, which lets the originator track his or her requests. Figure 6.17 shows the ActionItem Reply Form, which lets the recipient respond to the originator's request. When the recipient receives the original request, he or she can reply by clicking on the Reply button, which provides the form shown for taking action to fulfill the request.

3. *WorkBox list forms.* These forms help users keep track of all their work, plus outstanding work which is due back from others. Figure 6.18 shows an example of this. Every Metro user has an individual WorkBox. The WorkBox forms are simply HTML forms that tell the user about new, pending, and overdue work. The user sees what he or she has to work on, plus what others owe, and has a variety of ways to search and display the work.

With Metro, employees can do the following:

◆ Request action or information
◆ Track status
◆ Manage work lists
◆ Manage negotiations and agreements
◆ Build application forms for managing processes

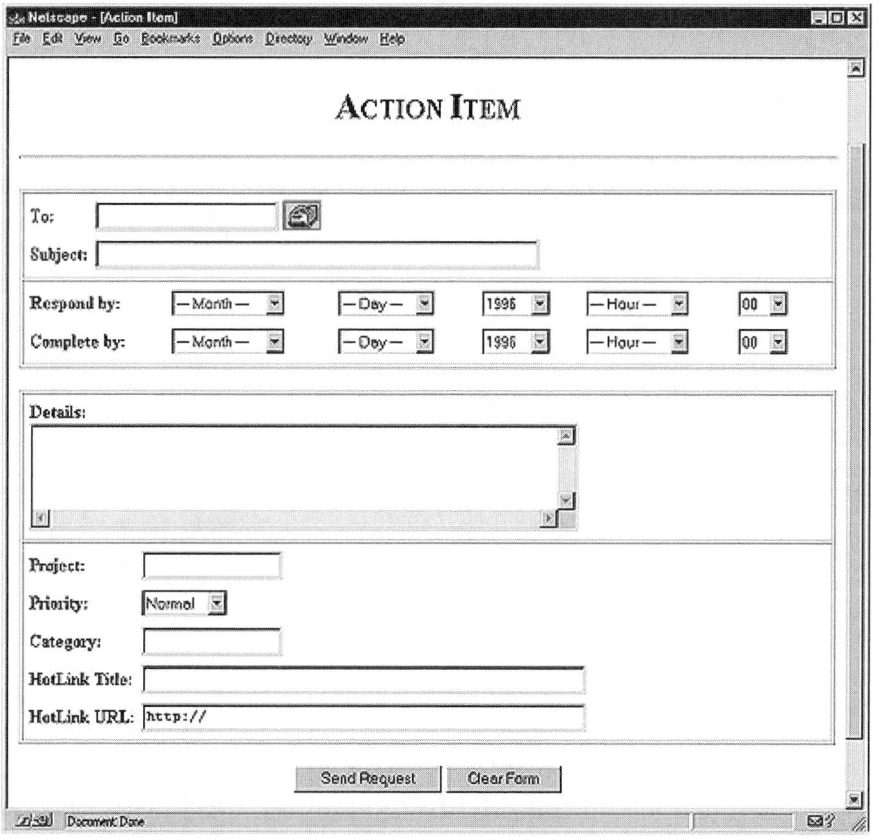

Figure 6.13 Action Metro ActionItem form (http://www .actiontech.com/Metro/info/whites/workflow/workflow_toc.htm). (Used with permission Action Technologies, Inc., Copyright 1996.)

In addition, you can extend workflow to your customers so they can process requests and track the status of those requests. They can do the following:

◆ Request service or initiate trouble tickets
◆ Manage and track projects, tasks, and assignments
◆ Arrange meetings
◆ Respond to RFPs, RFQs, and bids
◆ Apply for credit

Figure 6.14 Action Metro product order form (http://www.actiontech.com/Metro/info/whites/workflow/workflow_toc.htm). (Used with permission Action Technologies, Inc., Copyright 1996.)

◆ Submit orders
◆ Return products

Allaire: Forums and Cold Fusion

Allaire Forums is a Web-based discussion forum built from Allaire's Cold Fusion product. Cold Fusion is a tool for building workflow and groupware applications by combining HTML pages with database commands to retrieve information from relational databases and generate Web pages on the fly. Forums features threaded dis-

Figure 6.15   Action Metro New Hire Badge Request from Sandia National Laboratories (http://www.actiontech.com/images/badge. jpg). (Used with permission Action Technologies, Inc. and Sandia National Laboratories, Copyright 1996.)

cussions with advanced searches that let users filter messages by keyword, date, or topic. The use of *persistent cookies*—identification files stored on the user's computer—provides for transparent user identification. You can find more information about these products at Allaire's Web site at http://www.allaire.com/.

Amicus Networks: Community Builder

The Amicus Community Builder system is a suite of applications for on-line services. It includes CommunityACT, which provides chat, bulletin boards, and e-mail. You can get more information at the Amicus Web site at http://www.amicus.com/product.htm.

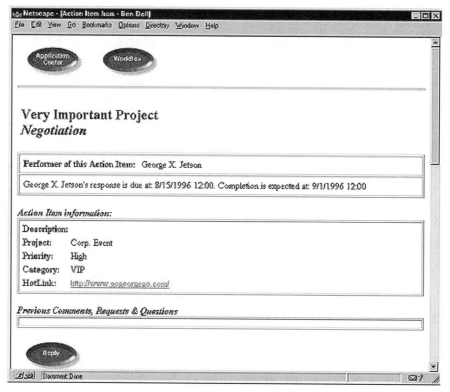

Figure 6.16 Action Metro status-and-review form (http://www. actiontech.com/Metro/info/whites/workflow/workflow_toc.htm). (Used with permission Action Technologies, Inc., Copyright 1996.)

Attachmate: Open Mind 3.0

Attachmate's Open Mind 3.0 provides conferencing and a knowledge repository, which are accessible from an HTML 3.0–compliant Web browser. You can get more information on the product at Attachmate's Web site at http://www.attachmate.com/. Open Mind 3.0 features include the following:

◆ Discussions
◆ Document management
◆ Replication of discussions, messages, and files

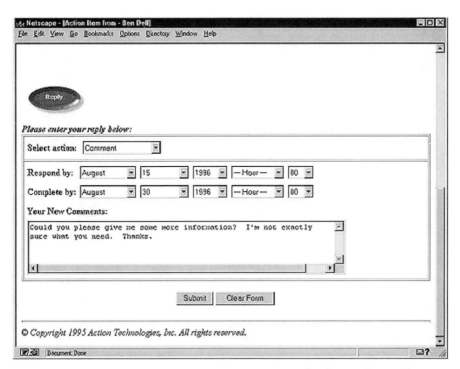

Figure 6.17   Action Metro ActionItem reply form (http://www. actiontech.com/Metro/info/whites/workflow/workflow_toc.htm). (Used with permission Action Technologies, Inc., Copyright 1996.)

- ◆ Limited group editing through checkout and check-in, with history and version control
- ◆ Viewers for Excel, Word, WordPerfect, 1-2-3, and other types of files
- ◆ Advanced searches
- ◆ User-created Open Mind accounts

Cap Gemini Innovation: WebFlow

Cap Gemini Innovation's WebFlow provides workflow and coordinated activity tracking by exchanging information among employ-

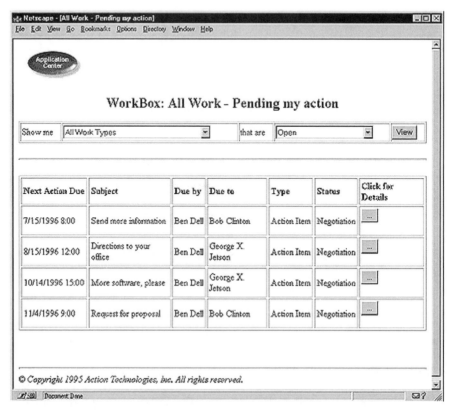

Figure 6.18 Action Metro WorkBox list form (http://www.action-tech.com/Metro/info/whites/workflow/workflow_toc.htm). (Used with permission Action Technologies, Inc., Copyright 1996.)

ees, suppliers, and customers. You can find more information at http://webflow.cginn.cgs.fr:4747/.

Connectix: VideoPhone 1.1 for Windows

Connectix VideoPhone 1.1 for Windows provides Web-based videoconferencing, voice conferencing, and whiteboarding. You can get more information at http://www.connectix.com/.

DataBeam: neT.120 Conference Server

DataBeam's neT.120 Conference Server 1.0 provides whiteboarding, or data conferencing, using Java-enabled Web browsers. The neT.120 Conference Server uses the international T.120 standard, and DataBeam bills it as the first standards-based, software-only server product for hosting multipoint conferences. It works on computers running Windows, UNIX, and Apple.

Figure 6.19 shows DataBeam's corporate look for conference-center home pages, which is where users go to set up or join in data conferences. Figure 6.20 shows an annotated data conference using a Java-enabled Web browser. Conferences can be used to

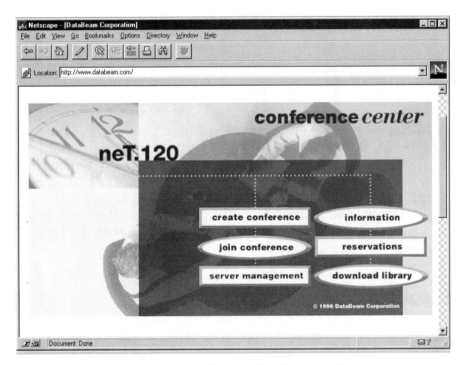

Figure 6.19 DataBeam neT.120 Conference Server corporate home page (http://www.databeam.com/Products/neT.120/screen-shots.html). (Used with permission DataBeam Corporation, Copyright 1996.)

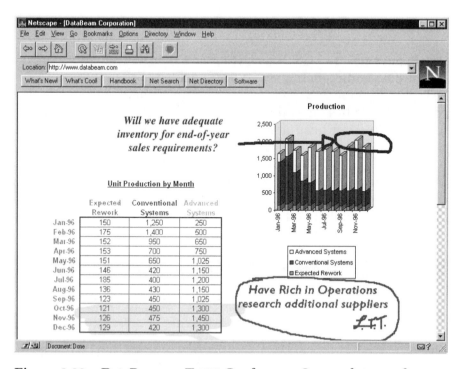

Figure 6.20 DataBeam neT.120 Conference Server data conference (http://www.databeam.com/Products/neT.120/screenshots.html). (Used with permission DataBeam Corporation, Copyright 1996.)

create, review, and present documents and presentations. You can get more information about neT.120 Conference Server at http://www.databeam.com/.

Digital: AltaVista Forum 2.0

Digital's AltaVista Forum 2.0 provides calendaring, conferencing, knowledge repositories, and support for chat and videoconferencing. Users can use most standard Web browsers for accessing Forum. It has no proprietary components, and works on UNIX and Windows NT servers. It's available in five languages. You can get more information about AltaVista Forum at the AltaVista Web site at http://www.altavista.software.digital.com/. AltaVista

Forum provides the following:

- *Discussion forums.* It allows your team to set up its own discussion forums and post or reply directly without using e-mail. Figure 6.21 shows the original post to start a forum at the AltaVista Roundtable, and Figure 6.22 shows a reply to it.

- *Web-based knowledge repository.* With the knowledge repository, you can share documents and organize the team's knowledge. Team members upload information they need to share, such as spreadsheets, graphics, or text files, into shared folders that support over 50 document formats. Authors can attach keywords and brief abstracts to their files so others know what to do with each document. The repository can also maintain multiple versions of files. Users receive e-mail notification of the addition of new documents.

- *Filtering of e-mail and news.* Forum brings in and filters news feeds from Individual, Incorporated, Associated Press, and other sources on the Web. It also provides information filtering from e-mail and HTML.

- *Search.* The AltaVista search engine provides full text indexing.

- *Home pages.* Teams can have home pages that link to the team's forum and to other important information. A community home page provides the links to all team-member home pages.

- *Polling.* Forum can poll team members for votes, thereby facilitating consensus among geographically dispersed teams. You can use this with customers and suppliers as well.

- *Group calendaring*

- *Supports chat and videoconferencing*

Future enhancements will include SMTP support, integrated chat, Web publishing tools, and access to databases and legacy applications.

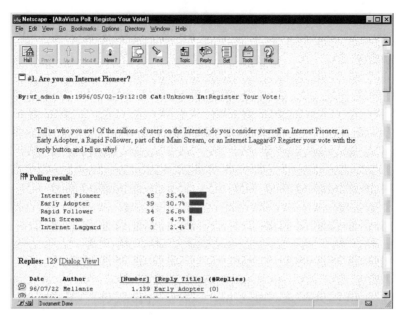

Figure 6.21 AltaVista Forum Roundtable poll—original post (http://www.altavista.software.digital.com/roundtable/nfintro.htm). (Used with permission Digital Equipment Corporation, Copyright 1996.)

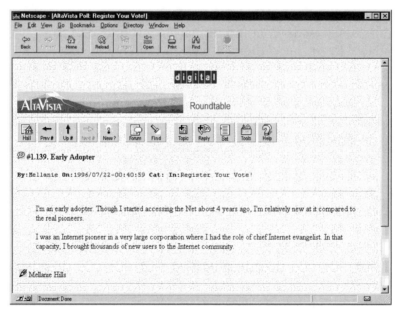

Figure 6.22 AltaVista Forum Roundtable poll—reply (http://www.altavista.software.digital.com/roundtable/nfintro.htm). (Used with permission Digital Equipment Corporation, Copyright 1996.)

ForeFront: RoundTable

ForeFront's RoundTable software, working in conjunction with the ForeFront Conference Server, provides chat and data conferencing. You can share images, documents, URLs, audio, video, and more. RoundTable works in any Web browser on the Windows 3.1, Windows 95, and Macintosh platforms. You can find more information at ForeFront's Web site at http://www.ffg.com/.

FTP/Campbell Services: OnTime Web Edition 4.0

Campbell Services' OnTime Web Edition 4.0 lets you use any Web browser for personal and group calendaring and task lists. You can find more information at their Web site at http://www.ontime.com/.

OnTime provides a day planner that lets you see appointments and tasks for a specific day. A week planner shows a week at a time, and the month planner shows free time for the month. You can search for specific appointments or details, and can view a public calendar list to see whose calendars are available. You can do this from across the Web so you can access your calendar from anywhere. OnTime also lets you embed calendars in Web pages if you wish.

Galacticomm: Worldgroup Internet Server

Galacticomm's Worldgroup Internet Server, along with its companion Worldgroup Manager plug-in for Netscape Navigator, provides browser-accessible e-mail, videoconferencing, conferencing and discussions, whiteboarding, chat, and knowledge repositories. You can get more information at http://www.gcomm.com/home.html.

JetForm

JetForm provides electronic-forms products that integrate work-flow into the Web. JetForm products include the JetForm Filler, for filling out forms embedded in Web pages, and JetForm Server, for processing the data and integrating with other JetForm work-flow products. You can use the Jetform Filler as a plug-in or as a helper application in a Web browser, depending upon what your browser supports. To use it, you simply fill in a form and send it to the server for processing. You can get more information about the JetForm products at its Web site at http://www.jetform.com/.

Lundeen: Web Crossing

Lundeen's Web Crossing provides public and private discussion forums that you can access from a Web browser. It's available for Windows NT, Macintosh, and some varieties of UNIX. You can get more information about Web Crossing at Lundeen's Web site at http://webx.lundeen.com/.

McCall, Szerdy & Associates: C.A. Facilitator for the Web

McCall Szerdy's C.A. Facilitator for the Web is electronic-meeting software that supports facilitated real-time meetings and unfacili-tated discussion groups. It supports most Web browsers and works on Windows and Macintosh-based Web servers. You can get more information at http://www.facilitate.com/.

Motet

Motet is a conferencing tool with a wealth of features, my favorite of which is the Bozo Filter, which lets you screen out postings by selected users. You can get more information at the Motet Web site at http://www.sonic.net/~foggy/motet/.

NetManage

NetManage offers a large family of standards-based collaborative products for use on an intranet. NetManage provides tools for calendaring and scheduling, voice and videoconferencing, whiteboarding, chat, e-mail, conferencing, and web-based knowledge repositories. You can get more information about its products from the NetManage Web site at http://www.netmanage.com/. NetManage has two major product families that provide these collaboration products.

1. *IntraNet Forum Server,* which is an NNTP server for hosting internal discussion groups.

2. *Chameleon,* which is the suite of products shown in Figure 6.23. It includes TCP/IP connectivity, the WebSurfer browser, Internet Relay Chat, e-mail, a newsreader, calendaring, a personal Web server, and a wide array of other Internet tools. It also includes SGI's InPerson, a whiteboard application for voice conferencing, videoconferencing, and whiteboarding over intranets and the Internet.

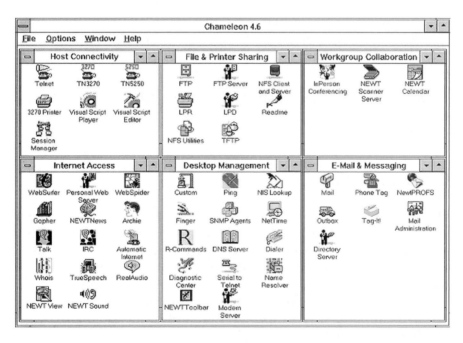

Figure 6.23 NetManage Chameleon (http://www.netmanage. om/netmanage/products/cham.html). (Used with permission NetManage, Inc., Copyright 1996.)

Now Software: Now Up-to-Date

The Now Up-to-Date line includes several interoperable, Web-enabled calendaring products, including the following:

- *Now Up-to-Date schedule and contact manager,* which lets you drag and drop events directly from the Web onto your calendar using your Netscape browser (Windows and Macintosh only). It saves links so you can return to the original location. It also provides automatic group scheduling and meeting notices.

- *Now Up-to-Date Web Publisher,* which lets you use drag and drop to publish calendars and address books on the Web without typing HTML.

- *AboutTime and AboutPeople,* which are plug-ins for Netscape Navigator that let you view calendars and address books published with Now Up-to-Date Web Publisher from within your browser.

You can get more information at the Now Software Web site at http://www.nowsoft.com.

Oracle: InterOffice

Oracle says that it built InterOffice from the ground up using open Internet standards and Web interfaces. InterOffice provides corporate intranets with e-mail, scheduling, workflow, and document management. Users can access it from a variety of platforms and tools, including Windows 95 and NT, Web browsers, and POP3 and IMAP4 clients. InterOffice works with UNIX and Windows NT, and supports SMTP, MIME, HTTP, and HTML standards. You can find out more information about InterOffice at the Oracle Web site at http://www.oracle.com/. InterOffice features include the following:

- *Messaging,* which includes public and shared folders, search, filtering, and support for disconnected users.
- *Directory services*
- *Personal and group calendaring and scheduling,* which includes to-do lists and support for disconnected users.
- *Document management,* which includes check-in and checkout, version control, and full-text searching.
- *Workflow,* which includes a graphical designer (for Windows 95) and an SQL engine.

O'Reilly: WebBoard

O'Reilly's WebBoard is a Windows NT or Windows 95–based conferencing and discussion forum product that users access from their choice of Web browsers. You can get more information at http://webboard.ora.com/.

Paradigm Software: WorkWise-Enterprise

Paradigm Software provides intranet-based workflow. Their WorkWise-Enterprise will provide a turnkey HR intranet that will let employees enroll in benefits plans, update their personal information, and route requests for information through the intranet. You can find more information on Paradigm's Web site at http://www.workwise.com/.

Proxima: Podium 2.01

Proxima's Podium 2.01 is conferencing and discussion software. Figure 6.24 shows a demo from its Web site using the frames version with a set of corporate icons. Proxima also has other libraries with cute and fun icons. You can get more information about this product at http://www.proxima.com/.

Quarterdeck/Future Labs: TALKShow

Quarterdeck provides a Virtual Conference Center on the Web using its TALKShow conferencing software. TALKShow provides conferencing and whiteboarding that lets multiple people exchange and edit documents and graphics. It works with Windows 3.1 and Windows 95. Quarterdeck also offers Global Chat, a chat tool that works with browsers for accessing chat servers, and WebTalk, an Internet phone product. You can get more information at http://www.quarterdeck.com/.

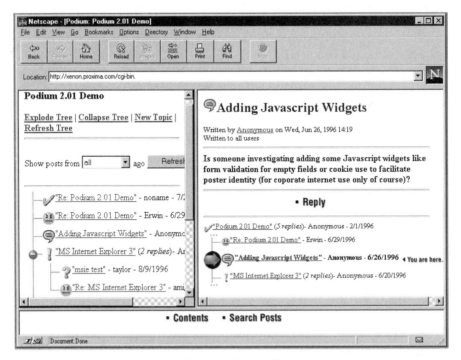

Figure 6.24 Proxima Podium demo (http://www.proxima.com/podium/). (Used with permission Proxima, Inc., Copyright 1996.)

RadNet: WebShare

RadNet bills its WebShare product as the first groupware product designed from the ground up based on the Web and open industry standards. WebShare is a tool for creating and customizing groupware applications. It comes with starter applications that provide calendaring, conferencing, and knowledge repositories. These applications include a threaded-discussion database, a problem-tracking application, a calendar, a newsletter, a contact-tracking application, and a document reference library. Users can access these applications from any Web browser and can create, edit, and delete documents, as well as upload file attachments and images.

WebShare also includes WebShare Designer, a visual design tool for creating forms, and WebShare Server, a groupware engine for storing information and managing the presentation of documents. The WebShare Server includes a Web server and an SQL database. WebShare integrates with MAPI and SMTP e-mail systems for sending messages. You can get more information about this product at the RadNet Web site at http://www.radnet.com/.

Screen Porch: Caucus 3.0

Caucus 3.0 provides Web-based conferencing and discussions, which can include text, HTML, hypertext links, images, JavaScript, Java applets, file libraries, audio, and video. It offers text searches and a personal *hot list.* Caucus conferences can be accessed from most browsers.

Caucus includes customizable templates in the Caucus Markup Language (CML), an extension of HTML that has 90 additional functions, including conditional logic and controls. It also includes development tools for creating custom applications. It's available for UNIX, with an NT version coming. You can get more information at http://screenporch.com/.

Searchlight Software: Spinnaker

Searchlight Software's Spinnaker Web server includes conferencing capabilities. You can get more information at http://www.searchlight.com/home.htm.

Spyglass/OS TECHnologies: WebNotes

WebNotes, from OS TECHnologies, which is now part of Spyglass, is a tool for Web-based conferencing. You can get more information about this product at http://webnotes.ostech.com/.

Symantec/Delrina: FormFlow 2.0

Delrina's FormFlow 2.0 now uses the Internet for sending forms. FormFlow works as a helper application in Web browsers, and Web page forms automatically launch FormFlow. Forms can be stored on FTP servers for easy access. FormFlow also includes tools for designing forms and automating business processes. You can get more information at the Symantec Web site at http://www.symantec.com/formflow/.

Thuridion: CREW

Thuridion bills its CREW product as the first interactive Web-based groupware suite. It provides group calendaring and scheduling, as well as knowledge-repository tools. Users can view and update their schedules, card files, and documents from a Web browser anywhere. CREW works under Windows NT or UNIX. You can check Thuridion's Web site at http://www.thuridion.com/ for more information about CREW. CREW's features are as follows:

- ◆ *Calendar.*   An integrated personal and group scheduler. You can easily keep track of individual calendars and to-do lists, and even schedule appointments via the Internet. You can view calendar information by day, week, or month, and view either individual or group schedules.

♦ *CardFile.* An address book and group organizer that makes it easy to schedule people and send them messages. You can use it to manage your contact list and resources via the Internet. You can attach images to cards for easy recognition, and they then become your business card on the Internet.

♦ *Messenger.* A universal in box that handles e-mail, voice mail, and faxes from within a Web browser.

♦ *Locker.* An Internet file system that uses a folder metaphor for sharing and transferring documents and files. The user is the only person who can grant access to information that's in his or her locker.

♦ *Office.* A start-up screen that lets users organize information their way and place their most frequent contacts and links to their favorite Web sites there.

UES: Track-It

UES Track-It provides workflow task lists and tracking that are accessible from Web browsers. Tasks can have documents attached to them for assignment to team members. Track-It also automates the routing of documents among team members. You can get more information at http://www.columbus.ues.com/.

Ultimus: WebFlow

Ultimus WebFlow is a Web-enabled workflow product. You fill out a form inside your Web browser and automatically transfer the contents into the workflow process. You can get more information from the Ultimus Web site at http://www.ultimus1.com/.

Ulysses Telemedia Networks/Intraprise Technologies: Odyssey

The Odyssey software suite provides Web-based groupware calendaring. It consists of Odyssey Calendar, Odyssey Contact Manager, and Odyssey Reminder. You can get more information at http://www.ulysses.net/.

WebCal

WebCal is a calendaring and scheduling product that works through most Web browsers. It lets you schedule personal and group appointments and to-dos, and provides day, week, and month views. It's available for UNIX, Windows NT, Windows 95, and Macintosh Web servers. You can get more information at http://www.webcal.com/.

WebFlow: SamePage

WebFlow's SamePage is a suite of information and project management tools built entirely for the intranet. SamePage provides group writing and shared editing, a type of conferencing, a knowledge repository, and some limited workflow. SamePage reminds people of their tasks. The company claims that "With SamePage, you stop the stalking and get more done!" You can get more information at the WebFlow site at http://webflow.com/.

When you put documents into the workspace for shared editing, SamePage dynamically converts them to HTML. You can also create new documents in SamePage. The document owner facilitates the shared creation and review process by selecting reviewers. All reviewers receive an e-mail when the document changes. Mandatory reviewers receive reminders when they haven't reviewed the document by a specified date.

Reviewers insert discussion comments into the document and view the comments of others. All changes and comments are objects that are dynamically assembled into views based on what the user requests. SamePage keeps track of all changes so that you can backtrack. Figure 6.25 shows a document containing discussion comments, plus a hyperlink to the history of other changes. There's also an assigned action item (AI#1) in a comment.

TakeAction! is the SamePage subsystem that manages action items and keeps track of assignment due dates. You can create action items within the document or from any page within TakeAction! Figure 6.26 shows the action item assigned in the discussion comment we saw in Figure 6.25.

SamePage is one of the few tools that permits simultaneous shared editing of documents on intranets. Its approach is somewhat unusual and changes our groupware paradigms. It effectively creates newsgroups within documents, and dynamically assembles those documents from the discussion threads. It's also some-

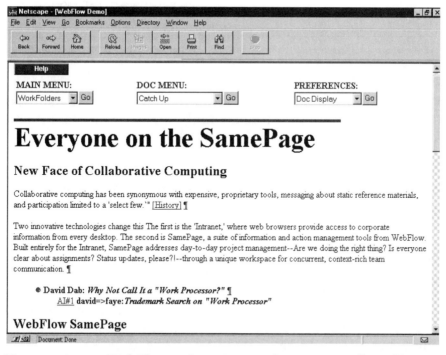

Figure 6.25 WebFlow SamePage discussion (http://www .webflow.com/demo.html). (Used with permission WebFlow Corporation, Copyright 1996.)

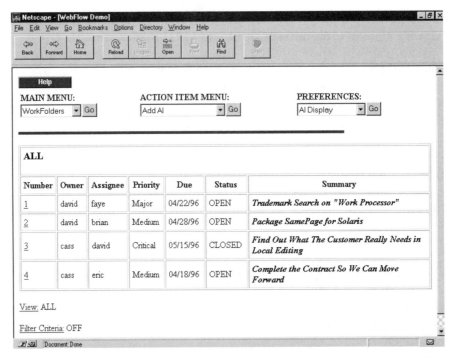

Figure 6.26   WebFlow SamePage TakeAction! action item list (http://www.webflow.com/demo.html). (Used with permission WebFlow Corporation, Copyright 1996.)

what unusual to have action items assigned from within a newsgroup or a document.

White Pine: Enhanced CU-SeeMe

White Pine's Enhanced CU-SeeMe is desktop videoconferencing software that provides full-color videoconferencing, voice conferencing, chat, and whiteboarding. You can use CU-SeeMe over the Internet or a TCP/IP LAN or Wide Area Network (WAN), which connects LANs in multiple locations. You can launch it directly from your Web browser, and it runs on both Windows and Macintosh. As I finish writing this book, White Pine has announced an agreement with Microsoft to incorporate Internet Explorer 3.0 and NetMeeting into the Enhanced CU-SeeMe to add full application sharing. You can get more information at White Pine's Web site at http://www.wpine.com/.

Miscellaneous

Many of the proprietary client/server workflow vendors are creating ways to tie the Web to their products. One example of this is Dun & Bradstreet Software's SmartStream Web Series. It consists of Java-based applets that let users execute electronic purchase requisitions from within a Web browser using D&B's proprietary SmartStream system.

All the products listed should give you a good idea of the intranet groupware products available. There are, however, others. I talked about CoolTalk and NetMeeting, but there are also many Internet phone products that don't incorporate data conferencing capabilities. These include VocalTec's Internet Phone, NetSpeak's WebPhone, and many more. At the time of this writing, Intel has introduced the Intel Internet Phone software, which is based on open standards and will let users of different types of software and computers communicate.

There are many tools that connect the Web to databases for building applications, as well as many document management systems for building knowledge repositories. To discuss them all would take an entire book, but wouldn't get us any closer to helping you implement groupware in your organization. So let's move on and talk about how we select the appropriate products.

chapter seven

How Do You Choose Intranet Groupware and What Are the Advantages and Disadvantages?

How Do You Choose Which Intranet Groupware Products to Use?

How do you figure out which groupware product is right for you? Since these products cover so much territory, and no one product can do absolutely everything, you may need more than just one.

My method of evaluating and selecting groupware may seem strange to those used to evaluating and selecting products based on their technical merits. For groupware, that's not necessarily the right way to go. The key to selecting a groupware product is to select a product that the users *want* to use. That may sound simple, but it isn't always.

Identify and Prioritize Needs

The first step is to figure out who has a problem. Groupware may be a tool to help solve that problem. Too often, we techies see some whiz-bang technology and decide that it's just what we need. Then we go out and try to find someone to use it or someone who has a need close enough for us to try it out. That's not the right way to do it. Groupware should fill a specific business need, and you must identify that need before you choose products. If we're implementing technology just for technology's sake, then we're doing a great disservice to our organizations. We really should fulfill specific business needs.

Start with the Users and Identify Their Needs

Let's presume that you have a group of users with a problem and they have come to you for help, or you've heard about their problem and offered to help. Before we can define what products to use, we need to start with the users and have them identify their needs.

What are the users' problems and needs? We sometimes think we know what their needs are without really asking them. That's a big mistake for groupware, because if the solution doesn't fit the users' needs, they just won't use it. How do we find out what their needs are? The best way is to get them together in a room to talk about what they need. You might consider bringing in a facilitator—that is, someone who's skilled in helping identify and prioritize needs. This is common in Joint Application Development (JAD) sessions, so you might consider using a JAD facilitator.

The first step in such a meeting might be a *dump* session. Users should talk about the way they currently do things and what impact that has. Then they should talk about their needs, problems, and frustrations. If you already have electronic-meeting tools, you should use them to capture the list. If not, the facilitator can record them on flipcharts. Once the group has dumped its problems, they should then list the things that work well and their ideas for how things could work better. This clears out all the emotional baggage and puts people in a positive frame of mind to start focusing on solutions. I recommend taking a break before starting into the next step.

Next, the group should take the dump lists and start categorizing items. Some things will fall into logical groupings. Other things may simply go on an issues list, which means that the group recognizes them but realizes that they're beyond the scope of the meeting. The group may wish to pass along those things that are administrative or policy decisions to the appropriate management for addressing. Other things may simply be gripes that the group decides to put aside.

The group should then discuss the specific categories of needs and record everything they can about them. Who has these needs? What are their jobs? How do they do these things today? Who does what? What kinds of computers and software do they use? With which groups must they coordinate to accomplish those jobs? Which computers and software do those groups use? Discuss additional ideas the group has for solving its problems, features and characteristics they need to solve these problems, and things they would put on a wish list if they could.

The next step is to distill everything into a list of requirements and needs and have the group prioritize them. Facilitators use a variety of techniques to help users prioritize lists.

Identify Infrastructure and Operational Needs

Along with the list of user needs and priorities there should be a similar list for the IT group. You may want to have a similar meeting in IT with those who would be affected by a groupware implementation. Identify what's important, such as the platforms on which the software must run. Are open standards required, or is a proprietary solution acceptable? Once IT has identified all of its needs, it should prioritize them as well.

Identify and Select Products to Present to the Users

The next step is to determine which products meet your needs. Here are some criteria for judging them.

- Platforms
- How open is it?
- Features
- Integrated or specialized
- Ease of use
- Training and support
- Cost
- Deployment
- Fit

- ◆ Stability
- ◆ Vendor support

Platforms

Which platforms do you have, and which platforms does each product support? These criteria may quickly eliminate some products. This is an area where intranet groupware has outshone proprietary groupware. Proprietary groupware may be difficult to install on a variety of different operating systems and network protocols; that is, if you can even get it for all the different platforms. Products based on open standards are generally available for most platforms.

How Open Is It?

How open is the product? This is a major battle being waged by some vendors. Netscape preaches this message every time it can. You must decide how open you want your products to be and examine the level of openness of any products you evaluate. Should you select only products based on open systems, or are proprietary products OK? Which products are based on open standards, and which are proprietary systems wrapped in open standards connections at their fringes?

In a recent conversation, Eric Hahn, Senior Vice President of Enterprise Technology at Netscape and founder of Collabra, made it clear that Netscape has a strong commitment to open standards. He clarified the importance of open standards by saying:

> There's a fundamental shift going on in that the future of groupware is on the intranet based on open standards. Our company is very clearly aligned behind that message. Our customers overwhelmingly tell us that they want the freedom and flexibility to have a choice of vendors and products, which open systems give them. They also want to dismantle the arbitrary barriers between the intranet and the Internet. There's a wonderful synergy when the same technology is used inside the corporation and on a planetary scale between corporations, because of things like virtual corporations, public demand cre-

*ation, and cybermarketing. All of those things are very easy
and cost-effective to do when the standards are the same, and
quite expensive and almost impossible to do when they're different. I would submit that there's a big distinction between the
way each vendor is getting to that "open standards nirvana."*

Hahn said that Netscape is sometimes hampered from going into
the market with a specific product because of the lack of a standard
for that product. I asked about calendaring products and he told me
that I might see something happening in that space very soon. A
few days later, Netscape, Lotus, IBM, Microsoft, NetManage, and 13
other companies convened at Netscape to start laying the foundation for development of a calendaring standard. We'll all benefit
from the ability of our tools to interoperate across the Internet.

Features

With the prioritized lists of needs as your criteria for judging
products, decide which products match your requirements. As
part of your evaluation, you'll develop spreadsheets that match
products to needs. You can share these with the users to help
them decide which tools are best for them. Here are the steps to
follow in evaluating features.

- Set up a spreadsheet listing the requirements, in their
  prioritized order, down the left side of the spreadsheet.
- List each product across the top of the spreadsheet.
- Below each product, indicate if it meets each specific
  requirement.
- Below, list the strengths and weaknesses of each product.
- Set up additional spreadsheets for feature-by-feature
  comparisons.
- Identify missing features and note whether you can
  modify the products to meet the needs or whether you
  can live without those features.
- List features each product has that you don't need. Iden-
  tify those that would come in handy and those that

would simply get in the user's way or cause unnecessary complexity.

You may need to weigh some user priorities and operational priorities when you make your decision.

There are some major differences in features between proprietary products, such as Notes, and intranet groupware. One difference is security—Notes is much more secure, but that will change with Netscape's addition of authentication by a certificate server and secured transactions with Netscape's Secured Sockets Layer (SSL).

Another difference is support for disconnected users. Proprietary groupware does replication, which lets you work off-line. Since we can dial in from remote locations and access information on the intranet, we haven't worried about replication. That's changing with the IMAP4 protocol, which supports disconnected e-mail use.

Since there currently isn't another product on the market that does what Notes does, the issue may come down to when you need groupware and if you can afford to wait. If you need all the features of Notes, and you need them now, you probably should go with Notes. If you can afford to wait, which you should be able to do if your workgroups aren't already screaming for groupware, then you may want to watch and evaluate intranet groupware. Rather than focusing on what each product has today, think about what each will have by the time you need it. It may take some time to get people collaborating, which you should do before introducing products. We'll talk about this in Chapter 10.

This isn't necessarily an either/or decision. Many companies are using a mixture of groupware products. They have Notes coexisting with their intranets. What I've noticed is that Notes implementation is rarely universal throughout an organization. There are usually pockets of Notes users. If you already have some Notes outposts in your organization, you're certainly not going to throw it away. You may want to consider making the information in Notes available to other users from their browsers. Those who are already familiar with Notes and who have extensive Notes applications built may want to use the newer Notes tools, such as

Domino or InterNotes Web Publisher, for publishing on both the internal and external Web. They can also make their Notes forms accessible from browsers so users can input to Notes databases and applications.

Let's look at how to evaluate each type of groupware product. For every product, you'll want to know which platforms they support and which browsers they work with. You should expect them to be graphical and intuitive, and to provide robust help and tutorials. Here are some specific things that are unique to the different types of groupware products, and what you should look for.

Calendaring and Scheduling

- ◆ Does it provide both personal and group calendaring?
- ◆ Does it provide individual and group address lists?
- ◆ Does it provide other tools, such as contact managers, phone books, and project managers?
- ◆ Can it find possible meeting times for all attendees?
- ◆ Can it schedule recurring appointments?
- ◆ Does it let recipients RSVP for meetings?
- ◆ How integrated are all the functions?
- ◆ How easy is it to use?
- ◆ Does it offer drag-and-drop features?
- ◆ Does it let you do searches?
- ◆ Can you access it over the Internet?
- ◆ Can you look at day, week, and month views and manipulate calendars in all views?
- ◆ Does it provide to-do lists?
- ◆ Can you assign tasks to others?
- ◆ Can you print reports in various formats?
- ◆ Which e-mail protocols does it support?
- ◆ Does it provide tools for migrating from other calendaring systems?

Voice Conferencing and Videoconferencing

- How many users can connect simultaneously?
- Does it run inside or outside a Web browser?

Electronic Meeting Systems

- How many users can you have?
- Which meeting tools does it provide?
- Does it provide tools to help sort items into categories and prioritize them?

Whiteboards and Data Conferencing

- How many users can connect simultaneously?
- How many users can share files simultaneously?
- Can you share applications and chat simultaneously?
- What kinds of files does it support?
- Can you share applications, such as Excel spreadsheets and Word documents?
- Which whiteboard tools does it provide?
- Can you capture, save, and print the marked-up file from the whiteboard?
- Can you save application changes from the whiteboard to a file?

Chat

- Is it intuitive and easy to use?
- How many users can it support simultaneously?
- Does it provide a transcript of the discussion?

E-mail

- Which protocols does it support?
- Does it integrate with calendaring and scheduling, conferencing, workflow, and electronic forms?

- Does it provide a universal in box?
- Does it provide off-line reading and message creation?
- Can users access their mail from their browsers?
- How easy is it to use?
- Does it provide filtering and search capabilities?
- Does it support attachments?
- Does it provide management tools?
- Is there a conversion tool for migrating existing e-mail messages and address lists?

Conferencing and Newsgroups

- Does it provide threaded discussions?
- Does it support public and private folders?
- Can you attach files and incorporate URLs in messages?
- Can you create HTML messages?
- What types of views does it support?
- Does it support full-text searches?
- Does it provide off-line reading and message creation?
- Does it support moderators, polling, and anonymous postings?
- Can new users enroll themselves?
- Does it provide gateways for Usenet newsgroups and electronic mail?
- Does it support mobile dial-up users?
- Does it store messages as threads in discussion databases, as documents in databases, or in folders? This can impact how easily you can maintain and delete messages.
- Does it require or include a Web server or will it work with yours?
- Does it provide selective replication for replicating only certain discussions, or do you have to replicate entire databases?

Knowledge Repositories

- Does it store documents as HTML or in their native format? If it stores documents as HTML, you must either use HTML to update them or reconvert them from their native format after updates.
- Do conversions happen on the fly? Converting on the fly can be slow.
- Does it provide tools for converting documents to HTML?
- Does it include authoring tools? Are they easy to use?
- Does it provide a variety of ways for users to load documents?
- Does it support or provide viewers for common word processing and other files?
- Does it do full-text searching?
- Does it handle checkout and check-in, version control, and archiving of documents?
- Can users replicate and synchronize databases for working off-line?
- Does it integrate with other tools to store discussions or support workflow?
- Does it provide migration tools for moving documents from other databases?
- Does it support programming languages and other tools for extending its capabilities?
- Does it support remote access via dial-up modems?
- Does it provide management tools?
- Does it come with a database or do you have to acquire and set one up separately?

Group Writing and Shared Editing

- How many users can work simultaneously on the same document?

♦ Does it allow for, and provide help with, resolution of simultaneous changes to the same information?

♦ Does it provide a history of changes that you can use to backtrack if necessary?

Workflow

♦ Does it work inside, or outside, the Web browser?

♦ Does it provide electronic forms?

♦ Does it include a forms design tool?

♦ Does it include customizable templates?

♦ Does it integrate with other applications?

♦ Does it utilize databases or messaging for routing?

♦ Does it provide for calculations and validation?

♦ Which programming languages and scripting development tools, such as Java, JavaScript, and ActiveX, does it support for enhancing workflow applications?

Integrated or Specialized

Intranet groupware today, with very few exceptions, requires you to mix and match to get all the features you need. This can be expensive and you may face compatibility issues.

There's a vast difference between Lotus, which covers many areas of collaborative computing, and smaller companies, whose specialized products focus on niche applications, such as calendaring or Internet phone. You'll need to determine whether you require an integrated product or whether you can put together specialized products for specific user populations. If you choose to go with niche products, will they work for your power users? Will you need to extend or replace them as your users outgrow them? How much pain will doing so cause?

The disadvantage of most integrated products is cost. With them, you'll pay for some features that not everyone will use. There are widespread reports that most Lotus Notes users use less than 20 percent of its features and capabilities. Most of them use the discussion databases and very little more. Collabra recognized this and billed its Collabra Share product as having 80 percent of Notes' functionality at 20 percent of Notes' price.

The disadvantage of specialized niche products is that they may not easily integrate and interoperate with the other products you have or those you'll add later. You may outgrow them and want to move up to something else. If they're fairly cheap, you won't lose much by throwing them away when something better comes along, especially if they're truly open, which means that you can easily migrate your existing information to a new product.

Ease of Use

How easily can your users get up and running on each product? Will they need to attend specialized classes, or can they figure it out by themselves? Getting products accepted and used often depends on how easy they are for users to figure out and use. A lot of users are just too busy to stop and go to classes, but if it's easy to figure out, they can do it themselves. Users these days have become very computer-savvy, as long as the technology isn't obscure. This is one of the reasons that intranets have been instant hits in most organizations—they're so easy to use that users have them figured out in no time. This makes any application you can run on a browser instantly compelling.

Training and Support

Proprietary groupware, such as Lotus Notes, requires an army of highly trained programmers and systems administrators, not to mention trainers and support people. In contrast, intranets are relatively cheap and easy to install, and don't require lots of trainers and support people. Users can download browsers from an intranet and use them with minimal training and support. In addition, though you'll need programmers for highly sophisticated applications, you can get by with fewer people for intranets than for products such as Notes.

How much training will users and developers need? What about support? These are factors that made Lotus Notes somewhat expensive. Notes hasn't been inherently intuitive, and has required expensive classes, even for users. By putting applications in Web browsers, you instantly minimize training because users

already understand the Web paradigm. They need to know only
how the application works.

Cost

How much will it cost? This is much less of an issue now with
intranet groupware. Since your intranet is probably already in
place, or soon will be, and many of these tools fit on top of or
inside the intranet, the incremental cost for new applications is
relatively small.

In the area of total cost there has been a lot of Lotus Notes con-
troversy. Notes has been a very expensive product to buy, implement, and maintain. For example, most estimates put the start-up
cost of Notes at about $2,000 per user, including training. If you
add specialized applications, you can expect to pay another few
hundred to few thousand dollars per user to get started. Because
of all the additional applications, one estimate says that most
Notes installations cost about $4,000 per user. Most caution that
you should budget several times the cost of the software for training and support. This may change as IBM makes Notes more price
competitive and as browsers become a standard user interface into
Notes.

Some of the integrated intranet groupware and document
databases for knowledge repositories can cost just about as much
as the Notes software. The difference in total cost comes from the
minimal amount of training and support required for getting users
up and running on these products, since they use Web browsers.
They end up costing one-half to one-third what Notes costs.

In evaluating products, look at how complex the product is and
how difficult it will be to set up. Will you need lots of technical
consultants to help you get it up and running? Will you need to
spend megabucks to train developers and users? Some statistics
have placed these costs at three to five times the cost of the software itself. Add all this up. What's the total cost? One analysis
said that only large organizations can afford Notes because it's just
too complex and expensive for small or medium-size businesses.

In *The Netscape Intranet Vision and Product Roadmap,* found
at http://www.netscape.com/comprod/at_work/white_paper/
intranet/vision.html, Marc Andreessen and The Netscape Product

Team compared Netscape solutions to prices for their proprietary competitors:

> *Netscape's intranet solution is significantly cheaper to acquire and to own than competitive systems. First, the software is significantly cheaper to acquire. (For example, the cost of acquiring Navigator and one SuiteSpot bundle and 1,000 clients is approximately $33,000. Current cost estimates for comparable Microsoft BackOffice and Lotus Notes packages are approximately $170,000 and $277,000, respectively.) Then, training and development costs are slashed through use of an industry-standard unified user interface—Navigator—and industry-standard APIs and scripting and programming languages. Finally, applications can be developed and deployed far more easily in the Netscape environment.*

As part of addressing cost, you'll want to look at resource issues related to adding these products. Will any of them cause you to have to add resources, such as servers, storage, bandwidth, or people?

Deployment

You'll want to consider how to deploy these new applications. Do they run on the server so users can simply access them with a browser? Do you have to deploy specific software to individual machines? This can make a major difference in the amount of work needed to roll out the application to all users. Do you have an easy way for your users to acquire the software they need? What about upgrades? How much work will it require to upgrade users' software and hardware?

Fit

It's important to assess how each product would fit in with your infrastructure. Does it support all the platforms you have, or will only users on certain platforms need it?

Stability

How stable is the product? Is it a brand-new product, or has it been around and been debugged? Products recently converted from client/server to the Web may have an edge when it comes to stability since they've only been converted to a different environment, not written from the ground up.

Vendor Support

In any assessment of software, you should consider whether the vendor has been around long enough and is likely to stay around. What is your experience with this vendor, and what is its track record for customer support? Check with others to find out their experiences with this vendor. Are you willing to try out a new vendor? There are advantages to working with small vendors that may try harder to satisfy your needs, and may even add your requirements into new versions. That may depend upon what kind of product it is and how you'll use it. It may not be desirable to stake your mission-critical applications, such as workflow, on a brand-new vendor.

Decide Which Products to Present to Users

Once you've gone through all the criteria in evaluating the products, you should be able to select those that will fit your needs and your environment. IT should select only the products that it can live with, because the next step involves letting the users choose the actual product. Select products with the entire organization in mind, because if all goes well, you'll roll out this groupware to the entire organization.

Show Products to the Users and Discuss Them

I believe the users should choose their own tools with guidance from the IT folks. At TI, for example, a specific group of users has a need for which IT is helping them identify the appropriate tools. That group of users is deciding which tool they want and funding the acquisition and piloting of that tool. You can feel pretty certain that this project will be a success because the users have identified their needs and are choosing and paying for the solution with help and guidance from their partners in IT. That's the way to do groupware!

You should put together a small demo of each product to show the users and help them understand what each product does. Be prepared to discuss the features of each, and maybe even give the users copies of your evaluation spreadsheets. You should talk about what each product can do for the users. Be sure to discuss cost and implementation issues that they should be aware of. They should have all the information they need to make a decision, but should rely on IT to have made the right technology choices. It's conceivable that you might want to lend your demo computer to the users for a few days or weeks to let them play with the applications before getting together to make a decision.

When you do get together to make the decision, it would be worthwhile to have a facilitator help the group walk through an analysis of how the products meet their needs, and to conduct a decision-making session. Once the group makes the decision, then it should decide upon the action steps for preparing and deploying the pilot application.

Advantages and Benefits of Intranet Groupware

Certainly the most talked about advantage of intranet groupware is the low cost. Since intranet groupware goes on top of an already existing platform, it's generally very inexpensive to deploy. Since much of it works with browsers, which users already know how to use, you have only to help users become aware of the nuances of the specific applications. This greatly diminishes the cost of training and support. Since many of these applications reside on the server and run from there, you don't even have to go around putting additional applications on everyone's computer.

As long as we're talking about costs, another advantage is the ability of intranet groupware to *save costs*. For example, we mentioned earlier that TI saved $100,000 by not purchasing a piece of equipment because they arranged to borrow one through a newsgroup. Applying this internally, if groups can share expensive resources, there's a huge potential for cost savings.

Another advantage is the ability to provide access to users on a wide variety of platforms. Doing this with proprietary groupware is especially challenging because many applications run only on certain platforms. Web browsers are universal, so you can deploy applications that run on browsers to everyone regardless of platform.

Groupware also improves productivity by creating better communication and coordination. Through conferencing software, you can decrease the need for meetings while still encouraging group decision making and teamwork. Data conferencing, videoconferencing, and chat tools help geographically dispersed teams to stay in touch and work together more effectively and productively. Those who are traveling or are telecommuters can still participate in decisions through these discussions.

In addition, groupware creates a valuable repository of corporate knowledge containing such things as lessons learned, best practices, ideas and experiences, and the expertise of company experts. This sharing of knowledge enables people to make the right decisions and do the right things.

Another advantage of some of the current crop of intranet groupware is that they obscure some of the more difficult tasks from the user. David Weinberger talks about this in "The Death (and Rebirth) of Document Management," a white paper from Open Text Corporation. (By the way, Weinberger has one of the best e-mail addresses I've seen—it's *self@evident.com*.) He says that in the past, document management systems have typically been only for full-time document professionals, and they've used document management systems for only the most complex and high-value documents. Open Text believes that document management and workflow should function without the users being aware of what they're using. Weinberger says that this overturns some of the fundamental assumptions of document management:

> *First, the traditional document management vendors have insisted that "Document management isn't about managing documents. It's about managing information." That contains an important insight about what is of value in a document. But, it is overturned by the fact that document management isn't even primarily about managing information. It's about enabling*

people to succeed at their jobs. It's about helping processes and interactions, not about managing a particular type of data.

Second, the industry has patted itself on the back because "Documents are the most complex data type." Well, yes, documents are far more complex than relational data. But they pale next to the complexity of people and projects.

One of my personal favorite advantages relates to conferencing tools, and this doesn't just apply to the intranet ones. Conferencing helps people participate by using their preferred thinking styles. According to the Myers-Briggs Type Indicator, a personal-style inventory, some people are introverts and others are extraverts. (Yes, Myers-Briggs spells *extravert* with an *a* instead of an *o*.) Extraverts tend to prefer to think out loud and in groups, and may do some of their best thinking in meetings where they can bat ideas about with others. Introverts are just the opposite, and may not contribute as many new ideas in meetings. They tend to want to take time to think by themselves before contributing to the group, and they like to know the meeting agenda and expectations in advance so they can prepare their ideas. Conferencing supports the preferred style for each type. Extraverts may tend to get right into the thick of the discussion, firing off one idea after another as they refine their thoughts and get input from others. If an impulse hits them, they have a message composed and sent before you can bat an eyelash. Introverts, on the other hand, will think through and refine their thoughts first, and maybe even go through several iterations, before finally submitting those ideas to the group. Conferencing makes it easy for both types to work the way they're most comfortable.

Disadvantages of Intranet Groupware

I won't get into the economics of intranets in this book since I covered that in my earlier book. I'll talk instead about the additional costs involved when adding groupware to the intranet. While intranet groupware is generally far less expensive than proprietary groupware, some of the new integrated tools have price tags that are pretty significant. However, even if the cost of the software is in the range of Lotus Notes, if you don't have to spend as much for training and support, you've still saved lots of money in the long run.

If we're going to store away lots of information for others to use, someone must take responsibility for cataloging information and making sure that outdated information gets purged from the system. Just as on the Internet, you can find information on intranets and in knowledge repositories whose authenticity and validity may be difficult to verify. With the lifespan of your products becoming shorter and shorter, information will also become obsolete quicker. It's important that you have a way to distinguish what's important and valuable from what's outdated and obsolete. This is something that few organizations have yet dealt with because most information on intranets is relatively new. Organizations have record-retention guidelines for paper and electronic media, and must soon do the same thing for their internal webs.

One of the serious disadvantages that we're just beginning to face is the problem of information overload. This is all so new that we haven't gotten too concerned about it yet. We can only drink from the fire hose so long before we realize that we must create more effective ways of dealing with too much information. We can expect a proliferation of agents in our groupware to help us filter information from both inside and outside the organization.

Security is currently an issue for intranets, but that will be solved soon. Right now on intranets there isn't a way to authenticate the person with whom you're interacting. By contrast, Notes passes a certificate to verify the identity of the user. The addition of SSL and certificate servers for authentication should solve this problem within the very near future.

As we've mentioned before, intranet groupware also doesn't currently support disconnected users, but that should be solved within the first half of 1997.

Finally, HTML doesn't provide the kind of rich interface that you get from proprietary products. With the addition of plug-ins such as Java and ActiveX, we'll see much more interesting applications, including more interactivity. Today, you have to configure plug-ins on each desktop, which negates one of the advantages of intranets. When browsers automatically load and configure plug-ins for us, that'll no longer be an issue.

Checklist: Choosing Intranet Groupware

Figure 7.1 summarizes the steps involved in choosing intranet groupware:

---

1. Identify and prioritize needs

   ◆ Identify user needs—facilitated meeting

      ◆ *Dump* session

         ◆ How things are currently done
         ◆ Needs, problems, and frustrations
         ◆ Ideas for how to do things better

      ◆ Categorize dump lists

         ◆ Who has these needs?
         ◆ What are their jobs?
         ◆ How do they do these things today?
         ◆ Who does what?
         ◆ Which kinds of computers and software do they use?
         ◆ Which groups must they coordinate with to accomplish those jobs?
         ◆ What features and characteristics do they need to solve these problems?
         ◆ What's on their wish list?

      ◆ Distill into list of requirements
      ◆ Prioritize requirements

- ◆ Identify IT infrastructure and operational needs

  - ◆ List what's important

    - ◆ Which platforms must the software run on?
    - ◆ Do you need open standards or is a proprietary solution acceptable?
  - ◆ Prioritize requirements

2. Identify and select products to present to the users—which products meet your needs?

   - ◆ Platforms

     - ◆ Which platforms do you have?
     - ◆ Which platforms does each product support?

   - ◆ Openness

     - ◆ How open is the product?
     - ◆ Should you select only products based on open systems, or are proprietary products OK?
     - ◆ Which products are open standards–based, and which are proprietary systems with open standards connections?

   - ◆ Features

     - ◆ Steps to follow in evaluating features

       - ◆ Set up spreadsheet listing prioritized requirements down the left column
       - ◆ List each product across the top
       - ◆ Below each product, indicate if it meets each requirement

- ◆ Below, list strengths and weaknesses of each product
- ◆ Set up additional spreadsheets for feature-by-feature comparisons
- ◆ Identify missing features and note whether you can modify the products or live without those features
- ◆ List features you don't need and those that would cause problems

- ◆ When do you need groupware, and can you afford to wait?
- ◆ Evaluating each category of groupware product below

  - ◆ Which platforms does it support?
  - ◆ Which browsers does it support?
  - ◆ Is it graphical and intuitive?
  - ◆ Does it provide robust help and tutorials?

- ◆ Calendaring and scheduling

  - ◆ Does it provide both personal and group calendaring?
  - ◆ Does it provide individual and group address lists?
  - ◆ Does it provide other tools, such as contact managers, phone books, and project managers?
  - ◆ Can it find possible meeting times for all attendees?
  - ◆ Can it schedule recurring appointments?

- Does it let recipients RSVP for meetings?
- How integrated are all the functions?
- How easy is it to use?
- Does it offer drag-and-drop features?
- Does it let you do searches?
- Can you access it over the Internet?
- Can you look at day, week, and month views and manipulate calendars in all views?
- Does it provide to-do lists?
- Can you assign tasks to others?
- Can you print reports in various formats?
- Which e-mail protocols does it support?
- Does it provide tools for migrating from other calendaring systems?

- Voice conferencing and videoconferencing

  - How many users can connect simultaneously?
  - Does it run inside or outside a Web browser?

- Electronic meeting systems

  - How many users can you have?
  - Which meeting tools does it provide?
  - Does it provide tools to help sort items into categories and prioritize them?

- Whiteboards and data conferencing

  - How many users can connect simultaneously?

- How many users can share files simultaneously?
- Can you share applications and chat simultaneously?
- What kinds of files does it support?
- Can you share applications, such as Excel spreadsheets and Word documents?
- Which whiteboard tools does it provide?
- Can you capture, save, and print the marked-up file from the whiteboard?
- Can you save application changes from the whiteboard to a file?

- Chat

  - Is it intuitive and easy to use?
  - How many users can it support simultaneously?
  - Does it provide a transcript of the discussion?

- E-mail

  - Which protocols does it support?
  - Does it integrate with calendaring and scheduling, conferencing, workflow, and electronic forms?
  - Does it provide a universal in box?
  - Does it provide off-line reading and message creation?
  - Can users access their mail from their browsers?

- How easy is it to use?
- Does it provide filtering and search capabilities?
- Does it support attachments?
- Does it provide management tools?
- Is there a conversion tool for migrating existing e-mail messages and address lists?

- Conferencing and newsgroups

  - Does it provide threaded discussions?
  - Does it support public and private folders?
  - Can you attach files and incorporate URLs in messages?
  - Can you create HTML messages?
  - What types of views does it support?
  - Does it support full-text searches?
  - Does it provide off-line reading and message creation?
  - Does it support moderators, polling, and anonymous postings?
  - Can new users enroll themselves?
  - Does it provide gateways for Usenet newsgroups and electronic mail?
  - Does it support mobile dial-up users?
  - Does it store messages as threads in discussion databases, as documents in databases, or in folders?
  - Does it require or include a Web server or will it work with yours?

◆ Does it provide selective replication or do you have to replicate entire databases?

◆ Knowledge repositories

◆ Does it store documents as HTML or in their native format?

◆ Do conversions happen on the fly?

◆ Does it provide tools for converting documents to HTML?

◆ Does it include authoring tools, and are they easy to use?

◆ Does it provide a variety of ways for users to load documents?

◆ Does it support or provide viewers for common word processing and other files?

◆ Does it do full-text searching?

◆ Does it handle checkout and check-in, version control, and archiving of documents?

◆ Can users replicate and synchronize databases for working off-line?

◆ Does it integrate with other tools to store discussions or support workflow?

◆ Does it provide migration tools for moving documents from other databases?

◆ Does it support programming languages and other tools for extending its capabilities?

◆ Does it support remote access via dial-up modems?

◆ Does it provide management tools?

♦ Does it come with a database or do you have to acquire and set one up separately?

♦ Group writing and shared editing

  ♦ How many users can work simultaneously on the same document?

  ♦ Does it allow for, and provide help with, resolution of simultaneous changes?

  ♦ Does it provide a history of changes that you can use to backtrack if necessary?

♦ Workflow

  ♦ Does it work inside, or outside, the Web browser?

  ♦ Does it provide electronic forms?

  ♦ Does it include a forms design tool?

  ♦ Does it include customizable templates?

  ♦ Does it integrate with other applications?

  ♦ Does it utilize databases or messaging for routing?

  ♦ Does it provide for calculations and validation?

  ♦ Which programming languages and scripting tools does it support?

♦ Integrated or specialized

  ♦ Do you need an integrated product?

  ♦ Can you put together specialized products for specific user populations?

- Will niche products work for your power users?
- Will you need to extend or replace them as your users outgrow them, and how much pain will doing so cause?

- Ease of use

  - How easily can your users get up and running on each product?
  - Will they need to attend specialized classes, or can they figure it out by themselves?

- Training and support

  - Does it require programmers, systems administrators, trainers, and support people?
  - How much training will users and developers need?
  - What about support?

- Cost

  - How much will it cost?
  - How complex is the product and how difficult will it be to set up?
  - Will you need lots of technical consultants to help you get it up and running?
  - Will you need to spend megabucks to train developers and users?
  - What's the total cost?
  - Will you have to add resources, such as servers, storage, bandwidth, or people?

- Deployment

    - How will you deploy these new applications?
    - Do they run on the server so users can simply access them with a browser?
    - Do you have to deploy specific software to individual machines?
    - Do you have an easy way for your users to acquire the software they need?
    - What about upgrades?
    - How much work will it require to upgrade users' software and hardware?

- Fit—does it support all the platforms you have, or will only users on certain platforms need it?
- Stability

    - How stable is the product?
    - Is it a brand-new product, or has it been around and been debugged?

- Vendor support

    - Has the vendor been around long?
    - Is the vendor likely to stay around?
    - What is your experience with this vendor?
    - What is the vendor's track record for customer support?
    - Check with others to find out their experiences with this vendor
    - Are you willing to try out a new vendor?

3. Decide which products to present to users—IT should select only the products it can live with
4. Show products to the users and discuss them

- Create a demo of each product to show users
- Users should choose their own tools with guidance from IT

  - Discuss the features of each
  - Give users copies of your evaluation spreadsheets
  - Talk about what each product can do for the users
  - Discuss cost and implementation issues

- Facilitated meeting to decide

  - Analyze how products meet their needs
  - Decide on products
  - Decide on action steps for pilot

Figure 7.1   Choosing intranet groupware checklist.

In Part 2, we discussed the nature of groupware and how to use it.

1. Chapter 4 defined groupware and explained why you need it.
2. Chapter 5 examined what groupware does and how we use it.
3. Chapter 6 looked at selected intranet groupware and workflow products.
4. Chapter 7 discussed how to choose intranet groupware and the advantages and disadvantages of it.

In Part 3, we'll discuss how to implement groupware.

1. Chapter 8 examines how to build your intranet—this chapter is for those who haven't read *Intranet Business Strategies.*
2. Chapter 9 discusses what makes groupware so hard to implement.
3. Chapter 10 explains two approaches to implementing groupware.
4. Chapter 11 examines the impact of groupware and workflow.

PART THREE

How Do You Implement Groupware and What Is the Impact of It?

chapter eight

Building Your Intranet

Two Different Ways You Can Get Started

This chapter is a very abbreviated version of the two ways you can build an intranet for your organization. It's for those who haven't read my *Intranet Business Strategies* book. If you've already read it, then skip to Chapter 9.

Of the 13 companies I worked with on these books, each took a slightly different approach to building their intranets, but there were lots of similarities. Some started with a formal program, whereas others started with an informal, grassroots effort. We'll look at two different ways you can create your intranet:

1. *Traditional model*—The formal approach
2. *Internet model*—The grassroots approach

Traditional Model

This approach is the way that we do expensive IT projects. It requires a formal request for funding, a specific plan, a cost-benefit analysis, and return on investment (ROI) calculations. Once you get approval, you move on to implementation. The steps in the traditional model are as follows:

1. Do you need an intranet?
2. Are you ready?
3. Develop a project plan and proposal.

4. Present the proposal and sell the concept.

5. Implement it.

6. Measure the results.

Step 1: Do You Need an Intranet?

First you determine why you need or want an intranet. You can hardly pick up a magazine without seeing an article about the use of intranets. Have your internal customers read those same articles? Are they asking you for an intranet? Is there a need in your organization that an intranet could meet? Intranets often start from grassroots efforts. Some employees see a need that an internal web can fill, and they put together a prototype to show to management, who creates a team to start working on it.

Start by determining the goals of your organization and what an intranet can do to meet those goals. If you aren't looking at meeting the needs and goals of your organization, then you're looking at this backward. This isn't hard. Can an intranet help you meet a competitive threat? Can it help you do things faster, better, and cheaper? Can an intranet provide the technology to help you reengineer a business process? It shouldn't be hard to spot opportunities for an intranet to make a difference.

Step 2: Are You Ready?

Once you've determined that you need an intranet, then you should determine what it would take to create one.

1. Which area or areas of the organization should be part of the initial intranet project? This could be enterprise wide, or just a workgroup or department.

2. Do you have the right infrastructure?

   ◆ Does this area have PCs, Macintoshes, UNIX machines, mainframe terminals, or no desktop machines at all? Will you need any computers?

   ◆ Is this area on a LAN or WAN? If not, what's necessary to put it on one?

◆ Does the LAN or WAN use TCP/IP? If not, you can:

  ◆ Load an Internet Protocol (IP) stack on each machine.
  ◆ Have IP reside on a gateway server.

If you're missing any of these components, you'll need to plunk down some serious money to change that. If you have TCP/IP in use, you're ready to move on.

3. Do you have the right skills and resources to set up internal web technology, e-mail, and the other intranet tools? You can hire the expertise, if necessary.

  ◆ Do you have expertise in setting up and running TCP/IP on the networks?
  ◆ Do you have expertise in UNIX or Windows NT?

4. Do you have the resources to handle the extra workload of an intranet?

5. Do you have someone who can take the lead in developing and maintaining applications for the internal web?

Step 3: Develop a Project Plan and Proposal

This step requires that you detail the problems your intranet will solve, determine the cost of building it, and detail the benefits you will derive. You'll use this information to create the proposal you'll present to request funding. You may find it helpful to bring in a consultant at this stage to help you develop the proposal.

Since technology projects often emerge from business process improvement (BPI) projects, let's say for illustration purposes that we've worked on a human resources BPI project for the Benefits Department and the team is recommending an intranet. We'll use this premise for our proposal. This is a highly simplistic example for illustration purposes only. In your own proposal, you'll need a lot more detail, complete with facts and numbers.

Sample Proposal: Benefits BPI Project

Figure 8.1 is a sample proposal for an intranet related to the Benefits BPI project. You may wish to look over each section of the proposal as I discuss it. This proposal focuses on the four BPI steps that come before the request for funding:

The Benefits BPI Team has reviewed the benefits process in great detail. We have talked with employees and members of the Benefits Department staff to discover the problems with the current process. We have looked at the best practices of other companies and have created a new process based upon implementation of an intranet.

Problems with the Benefits Process

There are two major problems with the benefits process which led us to investigate it. We interviewed members of the Benefits staff and other employees and verified these problems:

1. The Benefits staff feels that the current process of printing and distributing manuals is just too expensive, especially since changes are coming faster and faster these days. As soon as they get a manual updated, something else changes and they must start all over. They just don't seem to be able to catch up.

2. Employees feel that they have a hard time getting the benefits information they need. Their manuals are always outdated, and they can never find anyone in HR to answer their questions when they need help.

The Current Process and Why the Problems Occur

The current process flow (documented in the appendix of this proposal) shows some of the process steps that are part of the problem. For example:

- When there are *major* changes in benefits, the company rewrites the benefits manuals, prints them, mails copies to all locations, and warehouses sufficient copies to last until the next printing. This usually happens once per year per manual.
- When there are *minor* changes in benefits, the company publishes and mails revision letters with a page outlining the changes. Employees must insert these pages in their benefits manuals. Extra copies go to the warehouse for distribution with any manuals shipped in the future. This usually happens about three times per year per manual.
- Locations order extra copies of manuals and revisions from the warehouse to give to new employees.

The major process problems are:

- The process of making changes is very time-consuming.
- Things are changing faster and faster each year, and Benefits just can't seem to keep up.
- Because of the speed of these changes, manuals quickly become obsolete.
- The current process is very expensive because we have to print, distribute, and warehouse these manuals.
- Employees don't have easy access to this information, and they need the most current information.
- Employees can't always find someone to answer their questions or to update them on their status.
- It's hard for people to follow the manuals due to all the insert sheets detailing changes to the plan.

These problems occur because the Benefits Department just doesn't have a better way to distribute benefits information.

The Future Process That Will Solve the Problems

The BPI team proposes creating a new process (detailed in the appendix) for Benefits, including implementing an intranet, to solve the problem. An *intranet* is a private network that exists totally inside the company. A computer, called a *server,* will store all the benefits documents and make them readily available anytime someone needs access to them. We will place a piece of software, called a *browser,* on every computer. It will allow easy access to the benefits documents, regardless of the user's location.

An intranet will provide access for everyone to the latest information, and will be far less costly than the current process. Benefits can do updates quickly and easily, and everyone will have access immediately. The consequence of *not* doing this is that Benefits will fall further and further behind in disseminating changes, and employees won't have the most current information. Time lags in informing employees of changes could be costly to the company or to employees.

Implementation Plan for the Future Process

The team created a detailed implementation plan, complete with cost justification and a time line. You will find the detailed exhibits in the appendix.

Detailed Implementation Plan

The major steps in our implementation plan are:

1. Acquire and install server hardware and software.
2. Train administrators.
3. Acquire and install browser software.
4. Acquire and install publishing software.
5. Train Benefits staff on publishing software.
6. Convert benefits manuals and add revisions.

7. Create tutorials on the internal web.

8. Hold rollout meetings.

You can find the details of this implementation plan in the appendix.

Cost Justification

The cost justification consists of three parts:

1. Benefits and savings

2. Cost and expenditures

3. Summary and calculation of ROI

Benefits and Savings

The tangible cost savings from implementing an intranet will be approximately $199,000 the first year, as detailed in the appendix. (Figure 8.2 contains the cost justification that would normally appear in the appendix.) In addition, we expect to see intangible benefits in providing easy access to current information to all our employees. Not included are the savings to the Benefits Department from answering fewer phone calls. The time saved should allow them to do a better job of serving their existing customers. In addition, once the infrastructure for an intranet is in place, the entire organization can use it to achieve other significant cost savings.

Cost and Expenditures

The computing infrastructure and TCP/IP are already in place so the major expenditures are for servers and browsers. The costs of implementing the intranet total $79,500, as detailed in the appendix. (See Figure 8.2.)

Summary and Calculation of ROI

The first-year cost savings of $199,000 less implementation expenditures of $79,500 provide total savings of $119,500 the first year. (See Figure 8.2.) This yields an ROI of 150 percent.

Time Line

We will start immediately upon approval of this project. The detailed time line appears in the appendix. (Figure 8.3 contains the time line that would appear in the appendix.) We will order all hardware and software and begin training the first month. The process of converting benefits documents will begin immediately upon installation of the publishing software and completion of the training. The conversion process will be complete by the end of month 3, and rollout meetings will take place in month 4 to roll out the new benefits documentation to all employees.

Figure 8.1 Sample proposal: Benefits BPI project.

Identify the Problems with the Process   In this part of the proposal, we talk about the initial problems that led us to investigate the process. In the proposal we can see that the team has identified the two major problems with the benefits process:

1. The process of printing and distributing manuals is very expensive, and continues to get worse.
2. Employees aren't able to get the benefits information they need.

Define the Current Process and Why the Problems Occur   Next we talk about how the current process works and why it doesn't work any more. You should put your process flowcharts in the appendix of your proposal and refer your readers there for the details. For the sake of simplicity, I didn't include an appendix in this sample proposal. In the proposal, the team detailed the process for doing major and minor revisions to benefits manuals, which included writing, printing, and distributing the changes. Major revisions happen once per year per manual, and minor ones happen three times per year per manual. In addition, copies go to the warehouse to accommodate the addition of new employees.

Among the major process problems we detailed are that the changes are coming increasingly faster, making it difficult for the Benefits staff to catch up. Manuals are expensive to print and distribute, and become obsolete faster. This means that employees don't have the most current information. Benefits just needs a better way to distribute information.

Create a Future Process That Will Solve the Problems   In this part of the proposal we talk about the recommendations, explain what they are, and mention the consequences of not implementing them. In the proposal, the BPI team recommends creating an intranet to make benefits information available to everyone. There's a very simple explanation of what an intranet is. It explains that an intranet will provide the latest information to everyone, and that Benefits can quickly and easily update this information. The consequence of not implementing an intranet is that Benefits will continue to get further behind and employees won't have accurate information.

Develop an Implementation Plan for the Future Process   Next we talk about the implementation plan for the future process, which includes the cost justification and the time line.

Detailed implementation plan.   The implementation plan shows the eight high-level steps of the implementation and refers the reader to the detailed plan in the appendix.

Cost justification.   The cost justification has sections that talk about the benefits and savings, cost and expenditures, and the summary and calculation of ROI.

Benefits and savings.   In Figure 8.2, you can see the cost savings of $199,000 from implementing an intranet. In Figure 8.1, the proposal mentions additional cost savings. These include the potential created by having the intranet infrastructure already in place. Other areas of the organization can obtain similar savings with very little additional expenditure. Chapters 2 and 3 can give you lots of ideas for benefits from having an intranet.

Cost and expenditures. Figure 8.2 also shows the required expenditures to implement the intranet. The premise used is that the network infrastructure already exists and that TCP/IP is already on each machine. The required expenditure for server hardware and software, browsers, publishing software, and training amounts to $79,500.

Summary and calculation of ROI. Figure 8.2 shows that the result is an ROI of 150 percent!

Cost Savings from New Benefits Process		
Annual savings on the cost of preparing, printing, and mailing benefits manuals		
Major changes to manuals:		
4 manuals/yr. @ $12 per manual	96,000	
× 2,000 employees		
Minor changes to manuals:		
4 manuals × 3 changes/yr.	78,000	
@ $3.25 per change × 2,000 employees		
Eliminate one person from warehousing	25,000	
and mailing operation		
Total cost savings in year 1		199,000
Expenditures for New Benefits Process		
Server hardware and software	25,000	
Browser software @ $25 × 2,000	50,000	
Publishing software	1,000	
Training	3,500	
Total expenditures		79,500
Summary		
Cost savings in year 1		199,000
Expenditures		79,500
Net savings in year 1		119,500
ROI		150%

Figure 8.2 Sample cost justification: Benefits BPI project.

Time line.   Figure 8.3 shows the time line for implementing the intranet. The executives will pay close attention to this and will want to know when the project will be complete so you can start generating those cost savings. Make sure that your plan is realistic in this regard because if they remember nothing else, they'll remember your projected completion date.

Executive Summary: Benefits BPI Project

When you've completed your proposal, go back and distill it into a concise executive summary to attach to the front of the proposal. Executives won't have time to read the entire proposal, so give them a summary of what's most important. It should be no more than one or two pages. Give them the facts and sell them on the project.

Step 4: Present the Proposal and Sell the Concept

Next, you'll need to present this proposal to the executives who make the funding decisions. Make your presentation short and to the point, and remember to use simple and clear language. Intranets generate good ROIs, so it shouldn't be hard to get approval.

Steps	Month 1	Month 2	Month 3	Month 4
Acquire and install server hardware and software	███			
Train administrators	███			
Acquire and install browser software	█████			
Acquire and install publishing software	███			
Train Benefits staff on publishing software	███			
Convert benefits manuals and add revisions	██████			
Create tutorials on the internal web		█████		
Hold rollout meetings				███

Figure 8.3   Sample time line: Benefits BPI project.

Step 5: Implement It

Once you have approval, you can proceed with your plan. You may find it useful to do a pilot to work out the bugs before doing a full-fledged rollout.

Step 6: Measure the Results

Once you've implemented your intranet, look back at the results and compare them with your projections. You can also review what you've learned from the implementation to help you implement future applications such as groupware.

Internet Model

The second way to implement your intranet is the Internet model, which is an informal, grassroots approach. You allow the intranet to grow in the rapid, and sometimes chaotic, manner of the Internet. This way, your intranet will grow faster and quickly reach critical mass. If you have a network in place, you can use the Internet model because you won't have to go through formal approvals to get major funding.

Since the Internet model is very different from the traditional model we normally use, I'll go into a lot more detail about it. However, since the first two steps of both models are the same, I won't go into as much detail about them. The Internet model has nine steps:

1. Do you need an intranet?
2. Are you ready?
3. How do you proceed?
4. Build your intranet.
5. Create your audience.
6. Promote your intranet.
7. Create widespread enthusiasm and capability.

8. Make your intranet pervasive.
9. What lessons have we learned and where do we go from here?

Step 1: Do You Need an Intranet?

You first determine why you need or want an intranet. What are the goals or specific business needs that an intranet can help meet?

Step 2: Are You Ready?

Which areas of the organization need an intranet most? Those are good places to promote them. Do you need computers, networks, or network protocols? For purposes of this model, I'll presume you already have the infrastructure in place, or soon will. Also, do you have the expertise and resources to set up an intranet?

Step 3: How Do You Proceed?

This is where the two approaches diverge. You can do steps 3 through 6 of the Internet model concurrently.

Champions and Steering Committees

Once the CIO, or someone high in the organization, catches the vision of an intranet and becomes the champion, it becomes much easier. Most companies I spoke with had the CIO or someone else in IT as the champion or sponsor. In some cases, the champions included the CIO and his or her peers from corporate communications, human resources, or R&D. Some companies also had steering committees made up of the CIO and top IT management.

The goals of the champion and steering committee should be to determine where the intranet can best help the organization and to make sure it's deployed there. They also sponsor the intranet team, providing support, encouragement, and funding, and use their clout to overcome obstacles.

Often I hear that you must have support from the very top executives. In some organizations, that can be counterproductive because people won't put anything on the intranet without everyone's approval. If the top executives and management in these organizations will leave people alone to innovate and explore, the results may be amazing.

Should You Get Outside Help?

Once you have a champion, how do you proceed? First, identify your goals, and then decide what you need help with. This should dictate whether to hire some help or to go it alone. If you have the people and skills, you can certainly do it yourself. If you make mistakes, just try it again. Nobody gets the perfect intranet the first time —*don't expect to.* If you're running pretty *lean and mean,* you may want to bring in some assistance. If you hire some help, you'll get up to speed faster and avoid the pitfalls others have encountered.

What Should a Consultant Do?   Here are some of the things a consultant can help with or do for you:

- Help you identify your goals for the intranet
- Help you work through any organizational issues
- Meet with areas throughout your organization to help identify needs for an intranet and the types of information you should put on your intranet
- Help identify how people use the information and how you should provide it to them
- Help identify the sources and locations of information you need on your intranet
- Identify ways to get the information onto the intranet and determine any conversion that's required
- Identify any network infrastructure you need and help with the procurement and installation required to get the network ready for the intranet
- Identify the server hardware and server and browser software you need for the intranet and help with the installation

- Identify authoring and graphics tools for publishing web content
- Identify document databases, conversion tools, and any tools necessary to provide access to existing documents
- Assist with the development of the internal web structure and design
- Help develop guidelines and standards
- Help develop a publishing and approval process
- Help create demos
- Help promote the intranet throughout the organization
- Help form an intranet team and help them get focused
- Help develop applications and links to legacy databases
- Help figure out how to bring suppliers and customers into your intranet to provide opportunities for business partnerships
- Help identify and implement workflow and groupware
- Help identify and implement leading-edge technologies
- Help ensure you meet your intranet goals

With an intranet, you may not want to farm out quite as much as you would with an external Web site. You'll want to make sure your intranet fits your culture.

How Do You Select a Consultant?   How do you find and select a consultant to help you? Here are the steps.

1. *What kind of assistance is available?*   Hardware and software vendors offer intranet services and consulting, as do systems integrators. Recently there have been partnerships springing up to provide intranet services, such as HP and Netscape. There are also independent consultants who specialize in intranet and Internet consulting.

2. *How do you locate the kind of assistance you need?* Ask your hardware and software vendors about the services they provide, but remember that they also want to

sell products. Call the systems integrators you know. They focus on technology and solutions. You can find listings of intranet and Internet consultants on the Internet by using the search engines.

3. *How do you choose the right one for you?*   Ask whether these consultants can do the things for which you need assistance, or if they can help you find the resources to do so. What capabilities and alliances do they have? Large firms have lots of resources, but they can be expensive. Small firms may have alliances to bring you the things you need, and they cost less. Do you want one-stop shopping, or can you do some of the coordinating yourself?

4. *Talk to the people who would be working with you, not just the person selling the services.*   What have their intranet experiences been, and what is their perspective? Do they focus on the technology or on the solutions that an intranet can provide? Are you comfortable with them? Do they seem to know about your business and how it works? Do they understand your culture, and can they work within the constraints it imposes? Request the names of previous clients and talk with them to find out about their experiences. Did the consultant understand their needs? Were they happy with the consultant's work?

Your selection may come down to a *gut feel* as to which consultants will best fit with your culture and the people with whom they'll work. Make sure you and the consultant identify what you expect from each other and how you'll know whether the project was a success.

Step 4: Build Your Intranet

The role of the champion is to sow the seeds for the intranet. Now it's time for the champion to provide some initial funds to build a prototype or demo system, or even better, the real thing. The first thing you'll need to do is determine and develop your infrastructure needs.

Determine and Develop Infrastructure Needs

To run an intranet, you must generally have TCP/IP on your network. Do you have people with the skills to administer and support TCP/IP on your network? Do you have the network infrastructure to support the level of traffic you expect? Do you need additional bandwidth? As your intranet becomes larger and has more graphics, audio, and video, you'll need to increase network bandwidth. Take time now to project your needs and prepare for them. Should you outsource this to get bandwidth on demand? You may want to consider a network management tool, such as Network Health or Command, to document and analyze your WANs. Also, make sure that you teach web publishers how to create efficient pages.

How Will You Serve Remote Locations and Remote Users?

Make sure to consider how to provide remote locations and mobile users access to your intranet. Common ways to do that include the following:

1. Dedicated leased digital telephone lines
2. Nondedicated dial-up or switched access methods, from slowest to fastest, include:

    - Dial-up modem, which uses analog telephone lines
    - Integrated Services Digital Network (ISDN) modem, which uses digital telephone lines
    - Frame relay, which uses digital circuits
    - Asynchronous Transfer Mode (ATM), which is a new, high-speed switch technology

    There are three additional technologies to watch for possible future remote access:

1. Asymmetric digital subscriber line (ADSL) modem, which uses standard telephone lines
2. Cable modem, which uses television cable
3. Direct broadcast satellite (DBS)

Virtual private networks.   Virtual private networks (VPNs) let you use the Internet as though it were a private network for hooking up your remote locations. A VPN uses compatible firewalls on each end to encrypt transactions and permit access only to those with authorization. VPNs are less expensive and more flexible than dedicated lines.

Determine Security Needs and Implement Security

Security is a major concern when accessing the Internet or creating a VPN. Identify your security needs and determine how to implement them. Security is complex, and it changes quickly, so either read everything you can on the subject and proceed with care, or hire good help for setting up your Internet security. Check the appendix for the addresses of some security resources on the Internet. Security tools to consider include the following:

◆ *Firewall.*   To protect your network from intruders by monitoring the information passing through the firewall.

◆ *Encryption.*   Consists of *encrypting firewalls,* which let you exchange information confidentially across the Internet, and *message encryption,* which allows you to encrypt e-mail messages.

Also, consider having a clearly stated Internet security policy so your employees understand what things they should and shouldn't do. This should include regular use of virus-scanning and virus-protection tools.

Evaluate and Select an Internet Service Provider

In the appendix, you'll find lots of resources to help you locate Internet service providers (ISPs). Once you've located potential ISPs, you need to evaluate them and select one. UUNET Technologies provides an excellent list of criteria for selecting an ISP (*Selecting an Internet Provider,* at http://www.uu.net/ busguide.htm#selecting). I've paraphrased their eight criteria.

1. *Orientation.*   Does this provider focus on the needs of businesses?

2. *Quality of service.*   Is the service reliable, available, and high-performance?

3. *Points of Presence.*   Is the network Point of Presence (POP) close to your site? If so, it'll be less expensive.

4. *Service product range.*   Does the ISP provide a wide range of services that will meet all of your needs?

5. *Value-added capabilities.*   What value-added capabilities do they offer? Some of the ones that may interest you are setting up security and providing you with a domain name.

6. *Support.*   Do they have a 24-hour-per-day, 7-day-per-week Network Operation Center? Do they have personnel who focus only on the needs of business customers? Do they provide all the services you need?

7. *Experience.*   How long have they been an ISP? Is this their main business? How many business customers do they have and are those customers happy? Make sure you talk to some of those customers.

8. *Cost.*   While cost is important, it's only one of the criteria upon which to judge an ISP. It's best to avoid the cheapest provider because they must obviously scrimp somewhere to save on costs. Determine the range of prices and select a provider that isn't at either extreme.

Acquire an Internet Domain   Your ISP should be able to provide you with a domain name and get it registered for you. A domain name is nothing more than your address on the Internet. An example might be *yourcompany.com.*

InterNIC Registration Services provides U.S. and Canadian domain names. You can find the registration services for other countries through Yahoo's Domain Registration list at http://www.yahoo.com/Computers_and_Internet/Domain_Registration/. U.S. domain names cost $100 for setup and two years of use. After that, renewals cost $50 per year.

U.S. domain names (Table 8.1) end in a three-character code called a top-level domain name. These include **COM** for businesses, **EDU** for educational institutions, **GOV** for governmental organizations, **MIL** for military organizations, **NET** for network providers, and **ORG** for nonprofit organizations. Other countries have a two-character country code for the top-level domain name. Table 8.1 includes a sampling of country codes, such as **AU** for Australia, **CA** for Canada, and **DE** for Germany.

In the example *yourcompany.com, com* is the top-level domain name and *yourcompany* is the second-level domain name. This domain name is part of both your WWW address and your Internet e-mail address.

Select and Install Hardware and Software

The next step is to select and install your hardware and software, so we'll talk about the things you need to build your intranet.

Servers You can get started cheaply by using a spare or borrowed computer and free software downloaded from the Internet. Since intranets grow like wildfire, you'll need to get some serious equipment soon. The free software available from the Internet is generally quite good, but you may have concerns about support since the person who created the software may have moved on.

TABLE 8.1 Top-Level Internet Domain Names: United States and Selected Countries

Domain Name	Description
COM	U.S. Commercial
EDU	U.S. Educational
GOV	U.S. Government
MIL	U.S. Military
NET	Network
ORG	Nonprofit Organization
AU	Australia
CA	Canada
DE	Germany
FI	Finland
FR	France
JP	Japan
NL	Netherlands
SE	Sweden
UK	United Kingdom

Therefore, I'll concentrate on commercial products. While UNIX servers are predominant for external Webs, Windows NT already appeared to be leading the pack for intranets even before Microsoft started giving away its Internet Information Server.

You should select server hardware that will continue to meet your needs as intranet traffic gets heavier. There are several different kinds of server software, which you can put on separate machines or combine on a single machine. Performance may be an issue if they're all on the same machine. Servers include the following:

- *Domain name server (DNS).*   Sometimes called an Internet server, to handle domain names and other Internet services.
- *Web HTTP server.*   To provide HTML pages to Web browsers, and possibly to provide secure Web transactions. As of this writing, security comes in several varieties:

  1. *Secure HTTP (SHTTP),* incorporated in servers from Open Market.
  2. *Secure Sockets Layer (SSL),* incorporated in servers from Netscape, Microsoft, IBM, and Open Market.
  3. *Private Communications Technology (PCT),* Microsoft's enhanced version of SSL.
  4. *Secure Transport Layer Protocol (STLP),* which Microsoft has submitted as a draft proposal to the Internet Engineering Task Force (IETF). This protocol combines Netscape's SSL 3.0 with Microsoft's PCT 2.0, and is an attempt to forge an encryption standard from the competing protocols.
  5. *Secure Electronic Transaction (SET),* a joint standard developed by MasterCard and Visa. It should be in use soon after this book reaches the stores.

- *Proxy server.*   To allow access to the Internet from your intranet, while keeping the two systems separate. The proxy server will take requests from internal clients and request a specific address from the external server. This provides security because you don't reveal internal network addresses to the outside world.

- *Simple Mail Transfer Protocol (SMTP) server.*   For e-mail. This server may support the Internet's Post Office Protocol 3 (POP3) and Internet Message Access Protocol 4 (IMAP4).

- *Gopher server*

- *File transfer protocol (FTP) server*

- *Transaction server.*   For access to databases.

Some servers include other features and functions, such as firewalls, search applications, utilities for creating and authoring Web pages, and a graphical user interface (GUI) for managing Web page files. Some of the major players in the server market include Microsoft, Netscape, SGI, Sun, IBM, and Hewlett-Packard. Since server hardware and software change quickly, I've included in the appendix a list of resources on the Internet you can check out for the latest information about servers. Also, you can check out the many computer magazines for reviews and benchmarks.

Browsers   In addition to servers, you also need browsers. Let's defer our discussion of browsers to step 5, where you'll find a thorough discussion of all the issues and concerns.

Search Tools   Several of the companies that I spoke with said that they wished they had provided a search tool to their users sooner. It's a good idea to go ahead and evaluate search tools, whether or not you plan to install one initially. Some of the popular search tools are AltaVista, Excite, Open Text, Lycos, PLS, Verity, and WAIS.

Document Authoring Tools   When choosing HTML authoring tools, keep in mind who your web publishers are and what their preferences will be. Publishers may prefer what-you-see-is-what-you-get (WYSIWYG) authoring tools, such as Navigator Gold, Front-Page, Page Mill, or GNNpress, which show what a page looks like in the browser as you create it. Most HTML authoring tools are not currently WYSIWYG. Select tools that are easy to use and robust enough to do all the things that your publishers will want to do.

Document Conversion Tools   There are many tools emerging for converting existing documents to HTML, with more on the way. These should prove to be popular products as companies seek to convert their huge investments in existing documentation and manuals for use on their internal webs. Some examples include HTML Transit, Web Publisher, and Microsoft's Internet Assistants, which convert Word, Excel, and Power Point files into HTML documents.

Document Databases   Document databases store existing documents and can convert them to HTML *on the fly* for display in a browser. Some document database tools include Basis Document Manager by Information Dimensions, DynaWeb by Electronic Book Technologies, Folio Infobase Web Server by Folio, and Inter-Notes Web Publisher by Lotus.

Database Query Tools   Database query tools are in their infancy, but you'll definitely want to start evaluating and selecting some if you wish to offer intranet access to your databases. Some of the tools that allow you to program Web-to-database queries include Cold Fusion by Allaire, WebServer by Oracle, web.sql by Sybase, and Internet Information Server by Microsoft.

Plan for Maintenance of Your Intranet

As you select and install hardware and software, make sure to consider your needs for monitoring and maintenance of your intranet. Make sure that those who will administer your intranet have the tools and training they need to properly set up and maintain your intranet.

Step 5: Create Your Audience

Before people will be willing to publish content for the intranet, they'll want assurance that there will be an audience for their work. Your next step is to start creating that audience. Simply set up a Web server, put a browser on each computer, and turn people loose. If users have Internet access, they can surf the Net while your publishers start creating content for the internal web. All you really need to start your internal web is a simple but useful application. Set up your phone directory or employee locator as a starter application to get people coming to the internal web. If you give them something of value to them, they'll come.

What Tools Will Users Need?

When you do your demos, people will want access for themselves, and they'll want it now! You should prepare for this before you start doing your demos. Once you start those demos, you'll have an avalanche of demand for browsers. It's very easy for it to get ahead of you. People will start showing the internal web to their friends, who will also want access. It's like a grass fire—one spark starts an inferno. Be fully prepared to roll out browsers *before* you start presenting your demo.

Which tools should you choose? You'll need a browser, or client, to provide users with access to information on the internal web. There are lots of things to consider in choosing a browser:

- *User-friendliness.* Is it user-friendly? Is it easy to configure and easy to use?
- *Platforms.* Is it available for all the platforms you have?
- *Security.* Does it provide the type and amount of security that you need?
- *Cost.* How much does it cost? Though this is important, it shouldn't influence your choice, since the cost of most browsers is minimal.
- *Features and tools.* Does it include or support the features and tools you need?

    - *HTML.* Does it support the latest version of HTML? Do you even need the features of the latest version?

- ◆ *E-mail and newsgroups.*   Some browsers have e-mail and newsgroups built in, which makes it easier to set these up.
- ◆ *FTP and Telnet.*   Will your users need FTP to do file transfers, or Telnet to access mainframes? If so, do these tools come with the browser you're considering, or will you need to provide them separately?
- ◆ *Plug-ins, add-ons, and special features.*   Some browsers support plug-ins, add-ons, and special features. Others don't. If you need some of them, you'll need to choose a browser that supports them. You may want to consider what audio, video, 3D, phone, whiteboarding, chat, and plug-ins could do for your users.
- ◆ *Java, scripting, and ActiveX Controls.*   Do you plan to move beyond static pages to support applications? If so, some browsers support Java, scripting, and ActiveX. Others don't.
- ◆ *VRML tools.*   At some point you may also consider tools that use Virtual Reality Modeling Language (VRML). Does the browser you're considering support these tools?

The appendix provides a list of resources on the Internet for checking out the latest information about browsers.

Which Way Should You Go—Free or Purchased?   To quickly create your audience, you should make browsers and other intranet tools easily available and inexpensive. If you can use free tools, or if your champion will absorb the cost, you can make these tools free to users, which is even better.

There are a lot of free Internet tools you can use to build your intranet. Should you go with them, or should you buy tools? If the free tools meet all your needs, by all means go with them. If you need extra features that aren't available in the freebies, such as Netscape's security or special features, that's worth careful consideration. Netscape is quite inexpensive. For a small organization, the cost of licenses is fairly small. However, for an organization with thousands of users, Netscape can add up to some serious money. That's why the very large organizations that are deploying Netscape have negotiated worldwide corporate licenses. This move toward corporate licenses has made it less expensive overall, but it's still not cheap to bite the bullet and pay for it all up front. That's where the champion, and his or her budget, can help.

How Will Your Users Get the Software?

How can you make it easy for people to acquire the software? You can do the initial installations in three different ways.

1. You can have a person or group responsible for doing the installations if you have to install a TCP/IP stack on each machine, or if you have to install browsers and tools individually.

2. You can let people download their own software if everyone already has TCP/IP and you have a corporate license for your browser, or if it's free. EDS developed installation kits for the client software and added them to the product catalog so an EDS employee could install the software simply by selecting it from a menu.

3. You can let the system do the installations for you if you have an automated system.

You can handle upgrades to browsers, e-mail, and other tools by letting users click on an icon to download the upgrade.

How Will You Provide User Training and Support?

How will you provide the training? Since browsers are so easy to use, we structured our demos to serve as tutorials. We showed how to use the browser, the Internet, and the intranet, and we spent a few minutes talking about how to use e-mail and newsgroups. When people left the demo, they already knew what to do. You can also put a tutorial on your internal web to help people refresh their memories later.

How will you provide support to intranet users when they're using the browsers and applications you provide? Do you already have a help desk? If so, you can train the help desk staff to support the intranet. If you create a Web Services group, and they have responsibility for support, you can post their phone number and an e-mail *mailto* address on the intranet home page. You can also add a FAQ page and a newsgroup for posting questions.

Step 6: Promote Your Intranet

The next step is to start doing demos to show people what your intranet can do. You have to have something to show customers in order for them to buy. People can't see what isn't there so you have to build something to show them. You could describe it until you're blue in the face, and they just won't get it. Show them, and they'll understand.

Before you start to build your demo, you should have some goals in mind. What do you want to accomplish? For us, there were two goals. We wanted to show people the Internet and intranet in order to do the following:

1. *Recruit web publishers for the Internet Team.*   Web publishers are those who have content that they're eager to publish and share with others. The purpose of the Internet Team was to provide potential web publishers with the tools to get started, help in learning how to use those tools, and a means to support their efforts. In the demos, I asked for volunteers to join the team.

2. *Recruit an audience of users.*   Once people saw the intranet, they wanted it. We put browsers on their computers immediately to capitalize on their enthusiasm. The demos are an integral part of the strategy to create an audience for your publishers. As the audience grows, the content will grow as well, and the intranet will become more valuable.

We'll talk first about building your demo, and then about presenting it.

Build the Demo

After you've set your goals for the demo, you're ready to start building it. To make it easy for you to gauge the time frames involved, I've included a time line (Figure 8.4) showing what we did in the first six months of our intranet project. The steps and time frames involved in building the demo were as follows:

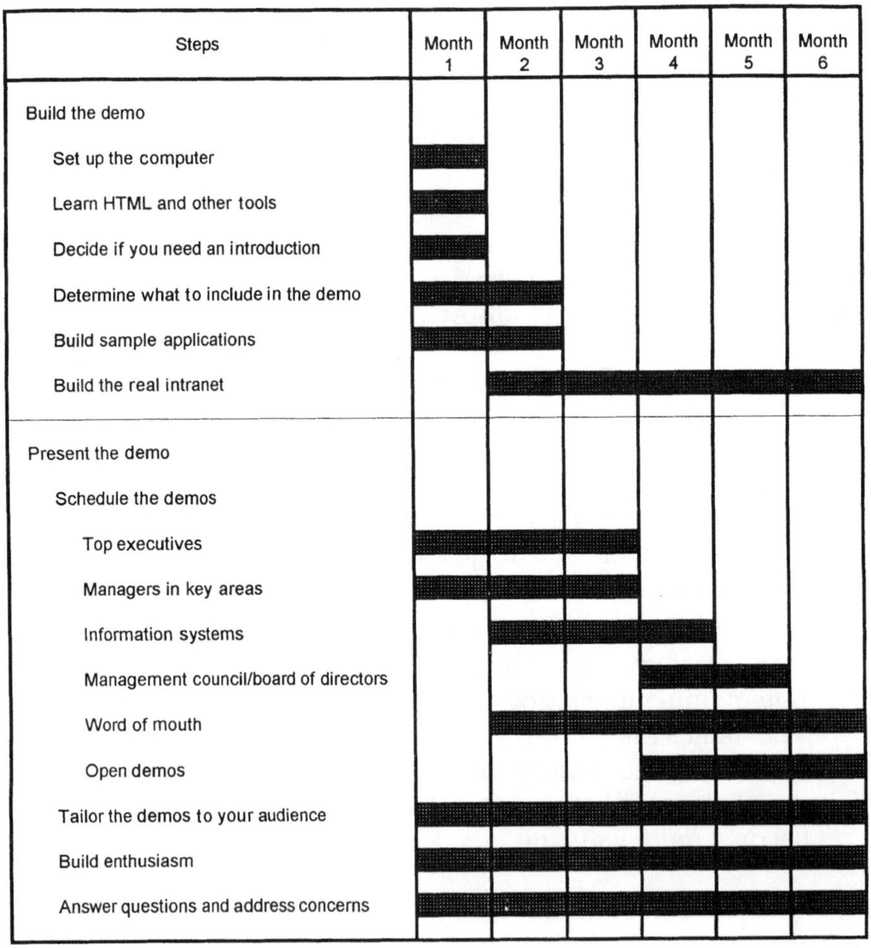

Steps	Month 1	Month 2	Month 3	Month 4	Month 5	Month 6
Build the demo						
Set up the computer	█					
Learn HTML and other tools	█					
Decide if you need an introduction	█					
Determine what to include in the demo	█	█				
Build sample applications	█	█				
Build the real intranet		█	█	█	█	█
Present the demo						
Schedule the demos						
Top executives	█	█				
Managers in key areas	█	█				
Information systems		█	█			
Management council/board of directors				█	█	
Word of mouth		█	█	█	█	█
Open demos				█	█	█
Tailor the demos to your audience	█	█	█	█	█	█
Build enthusiasm	█	█	█	█	█	█
Answer questions and address concerns	█	█	█	█	█	█

Figure 8.4   Demo time line—promote the intranet.

1. *Set up the computer.*   Completed in month 1.
2. *Learn HTML and other tools.*   Completed in month 1.
3. *Decide if you need an introduction.*   Completed in month 1.
4. *Determine what to include in the demo.*   Spanned months 1 and 2.
5. *Build sample applications.*   Spanned months 1 and 2.
6. *Build the real intranet.*   Started in month 2. We rolled out the real intranet in month 4 and continued to expand it through month 6 and beyond.

Set Up the Computer   To build your demo, you really need little more than a browser on a computer. Here are the things you need:

1. *Computer.*   If necessary, use a spare computer or borrow one.
2. *Internet access.*   You can set up a server and arrange for Internet access, or you can get on the Internet cheaply with a modem and a dial-up account.
3. *Browser.*   You can download Mosaic or Microsoft's Internet Explorer from the Internet for free, or you can purchase Netscape directly over the Internet.
4. *HTML authoring tool.*   There are free and shareware HTML authoring tools available on the Internet. See the appendix for Internet references about HTML authoring tools and other tools.
5. *Graphics tool.*   You can get a commercial graphics package or download a shareware tool such as Lview.
6. *Caching tool.*   If your demo will include the Internet, you may need a tool that allows you to cache pages in case you lose your Internet connection during a demo. Web-Whacker and WebEx will automate this process for you.

Learn HTML and Other Tools   Once you have the tools, you need to learn HTML and how to use the tools. There are lots of good books on the subject and numerous resources on the Internet, some of which you can find listed in the appendix.

Decide If You Need an Introduction   Before you build your sample applications, you need to decide how you wish to help your audience understand the basic concepts. You may need a simple introduction to explain what the Internet and the WWW are all about. You may wish to give a short introduction in very simple language that covers the following:

◆ The Internet and its history
◆ The World Wide Web and where it came from
◆ Browsers
◆ Hypertext linking and HTML

With all the articles in the general media today about the Internet and intranets, you may not really need an introduction. To find out, call or have lunch with some of the people that will be in your demos, and find out how much they know about the Internet. If your organization already has Internet access, then you probably don't need an introduction and can go straight to the meat of your demo.

Determine What to Include in the Demo   Next you'll need to identify what to put in your demo. You should incorporate the needs of your business so you can show people how an intranet can help.

Identify needs.   Start to identify your needs and contact business partners to provide information for the demo:

1. *Brainstorm.*   Identify as many things as you can that would add value if they were on the intranet.

    ◆ *Paper.*   You might start with information in paper form which costs the company lots of money to print and distribute, such as telephone directories, procedures manuals, and benefits information.
    ◆ *Disparate systems.*   Look for where you have information accessed from different types of equipment and operating systems.

2. *Identify contacts.* I called my IS colleagues who worked with specific areas of the business to find out who to contact.

3. *Contact business partners.* Once I knew which business partners to contact, I called them, explained what we were doing, and asked for copies of real information to use in the demo.

Involve others. Involve everyone who can help you to determine the critical business needs.

1. *Informally.* Talk to everybody you can, stopping them in the hall or asking them over lunch about how an intranet could help them and which applications would be of value.

2. *Formally.* Consider having Joint Application Design (JAD) sessions to brainstorm and identify uses. Soon, you'll have a long list of applications, along with real information, to start putting into the demo.

Build Sample Applications For your demos, you'll want to build something to hit the *hot buttons* of every area. Here are some things you can do to help nontechnical people understand what you can do with the Internet and intranet.

1. Create a home page for your department that includes lots of useful information.

2. Create an employee locator to search for locations, telephone numbers, and e-mail addresses.

3. Set up a variety of HTML pages showing procedures manuals, benefits information, and samples of other information you've gleaned.

4. Tie HTML pages to databases to show how people can have timely and easy-to-use access to information. Create a mock-up if necessary.

5. Add some graphics, sound, and video clips.

Build the Real Intranet As soon as we had built our demo, we started building jWeb, our real intranet. Many of the sample applications used in the demo were real information. All we had to do was to incorporate them into the new look for jWeb. Soon, we had a real intranet with lots of applications to roll out to the company. Then we started using it for our demo. Some of our early applications included the following:

♦ Phone directory

♦ IS departmental home pages with contact information, organization charts, and documentation

♦ Training schedules and registration for classes

♦ Software downloads

Present the Demo

Once the demo is built, it's time to start presenting it. From the time line in Figure 8.4, you can see that our demos started immediately and ran through month 6. In that time, I did over 100 demos and presentations to groups ranging from two or three to several hundred.

Schedule the Demos We started scheduling our demos by having senior IS management arrange them for us. The CIO lined up demos with the top executives, and senior IS managers lined up demos with their customers. Here's how our demos proceeded, along with the times from Figure 8.4.

1. *Top executives.* Months 1, 2, and 3.
2. *Managers in key areas and their staffs.* Months 1, 2, and 3.
3. *Information systems.* Months 1, 2, and 3.
4. *Management Council and Board of Directors.* Months 4 and 5.
5. *Word of mouth.* Months 2 through 6.
6. *Open demos.* Months 4 through 6.

Tailor the Demos to Your Audience   For each demo, we customized the presentation to the interests of the group or department we were working with. It was important to tailor each and every presentation so the audience could see things of value for them. We set up an Interesting and Useful Web Sites page on our intranet to make it easy for our audience to link to these locations later.

For the presentation to the Management Council, we were especially careful to communicate in their language and to choose sites they would be interested in. We also discovered a great way to get their attention by showing the alma mater of our Chairman of the Board. It had a page with information about the Oklahoma Business Conference and a picture of the Chairman, who was the featured speaker. When we showed that page, and the Chairman's picture, the murmur in the room told me we made an impact. Who could argue about the Internet when the Chairman was already on it?

One of the most important things I've learned in presenting demos is that *it's more important to communicate than to be technically correct.* If you're technically correct, it may only confuse them. Your goal is to communicate so that they understand.

Build Enthusiasm   At every demo you'll hear more and more ideas of ways you could use the intranet. Collect those ideas and use them to enhance your demo with new applications. Give those who had the ideas credit for them in your demos.

Answer Questions and Address Concerns about the Internet and Intranet   Your demo should stimulate lots of questions. Here are some that we encountered most frequently. You'll need to have your own answers ready for them.

- What will happen to productivity if we give employees access to the Internet?
- How secure is the intranet?
- If we access the Internet, won't we bring in viruses?

- How much does it cost the company to access the Internet?
- How do I get my department on the intranet?

Other Ways to Promote Your Intranet

At some point, you'll want to use other means to promote your intranet. Some ideas follow.

Web Fair To further heighten the enthusiasm, our Internet Team staged a Web Fair that was open to all employees. It was a wonderfully lively, all-day event, with a surfing theme. There were surfboards and other props all around the auditorium. Computers were set up to showcase various departments' web sites and to let people surf the Internet. There were mini–training sessions on HTML, CGI coding, and various Web publishing tools. Some vendors, including Netscape, had booths and gave away T-shirts, books, and software. The turnout was so incredible that the refreshments disappeared in the first hour. People came in waves, and every few minutes the CIO had a different senior executive with him. The excitement spread browsers and the intranet to thousands of employees.

Advertising Campaign Turner Broadcasting had a very interesting way to promote their intranet: the Turner Employee Services Network (TESN). TESN grew from a project where the VP of Human Resources created and sanctioned a cross-functional team to develop ideas on better ways to serve internal customers. They held focus groups with employees to identify what employees needed. The team worked with an outside company to design the internal web site and create the content. To promote TESN to their employees, they worked with an ad agency to build an ad campaign. The ad agency came up with the network idea and created a teaser campaign, which consisted of the following features:

1. *Posters.* They created posters, which they hung in the break rooms at all locations.
2. *Mailing.* They treated the ad campaign like a consumer campaign for a network. They sent a small copy of the

posters to employee's homes with a message from Allan DeNiro, Vice President of Human Resources, and an invitation to the launch meetings.

3. *Launch meetings.*   Turner held launch meetings at the CNN Center in Atlanta and at other Turner locations. The meetings featured a wonderful, professional video-tape which showed the following:

- ◆ Allan DeNiro talking about how he had created the team to come up with ways to treat each employee as a customer and to create the greatest customer-service organization.

- ◆ The team explaining how they had talked to employees to find out what they wanted and needed. They decided to:

    - ◆ Create an internal web to serve employees as customers.
    - ◆ Offer kiosks for employees without computers.
    - ◆ Provide a 24-hour service hotline for employees.
    - ◆ Give each employee a personal service representative in HR.

- ◆ A special report, with an overview of TESN, by CNN news anchor, Lynne Russell.

They had a great turnout for these launch meetings. According to Jimi Stricklin, Director of Employee Services Development, the ad campaign worked extremely well: *People came in droves, and were excited because it was for them.*

Step 7: Create Widespread Enthusiasm and Capability—The Role of the Intranet Team

Why do you need an intranet team and what will they do?

Why Do You Need an Intranet Team?

When you build an intranet, there are lots of things you must do, including the following:

- Set the organization's direction for the intranet.
- Guide the intranet in moving in that set direction.
- Create the infrastructure.
- Evaluate and select hardware and software.
- Install and maintain servers.
- Install intranet tools for people.
- Create training for web publishers.
- Design the structure of the internal web site.
- Design the home page.
- Develop content and design.
- Create publishing guidelines.
- Encourage web publishers to publish.
- Approve content for the intranet.
- Advertise and promote the intranet.
- Encourage and support people in their use of the intranet.
- Create applications.
- Update publishers on new tools.
- Keep it all moving forward.

These things require lots of different people with lots of different skills, which you don't usually find in a single department. You need programmers, systems administrators, communicators, artists and graphic designers, marketers, technical support, trainers, and others. These people come from all across the organization. How do you coordinate all these activities and get them accomplished? That's the role of the intranet team.

The team sets the direction and coordinates and communicates all the necessary steps required to start up and maintain your intranet. The team does everything on the preceding list, and more. At JCPenney, we called ourselves the Internet Team because we focused on both the external Internet and our internal internet, jWeb.

Cathy Mills, VP and Director of Company Communications at JCPenney, and owner of jWeb, says that the Internet Team was the driving force in the development of jWeb. She belongs to several organizations of directors of corporate communications, where she's often asked how to create an intranet. She tells them to put some young people together in a room—young communicators, young artists, and information systems folks. She jokes that you should lock the door so they can't get away, because they won't enjoy this interaction until they find a common ground. She believes the team is the only place folks from such different areas of the company can come together and work on something of common interest, and that this was critical to the development of jWeb.

Should the Intranet Team Be Combined with or Separate from the Internet Team? It really doesn't matter whether the team deals with both the Internet and intranet or just the intranet. In most of the companies I talked with that had teams in place, the team had responsibility for both. With a single team, there may be many issues that overlap, so you don't have two competing bodies trying to make decisions. Since the tools are the same, you gain leverage in training publishers. Sometimes, though, things can seem a bit fragmented when you focus on several different audiences. You might consider having subteams focused on the different audiences and different issues.

Composition of the Team The team should be cross-functional, with representatives from all areas of the organization. It should include the following:

- *Team leader.* The team leader represents the champion and keeps communication flowing between the team, the champion, and the steering committee. The team leader has responsibility and authority to keep everything moving, resolve issues, and ensure that the team meets its goals.

- *Web architects.* These folks develop the structure and flow of the internal web.

- *Web services.* These are the folks who evaluate and select Internet and intranet tools, build Web applications, train and support web publishers, and keep everyone up-to-date. They make sure the team is aware of technical issues, new software, and the tools and techniques available to web publishers and developers.

- *Webmasters.* These are the folks who set up and administer Web servers and maintain their content. They keep the team aware of capacity issues and changes that will impact the web publishers.

- *Programmers and applications developers.* These folks hook the databases to documents and forms and do fancy things such as develop Java applications.

- *Graphic artists and designers.* These folks develop the home pages and graphics for the internal web. They may create libraries of graphics, icons, bullets, and navigational tools for all web publishers to use.

- *Communicators.* These are the folks who are responsible for the image and message of the company and for all internal communications with employees. They already know how to communicate with employees, including what to say and how to say it.

- *Web publishers.* These folks generally come from all areas of the organization. They're enthusiastic about the Web and develop and oversee the content of their departmental web sites.

- *Technical support.* These folks install, or help to install, TCP/IP, browsers, and other applications for users.

- *Trainers.* These folks develop and deliver training for web publishers and end users.

- *Help desk and support.* These folks support your audience as it grows, and should be brought into the planning early in the process.

- *Legal.*   These folks deal primarily with the external Web site, but need to be aware of anywhere the intranet interfaces with suppliers, customers, or others outside the company. Have them involved, but make sure they understand that their role is not to delay everything.
- *Facilitator.*   The facilitator plans for and runs the team meetings to ensure that they are as productive as possible.

Does the Team Really Need a Facilitator?   A facilitator is some-one specially trained to run meetings effectively, and who may also be skilled in team building and team dynamics. A facilitator is skilled in bringing teams to consensus, allowing everyone to buy into the decisions. If you think that's a frivolous role, then try visualizing a meeting of 40 to 50 techies, artists, and businesspeo-ple without a facilitator. It won't be an effective meeting. Facilita-tors are invaluable when you have meetings with a large number of participants and have a desired set of results to achieve.

To find a facilitator, you might check with your HR department, Total Quality Management program, or business process improve-ment or reengineering program. Other options include checking with consulting firms, searching the Internet for facilitation com-panies or facilitation brokers, or sending a message to the modera-tor of the Internet misc.business.facilitators newsgroup asking for help in finding a facilitator. Money spent on facilitators is money well spent.

Team Meetings

The following activities were generally included in the team meet-ings:

- Welcome and introductions
- Recognition for team members
- Guest speakers
- Demos of applications and tools to keep everyone up-to-date
- Updates on Internet and intranet plans and results
- Team-building and creativity exercises

- Brainstorming and discussing expectations, vision, mission, goals and objectives, and how the team should work
- Subteam reports on progress and plans
- Reports from conferences and shows
- Setting logistics for future meetings

What Are the Team's Objectives?

The team decided to create five subteams to work on its five objectives.

Internet Team Home Page and Communications   Since the team consisted of people from many different areas of the business, communication was a critical issue. Techies on the team had to truly listen to others and learn to communicate without technical jargon. Everyone else had to learn to listen carefully and try to understand what the techies were saying. Team building helped to create communication. The team even decided to create a subteam focused on continuing the communication among team members.

The team started out with a newsgroup for fostering communication, and then moved some of the content over to a team home page on the intranet. They posted the vision, mission, objectives, roster, subteams, meeting minutes, agendas, and decisions. Subteams posted their information as well. Team members posted bios, questions, ideas, tips, comments, requests, and reviews.

Promote jWeb to Employees   This subteam, which focused on promoting jWeb to employees, sponsored the Web Fair and focused on promoting use of the intranet to all employees.

Promote the Effective Use of the Internet and jWeb   This subteam focused on training users and helping them use jWeb most effectively. Since we already had so much training in the demo, this subteam focused on other ways to help employees get the most out of jWeb. They built the jWeb tutorial, which you could access from the home page. They also developed tip sheets and handed them out at the Web Fair to help people get started. Since browsers are so easy to use, this provided most of the training users needed. This subteam also focused on finding and sharing anecdotes of how individuals and departments were using jWeb and the Internet most effectively.

Identify and Spread Tools and Best Practices   This subteam focused on identifying the tools that worked best for certain applications and identifying techniques to make the job easier for web publishers and developers. They published their findings and recommendations on their section of the team's jWeb site.

Develop and Communicate Guidelines, Standards, and Policies
This subteam, which focused on developing and communicating guidelines, standards, and approval policies and procedures, had the greatest challenge. They designed the structure and flow of jWeb, and worked on the following areas related to jWeb.

Set direction and guide development of the internal web.   There were four major issues the subteam wrestled with in guiding internal web development.

1. *Should there be web publishing standards?*   Common approaches include the following:

   ◆ *Standardized and controlled.*   By having a consistently applied standard, everyone knows where to look for certain types of information on every page, and navigation is consistent. Everything must be approved before it goes on the intranet. If everything looks the same, the results may be boring, and you won't get interesting and exciting things because you don't allow them.

   ◆ *Loose and chaotic.*   By letting people experiment, they learn what works well and what doesn't, and they may create interesting and exciting things. Since content doesn't go through approvals, some things may not be as businesslike as you want. The creativity and innovation spawned by lack of standards will more than make up for a few ugly pages.

The subteam decided to let people experiment, learn, and make mistakes. In those areas where management insisted upon a consistent appearance among all groups, the results were often rather boring.

2. *What approvals and authorizations are necessary?* Some companies have formal procedures for approvals, but my gut feeling is that with most the decision tends to reside, as it did with us, at the level of the publisher and his or her manager. If you would have your manager approve a memo you send, then you will probably have that same manager approve your content. It may be worthwhile to have someone in employee communications to go to for guidance if there's something about which you're unsure.

3. *Should you allow personal home pages?* If you allow or encourage home pages, will you teach everyone how to do HTML, or can you do something to make it easier for them? Some companies encourage everyone to have a home page, believing that people learn valuable new skills. Home pages also make it easy to find people with the specific skills you need. Some companies discourage personal home pages. They worry that people will waste time trying to outdo others, which may impact productivity. This is a decision that every company with an intranet must make.

4. *Who should ultimately own the intranet?* When we started, IS took responsibility for both the external Web site and the internal web, and we knew we would turn it over to some other area of the company when that was appropriate. We eventually turned both of them over to Company Communications, who were the folks responsible for speaking on behalf of the company and communicating with employees. That seems to be a trend among other companies, as well, though the IT group still owns the infrastructure.

Set internet policies. One common theme from companies I worked with is the fear of opening up access to the Internet. You'll want to create an Internet policy and publish it on the internal web. What your Internet policy says is less important than actually having one and making everyone aware of it. Here are the three basic issues:

1. *Should you allow universal access to the Internet?*
    Should you give everyone access to the Internet, and what will happen to productivity if you do? Managers worried about how they would keep their people from playing all day. This really isn't a new issue, since people have always found ways to waste time. In my experience, when people first got access to the Internet, they were like kids with a new toy. When the novelty wore off, they used it for business use, maybe some personal use at lunch, and all the playing was simply inexpensive training.

2. *Should you allow personal use of the Internet?*

    ◆ Should you allow personal use of the Internet? If so, how much? Do you allow your employees to use the telephone to make and receive personal calls during office hours? If so, does the same policy apply to using your company equipment to access the Internet? Some CIOs simply dismiss this as a nonissue.

    ◆ What should you do about access to sexually explicit sites? Companies take several approaches:

        ◆ *Total laissez-faire.*   We won't worry about that.
        ◆ *Total control.*   We only allow access to certain sites from our computers.
        ◆ *Middle of the road.*   We trust our employees to use good judgment and will block a few really offensive sites so employees don't accidentally stumble across them.

    ◆ What should you do about what employees say while using the company e-mail address? Some organizations simply ask their employees to use good judgment, while others have a formal policy requiring employees to include a disclaimer in their messages.

3. *How do you help people understand what is confidential?*
Those who are publishing content need to be aware of what not to put on the external Web site. This applies to e-mail as well. You may wish to train users in this.

Train and support web publishers.   One of the keys to making jWeb successful was having lots of useful content. To get there, we needed to provide publishers with the tools to publish, train them in how to use the tools, and keep them updated on what was happening with tools and procedures.

When books on HTML started appearing, we bought every copy we could get our hands on and started giving them to those who were ready to start publishing. We put together a class to teach people how to author in HTML, how to use graphics, and how to link their content into the corporate intranet. We put some members of the Internet Team and anyone ready to start publishing content through the first few classes. To train more publishers, we put the schedule of HTML classes on the intranet and offered them at no charge.

Encourage publishing.   To make it easy for publishers to get started, departments could put their own content on the IS server. It was only when they wanted or needed control that they put up their own servers.

Within a couple of days after the very first HTML class, the first non-IS departmental home page appeared. The publisher received lots of attention and recognition, and I included his site in my demos along with mention of his name. All the hoopla paid off—within days, several more departmental sites appeared.

Step 8: Make Your Intranet Pervasive

When publishing starts taking place on the internal web rather than elsewhere, and people start expecting to find the information they're looking for by going to the internal web, you're getting where you want to be. The intranet is starting to become ingrained in the culture. How do you get there?

How Do You Make the Intranet the Universal User Interface?

1. *Design it for users.*   Make your intranet user-friendly. Make the icons intuitive and the flow logical. Put information where people expect to find it. Make the navigation easy and logical.

2. *Keep it fresh and new.*   Just as with external Web sites, you need to keep internal webs fresh and new so that people will continue to come back and use them. Here are some ways to accomplish this:

   ◆ What's new sections
   ◆ Announcements and bulletins
   ◆ Newsletters
   ◆ Useful information
   ◆ New content
   ◆ Database information
   ◆ Graphics
   ◆ What's interesting on the WWW
   ◆ Publicize great internal pages
   ◆ Interactivity
   ◆ Sports and clubs
   ◆ Services, such as the cafeteria, fitness center, and others

3. *Review your bandwidth needs frequently.*   As you get more information on your intranet and more users, you'll need more capacity. Plan to monitor capacity constantly and schedule frequent reviews, and even upgrades, if necessary.

4. *Add new tools.*   Make sure to add new tools to help your publishers do a better job of publishing and your

users to get more value from your intranet. Remember to teach them how to use them.

5. *Continue to coordinate the team's efforts.*   Whatever you do, make sure to keep the team going. The team should review the status of the intranet on a regular basis and set new goals for the future. It's time to start thinking about workflow for streamlining your business processes and how you can use groupware for collaboration and communication.

What Are the Critical Success Factors?

To ensure your intranet's success, here are some things it should do:

1. Provide value to the business
2. Communicate throughout the organization
3. Provide valuable and relevant content
4. Provide value to your people
5. Train and develop your people
6. Help develop your products
7. Perform customer-related tasks
8. Involve lots of people so you have a diversity of ideas
9. Change your business culture

Step 9: What Lessons Have We Learned?

The 13 companies that I worked with were very generous in sharing their experiences. They talked about what worked well, and what they would do differently if they had it to do over again. Here are the 20 lessons they learned:

1. Start it as a grassroots effort.
2. Have a champion and/or steering committee to push it forward.
3. Have business goals drive it.

the traditional model or the internet model:
to bureaucratize or not?

229

4. Choose your technology early and carefully.
5. Get the network in place as soon as you can.
6. Plan capacity ahead of demand.
7. Determine who owns the intranet and how much the IT folks should be involved.
8. Involve all stakeholders and get them to work together.
9. Have someone in charge.
10. Decide if you want standards and, if so, create them.
11. Start small and start quickly—you can always change it later.
12. Create the support structure early.
13. Focus on compelling content.
14. Modify the processes from paper-oriented to on-line.
15. Develop the skills you need.
16. Promote and advertise it.
17. It isn't easy to keep content up-to-date.
18. Beware of legacy applications.
19. Be prepared for concerns and fears.
20. Make sure the business knows what's possible for the intranet.

The Traditional Model or the Internet Model: To Bureaucratize or Not?

We've talked about the Internet model and the traditional model, which I also refer to as the *bureaucratic* model. Bureaucracy is a fact of life today in most established businesses. It lends order and control to what could otherwise be chaos. However, bureaucracy can stifle innovation and creativity. It makes businesses slow to react to customer needs and changing customer expectations. Many nimble new businesses are popping up to fill the voids created when customer needs change and bureaucratic companies aren't agile enough to accommodate those needs. This new competition is causing some businesses to realize that they must move away from bureaucracy and toward empowering their workers. That's why trying the Internet model for creating your intranet makes a lot of sense.

Given a choice between the traditional model and the Internet model, how do you decide which way to go?

1. *Traditional model.* If you don't have the infrastructure to support an intranet, you probably have to use the traditional model because of the expense involved. However, you can keep your infrastructure project separate and use the Internet model for the rest of your intranet.

2. *Internet model.* If you already have the infrastructure, you can choose to use the Internet model. The decision probably depends on your culture. If your organization allows, or even encourages, grassroots efforts, then you should use the Internet model.

chapter nine

What's So Hard about Groupware?

The People Part Is Hard

Before we start looking at how you implement groupware, let's take a look at what makes it so hard to implement, and sometimes even causes it to fail. What's so hard about groupware? Very simply, it's people. They're not only the hardest part, they're also the most important part. It's these people issues that make IT folks very uncomfortable. We can deal with the technical stuff, but it's much harder to deal with the people issues. That's why most IT groups are unprepared to implement groupware, and why these projects so often fail. We figure that if we build it, people will use it. That's just not the case. You have to understand people, and the dynamics of working in teams, to understand how to implement groupware. This book will help with that.

Groupware projects fail when companies try to use them after downsizing to *replace people* and to improve productivity. That's a mistake, because *groupware works only when employees feel secure.* After downsizing, the survivors are the real victims. Employees feel threatened and insecure, wondering if they're next. To make matters worse, the treadmill speeds up and they just can't seem to keep up. This is when people need to know that they have the organization's support. They don't need to get some technology shoved down their throats to cause them even more anxiety. Employees will believe that groupware is just another ploy by the organization to get more out of them and to siphon off their knowledge before the next wave of downsizings. They'll resist in every way they can. Then we'll chalk it up as another groupware failure and never really understand why. It's important for employees to know that the organization is implementing groupware to help them and support them. Groupware will succeed only if employees are willing to use it and if they feel that the organization supports them.

Groupware depends upon sharing, which is an alien concept in most corporations today. Your employees may have forgotten how to share because of what they've been taught. Most of us learned to share when we were little. When we started to school, we were told that sharing was *cheating*, and we couldn't do that. All through school we competed for grades, and when we started to work we competed for raises and promotions, all based on our individual achievements. Now things are changing and we're being told to share. No wonder employees are confused. They haven't had to share since kindergarten, and may not even remember how. To make matters worse, the system still rewards individual achievements, not sharing. The first step, long before you think about the technology, is to figure out how to get people to share all the things they've accumulated over the years and have become so good at hoarding. This is the basis for much of the resistance we see when companies try to introduce groupware. It's premised on the concept of sharing, which is the very antithesis of what we've trained people to do. So we must first retrain them.

People understand the concept of working together and collaborating, but many just aren't comfortable with it because of how they've been managed. For years, an autocratic style of management has been predominant. Managers have told employees what to do, and they probably didn't tell them why. Today, managers must empower their employees and encourage them to make their own decisions. Companies have finally started to realize that knowledgeable employees are good for business. They're even starting to share information with them. They're letting them make decisions and expecting them to work together to accomplish more than they can accomplish individually. It'll take time before people know what to do and how to perform now that we're empowering them.

As companies start to implement groupware, they see people resist, and even sabotage, the groupware project. Why would they do that? Those most likely to do that are those with something to lose:

- Employees who value their autonomy and feel that groupware brings *Big Brother* down upon them. For them, their schedules become public knowledge and available for other people to manipulate.
- Employees and managers who hoard information and believe that it gives them power. When everyone has information, they lose that power and no longer have an edge over their competition.
- Secretaries and clerks who have everything under control. Their efficiency gives them power, but when orderly files no longer matter, they risk losing their power base.

When you consider implementing groupware, you'll need to figure out who the resisters may be. Try to get them involved early so they'll become your groupware evangelists. Groupware can be so hard that some organizations have simply opted to postpone implementing it until they've reengineered their processes, reorganized into teams, and solved their organizational issues. You'll need to address all these people issues, and more, before you even think about the technology. That's pretty scary for us techies, but the reward from a successful groupware project will make it worthwhile.

Change Is Hard

Part of the reason we see resistance to groupware is that change is hard on people. Even *good* change is hard for them. People are comfortable doing things as they've always done them, and it takes a lot of energy to disturb that equilibrium and get them into motion. It's not that people don't want to change; it's that they resist disruption. Anything that's disruptive is scary because of the fear that you'll be worse off, rather than better, after the change. If you've ever found yourself scared over a good change, such as a new job or a household move, then you can understand the disruption caused even by a good change.

Stages of Change

Regardless of whether change is positive or negative, there will be an emotional response of some kind. The emotional response to positively perceived change is different from that of negatively perceived change. It doesn't matter whether the *actual* change is good or bad—what matters is how it's *perceived* by the person affected by it. Let's look at the five stages of emotional response to positively perceived changes.

1. *Uninformed optimism.* When you first hear about the change, you presume that everything will be fine.
2. *Informed pessimism.* Once you know the details and can see how the change will impact you, you become pessimistic because it disrupts what you're used to.
3. *Hopeful realism.* Once you know that everything's going to be fine when you get through the change, you start to accept it.
4. *Informed optimism.* The further you get into the change, the more sure you are that everything's going to be fine, so your optimism returns.
5. *Completion.* Once you've completed the change, this becomes the new normal state.

There are eight stages of emotional response to negatively perceived changes.

1. *Stability.* Before you actually find out the details of the change, there's stability.
2. *Immobilization.* The first emotional response is immobilization. At this stage, people are like deer frozen by oncoming headlights—unable to respond in any way.

3. *Denial.*   Once the impact of the change starts to sink in, there's a refusal to accept it and a desire to return to the way things were before the change.

4. *Anger.*   Next comes anger, with its heightened emotional response. This happens when you recognize that the change has happened and there's no going back.

5. *Bargaining.*   Anger leads to bargaining, which is an attempt to return to the way things were.

6. *Depression.*   Once it's obvious that you can't return to the way things were, depression sets in.

7. *Testing.*   As you move out of the depression stage, you start testing to see what can be done and to determine how to adjust to the change.

8. *Acceptance.*   Finally, you accept the change and move on from there.

Not only do people go through these stages of change, but so do organizations. The dynamics of the marketplace may cause all of these emotional responses in organizations. After seeing these stages of change, you'll understand why David Coleman, Managing Director of the Collaborative Strategies Division of GroupWorX, has created Coleman's First Law: "People are resistant to change, and organizations are exponentially more resistant." His two corollaries follow: "The larger the organization, the greater the exponent number" and "the bigger and more complex the project, the greater the exponent will be." (From *March '96 Hot Tip: Groupware Tools for De-Engineering* at http://www.collaborate.com/tip0396.html.)

How to Manage Change

Managing change is an important part of any groupware project. Before you start implementation, you must be aware of the concerns of those who will take part in the project and make sure to address those concerns. You should also be aware of any concerns the organization may have and plan to address those as well. This should be part of any systems implementation, but is even more critical for groupware. Failure to do so may doom your project.

As you get started, you should prepare people and the organization for changes that groupware may bring. People need to be ready for the initial commitment of time that groupware may entail. Also, because of groupware, people will work differently. Those involved will become more reluctant to attend meetings held simply to communicate information. They'll prefer that you send them the information electronically rather than wasting their time.

An important lesson from projects that have failed is that you can't just parachute in groupware and manuals and expect people to use them. You must put energy into preparing people for the change, training them, and helping them through the rough spots. You have to help them understand why it's worth their time to learn to use groupware. You should involve them in planning so that they know what to expect and will want to participate. Groupware can cause revolutionary changes for some individuals and departments. Participants must be willing to commit to experimentation to find what works best for them, and to revise their workstyles accordingly.

Tom Davenport, author of *Process Innovation: Reengineering Work Through Information Technology* (Harvard Business School Press, 1993), wrote in "Software as Socialware" (*CIO,* March 1, 1996, pp. 24–26) about creating the role of Social Systems Analysts (SSA) to help manage change in software development projects. Davenport suggests that "If software is to be successful, it must include social and behavioral change. Just as there are information inputs and outputs, there are human inputs and outputs." Davenport said that a recent study suggests that the failure rate for business-critical systems projects is greater than 90 percent, and he suspects that the failure rate for groupware projects is even higher. To remedy this, he advocates having SSAs who would be responsible for changing the information behaviors of individuals and groups. He suggests that primarily they must be skilled in managing change, but must also be able to talk with techies. Large projects would need a full-time SSA, while smaller ones could use one part-time.

Davenport suggests that an SSA should do the same kinds of things we do in business process improvement projects. They should shadow people to determine how they use information, identify their needs, determine current processes, help in the design and buy-in of systems, make sure systems fit the culture, and work on implementation, rollout, and training. Part of their role is to be good change managers, which isn't easy to do. He suggests that they need experience, and maybe even some gray hair. Using checklists and guidelines isn't enough—you can check everything off and still find that it doesn't work. That's because no one found out just how much change the executives would accept. Much of change management happens behind closed doors. He suggests that this role shouldn't be hard to justify—just add up the number of failed systems and you can certainly pay for SSAs. This is the kind of role that might be useful in implementing groupware. SSAs could get teams to collaborating before adding technology to the mix.

A common trend in organizations is to implement groupware as part of reengineering their processes. David Coleman, in *March '96 Hot Tip: Groupware Tools for De-Engineering* (http://www .collaborate.com/tip0396.html), has proposed an interesting theory for a different approach. He calls his concept of organizational change *de-engineering*. He bases some of his ideas on the five laws of chaos, which he learned from Chaos Theory expert Dr. Laurie Fitzgerald. These laws are controversial, but they also make sense, and are backed up by complex mathematics. Here's my abbreviated version of the explanation of the Five Laws of Chaos:

1. *Consciousness.* Everything is possible, which implies that we can choose our reality, which then becomes permanent.
2. *Connectivity.* Everything affects everything else in many complex ways.
3. *Complexity or indeterminacy.* Systems are too complex to predict.
4. *Dissipation.* Everything is falling apart, and some of the components will become part of the new structure.
5. *Emergence.* As systems and organizations dissipate, they also reorganize more harmoniously.

Coleman believes that within most dissipating organizations there are the seeds of a new organization, and most people, processes, and organizations can self-organize, which is preferable to reengineering:

> Today, the BPR philosophy focuses on control and structures rather than on purpose and direction. We no longer let the structure emerge the way a stream finds its course down a hill. Instead, we try to structure a process or plan the outcome.
>
> The fact that BPR has not met with great success leads us to believe that we may be taking the wrong approach; rather than imposing a structure (re-engineering) on a business or process, it might be better to provide a direction (like the stream) and some tools to help the organization move in that direction and then let the people re-engineer themselves.

He suggests that rather than controlling change through reengineering, those who favor self-organization will go with dissipation, and will preserve the people, processes, knowledge, and experience for the new future organization. Groupware is the tool for preserving that knowledge and experience.

This idea of letting an organization fall apart is pretty scary, but Coleman says that it helps if management is willing to do so in a way that preserves existing knowledge, energy, and people for the new organization. An example of this might be when an organization spins off a new, entrepreneurial business which is unencumbered by the bureaucracy of the parent organization. The new organization self-organizes in a new and harmonious way based on its knowledge of where it wants the new business to go.

Coleman believes that empowered people equipped with groupware can reengineer themselves and be more successful. It is pretty strong stuff to espouse that organizations don't need to reengineer and that they should instead equip their people with tools to allow them to self-organize. This suggests that as we turn people loose with groupware, we may start to see some very fundamental and unique business transformations.

Factors That Contribute to a Successful Groupware Implementation

Here are some of the things you can do to make your groupware implementation successful.

1. First and foremost, have people start collaborating before you even think about adding the technology. Try to build teamwork and a collaborative culture, and then you can add the tools to assist them. It helps if people already know each other, like each other, respect each other, and even trust each other before they start to collaborate. Team building is a useful prerequisite, and is certainly less expensive than the cost of a failed system.

   This may seem like heresy to IT folks, since we look at technology as the solution to all problems. However, lack of collaboration doesn't come from a lack of collaborative tools. It comes from a lack of interest in collaborating or not knowing how to collaborate. You have to get people working together and cooperating before groupware will work. The purpose of groupware is to make it easier for people to do what they're already doing.

2. Change the culture to support collaboration.

3. Make sure employees feel secure and supported by the organization, because groupware only works when employees feel secure.

4. Make it the users' project. Business users should own it and make the product decisions.

5. Ensure good communication among everyone participating in the project. Start the communication early and keep it up.

6. The role of IT is to support and coordinate, not to dictate and control. IT should create and support the network infrastructure, provide communications, and provide the resources necessary to make the project successful.

7. Don't dictate or decree anything.

8. Executive leadership and support can help to start the change process and eliminate obstacles. You don't necessarily need executive leadership at the very beginning when you do pilots, but it can be helpful later to eliminate the inevitable resistance. If senior managers make it known that the best way to contact them is through a specific groupware tool, then others will start using it as well.

9. Enroll the thought leaders and influencers early.

10. Plan to help people with change.

11. Help people to see why they should want groupware.

12. Have evangelists promote the idea at every opportunity.

13. Plan for any training and support that you need. Do you need more people or specialized training programs? If so, get them. You won't get the results you expect unless you anticipate and cover all the users needs.

14. Plan for growth and be prepared to ramp up quickly, just as with the intranet.

15. Groupware must provide benefits every day to users and should be so compelling that they want to use it because it improves their work life.

16. Apply the lessons learned at each stage to the next roll-out or application.

17. Measure the results if you can, but don't rely upon results to sell the project. Many of the results are intangibles.

chapter ten

Two Approaches to Implementing Groupware

Introduction

We've looked at what groupware is and why you need it, reviewed some of the intranet groupware products and how to select the right ones, and discussed the challenges of implementing groupware. Now it's time for us to look at implementing intranet groupware. I recommend two approaches to implementing groupware. The first approach involves working with users to identify their needs and to help them select an appropriate product. I call this the *user-focused* approach. The second approach is part of implementing a *business process improvement (BPI),* or reengineering, project. I call this simply the business process improvement approach. Some companies have tried a third approach that decrees that everyone must use groupware. We won't bother with the third approach because it's very ineffective. In this chapter we'll look first at the user-focused approach, and then at the business process improvement approach.

The User-Focused Approach

Generally, groupware projects emerge from a user-focused approach, which works best for an off-the-shelf solution. Workflow projects tend to emerge from the BPI approach, which works well for customized solutions. However, you can do either project with either approach. The seven steps in the user-focused approach are as follows:

1. Are you ready?
2. Select a group and have them start collaborating.
3. Start changing the rewards system.
4. Identify your groupware needs.
5. Do an initial pilot.
6. Start other pilots.
7. Create enthusiasm to reach critical mass.

Step 1: Are You Ready?

The first step in the user-focused approach is to assess the company culture, the business environment, and the technology environment.

How's the Company Culture?

Here's a checklist of some things to think about if you want to implement groupware. This is the most important of the three assessments we'll look at. If you answer *yes* to any of these questions, you should think seriously about changing the culture before you try groupware. A *yes* should be considered a red flag. You need to change these things for groupware to have a chance of being successful.

- Is there an entrenched hierarchy?
- Is it a highly command-and-control environment?
- Do all decisions come from the top?
- Does the organization consist of many highly competitive employees?
- Are department heads protective of their turf, and do they refuse to allow others to "play in their sandbox"?
- Do some departments hide and protect their information from others?

- Are meetings mostly one-way flows of information instead of being participatory?
- What happens when something fails? Does the person who's responsible get banished to *corporate Siberia* instead of being rewarded for trying something new and risky?
- Does the company reward individual achievement and even discourage collaborative efforts and teamwork?
- Are there hundreds of policies and procedures that forbid or discourage employees from trying something new?
- Do some employees, especially managers, hoard information? Would these employees feel powerless if everyone else knew what they knew?
- Are managers constantly checking up on employees as though they don't trust them to get their jobs done?

It may be difficult, if not impossible, to have a successful groupware effort if you answered *yes* to most of these questions, and you'll need to work on changing the corporate culture. If you answered *no* to most of them, then your organization may be a good candidate for groupware. Other indicators that you may be ready for groupware are as follows:

- Is the culture open and participative?
- Is the organization flexible and adaptable?
- Does the organization encourage collaboration and sharing of knowledge?
- Does the organization encourage and reward learning and trying new things?
- Are there teams in place and is there team-based compensation?
- Is senior management willing to try new things—even to lead the charge?

If you can answer *yes* to most of these questions, then your organization is a really good candidate for groupware.

How's the Business Environment?

If the culture is ready, then is there anything in the business environment that's encouraging you to consider groupware?

- Are your competitors already using groupware?
- Do you need tools to help manage large-scale projects?
- Is your organization experiencing major business change?
- Are you experiencing the need to change your business processes to improve cycle time, cost, quality, or customer service?

Groupware can help you with all of these. It is most valuable if it fulfills a business need or goal.

How's the Technology Environment?

If both the culture and business environment favor groupware, your next assessment is to determine if you have the right infrastructure to support it.

- Do you have a LAN in place?
- Do you have your remote locations connected into a WAN?
- Do you have an intranet?
- Are your networks stable and well managed?

If you don't have all of these, then that's where you need to concentrate your effort. Chapter 9 gave you lots of information about how to create the intranet part of this. If you do have all of these, you're ready for step 2.

Step 2: Select a Group and Have Them Start Collaborating

If the environment is right and you're ready to start moving toward groupware, the next step is to select the right group of people and have them start collaborating. No, I didn't say to pick the product next—I said to start people collaborating. If that's already happening in your organization, and everyone's comfortable sharing and working together, then the hard part's done for you and you can go on to the next step. However, if that's not the case for you, then you have a lot of work to do. You shouldn't proceed until you have accomplished this. *Don't skip this step!*

Nothing is more critical to the success of groupware than creating the environment in which it can succeed. Farmers don't just go out and poke seeds into the soil and hope they'll grow. They take the time to till and prepare the soil before planting seeds. After that, they water and tend and fertilize the plants until they produce. That's exactly what we must do if we want to harvest the results of a successful groupware project. This step involves taking the time to choose the right group and to build team bonding. Team bonding takes time and costs money, but in the long run it's a lot cheaper than a failed groupware project.

How Do You Choose the Right Group?

How do you choose where to start and whom to start with? Do you seek them out or do they seek you? Either way will work as long as they meet the criteria I'll outline below. You may be approached by a group that's heard about Lotus Notes and wants it or something like it. They know they need a solution that will help them work together and they know that such solutions do indeed exist.

The other way is for you to seek them out. It's a good idea to look for a group that's heavily involved in meeting the goals of the business. It's especially good if you can find a group that has something very important to do for the organization, because that kind of success is worth a lot when you want to sell the idea to the rest of your organization. It's nice if you can find a high-profile project or group and can help them to accomplish their goals more easily and better.

It's best to start with a group that already works together, or is just starting to do so. It's even better if it's a cross-functional team. For this reason, you might consider a BPI team or your intranet team, as both are typically cross-functional. BPI team members are chosen for their open-mindedness and willingness to be creative and innovative. As a result, they tend to be good choices for groupware. Intranet team members are typically very open to trying new things, especially if they volunteered for the intranet team. You could also consider groups involved in core business processes that focus on meeting the needs of your customers, since helping them to work together better should yield a high payback. For example, product development teams or customer service teams may be more receptive to groupware and collaboration. Product development teams usually have engineers and researchers, both of whom are receptive to technology. Scientists are taught to collaborate, so they should be comfortable working with groupware. Customer service is another area where the people should be receptive to groupware. Customer service tends to attract people who like other people and are comfortable working together, sharing, and helping others. Sales is in a core process area that's less receptive to groupware because of their compensation systems. As long as you compensate salespeople with commissions based on their individual sales, you won't have much collaboration. If, however, you change the structure and compensation to revolve around teams, you may find that sales is another good potential area for groupware.

One potential area of concern when working with teams that have tight deadlines is that they may not have time for the testing and problems that will inevitably occur in a pilot environment. If they have more flexibility in their time frames, especially with longer-term projects such as may occur in product development, they may be able to quickly recoup the lost time through greater productivity and better tools. That's something you just have to explore with them. You could also try working with more than one group at a time so you can evaluate multiple solutions simultaneously to determine which products work best for your organization.

What are some of the characteristics you should look for in the individuals and teams that you want to work with on your groupware project?

1. *Cross-functional.* A cross-functional team works best since it has people with a variety of skills, interests, and needs and provides a good cross section of your organi-

zation. If a team is physically located together, members will need to try much harder to change the way they already do things, but that's not such an issue with a team that's flexible and adaptable.

2. *Geographically dispersed.* Smoothly functioning, geographically dispersed teams are a good choice because you can offer them so much value to compensate them for the time it takes to participate. Geographically dispersed teams may welcome new tools that make it easier for them, and therefore this is the ideal test area for a groupware project.

3. *Represent a dominant functional area.* If you can't get a cross-functional or geographically dispersed team, then it's best to choose a functional area that represents a large portion of your population and their needs. You could also choose several areas that normally work together so they get a chance to wring out all the features under both the best and worst conditions.

4. *Team size of about 6 to 12.* The ideal size group will be from about 6 to 12, although you can certainly use larger groups if necessary. Groups that are smaller may not have enough participants to really change the way they work.

5. *Individuals who can be freed up.* A groupware test can be time-consuming, so it's best to have individuals who can be freed up from some of their current responsibilities.

6. *Natural leaders.* Participants should be the thought leaders and influencers who are well regarded by others.

7. *Flexible, adaptable, and persistent.* Participants should be willing to try new things and be flexible enough to find solutions to any problems that arise. They should be willing to keep records of what they've learned along the way in order to benefit others.

8. *Individuals with the right equipment.* All participants should be on the intranet and have the appropriate equipment.

How Do You Create the Team?

One of our goals is to turn this group into a performing team. We often see the terms *team* and *group* used interchangeably, but there is a big difference. I once attended a class that used an exercise to illustrate the difference. The instructor had a shallow box containing 50 common objects—business card, ballpoint pen, paper clip, thimble, eraser, push pin, nail file, plastic fork, napkin, screwdriver, and lots more. The instructor brought the box around and showed it for a few seconds to groups of three. Each individual then listed the things he or she saw and counted the number of items. We listed each person's count on a flipchart. Each group then combined their individual lists and counted the number of unique items they saw. We listed the group totals on the flipchart. Then we threw away all individual and group lists. We began again, with each group deciding how it would approach the task. This time, the instructor stirred the contents to reveal different items. The goal was to see which team could identify the most. Each team approached the task differently. One team divided the box into thirds, with each member responsible for a third. Others had each member responsible for certain colors or types of objects. Each team listed and totaled its items. This time, each team had two to three times more items than before. We reasoned that some people remembered items from before and added those to the ones they saw the second time around. Our subsequent experience, however, has shown that the mind holds only so many items at a time, with few items being repeated from previous lists. The message you get from this is that groups are often people working together without a common goal. When you give groups a common goal and an opportunity to decide how to approach that goal, they become a team. Team performance is usually superior to group performance.

Organizations create teams to generate a collective knowledge and wisdom and to accomplish much more than individuals alone can. Groupware supports these teams by giving them tools for communicating and collaborating. In some cases, these may be virtual teams, which makes the tools that much more important. Most important, teams must have a shared objective.

It's so important for group members to know one another, respect one another, and even like one another, before they get started. With geographically dispersed teams, it's very important to get them together to get to know one another when they first start working together. It's really important to establish that face-to-face relationship first. Once they know each other, it's much easier to work together using e-mail and groupware tools.

Four Stages of Teams   Teams go through four distinct stages, and every team goes through all four of them. The facilitator can help the team move easily through these stages.

1. *Forming.*   The first stage is forming, where the team starts getting organized and figuring out what to do. Everyone is a little cautious in this stage and people are reluctant to let their hair down.
2. *Storming.*   As they move into storming, team members have started getting comfortable with each other and may even start to openly disagree. This is a normal, healthy stage for the team to go through.
3. *Norming.*   As team members get more comfortable with each other, they start to develop team behavioral norms. Each team member takes a specific role and they start working together more effectively.
4. *Performing.*   By the performing stage, team members are working together cooperatively and effectively, and members start to really care about each other. The team becomes more than just the sum of its members.

Any team can revert to any of the previous stages at any time.

Team Building and Bonding   How do we start creating a team? When you mix people from different areas, they may not know how to communicate with each other since their vocabularies may be different. You start creating a team by getting people communicating.

It's at this early stage of team development that it may be useful to identify team members' personal styles through instruments such as the Myers-Briggs Type Indicator (MBTI). These instruments help team members identify their own and others' preferred styles so they can know how to best work with and communicate with each other. The MBTI defines four personality dimensions, with two opposite styles for each dimension.

1. *Introverts (I) or extraverts (E).*   Introverts draw their energy from inside and focus on ideas and emotions, while extraverts (yes, in MBTI that's an *a* rather than an *o*) draw their energy from outside and focus on people and things. Everyone will tend toward one or the other.

2. *Sensing (S) or intuition (N).*   Sensing involves use of all five senses to absorb information. Intuition involves absorbing information with a sixth sense while focusing on what's possible.

3. *Thinking (T) or feeling (F).*   Thinking is making logical decisions, while feeling is making decisions based on values.

4. *Judging (J) or perceiving (P).*   Judging is planned and organized. Perceiving is flexible and spontaneous.

These four dimensions combine to form 16 personality types. For example, an ESFJ—Extravert Sensing Feeling Judging—the most common type in our general population, is warm and thoughtful with good people skills. ESFJs are the most cooperative of the 16 types. They like to do nice things for others. They work well when encouraged and praised, and have little interest in technical subjects. They want to positively impact others' lives. You won't find many ESFJs in IT departments.

By contrast, the most common type for computer professionals is ISTJ—Introvert Sensing Thinking Judging. These folks are quiet and serious, orderly, logical, dependable, thorough, and well organized. They work steadily in spite of distractions. Just from this you can easily see why inner-directed IT professionals may have a difficult time talking with outer-directed business people! ISTJs are more thinking-oriented, whereas ESFJs are more feeling-oriented.

Knowing personality types of team members makes it easy to figure out who may be most comfortable with particular communication and work styles. This tool can be very helpful in getting the team started and figuring out which roles are best for which team members. Some people consider Myers-Briggs to be controversial, so you have to judge it by the value you seek from using it. Using it to pigeonhole people is a bad use of the tool. Using it to learn how people feel about different tasks and what they're most comfortable with is a good way to use it. By learning team members' styles, you can more easily divide up responsibilities among team members. In addition, by learning the kinds of interactions they prefer, you can more easily identify the tools they will be comfortable using. Since introverts like to go off and think about a problem and come back with ideas or solutions, while extraverts like to brainstorm in groups, discussion databases will work well for both because they can respond whenever it's most appropriate for them.

When you know the team's MBTI styles and are ready to start team building, you'll want to have a skilled facilitator, or SSA, as suggested by Tom Davenport, to help create communication and break down walls between team members. It's important to build team relationships. Team bonding is a sense of unity and caring among team members. It takes time to build, but you can speed it up by giving the team opportunities to get to know one another personally. Here are some techniques for team bonding:

- *Experiential programs.* The most common team-building technique is the use of experiential programs, such as Outward Bound. These programs build team trust and communication. Some people can become very uncomfortable in these situations, so they can backfire on you. Be very careful if you choose this.

- *Trips.* Taking the team on a trip is my favorite because it's worked successfully for me. My co-facilitator and I took our BPI team on a best-practice visit to a company known as *best in class* for the process we were working on. The trip was great for building relationships and communication. Throughout, team members did little things for each other. Some checked in baggage while others parked the cars, and some retrieved baggage while others picked up the rental vans. During meals and while traveling in the vans, there were lots of opportunities to get to know each other better and learn about each others' families and interests. This team became a very high performance team and supported each other through a very challenging project.

If possible, get your team out for a trip somewhere. Pile them into a van or some cars and go visit other companies that have implemented groupware to find out about their experiences. Go to a vendor seminar to look at groupware products. The destination doesn't matter—it's just important to get people out of the office and give them a chance to get to know each other and share a common experience.

◆ *Social events.* Getting the team together for a meal or social event is another good technique, and unless you go to an expensive restaurant or country club, it shouldn't be very expensive. It's preferable to go someplace relaxed, where everyone can dress casually, let their hair down, and just get to know each other. However, pool parties don't work well for this!

How Do You Start the Collaboration?

Most people have a misperception of collaboration. Michael Schrage, in *Shared Minds: The New Technologies of Collaboration,* Random House, New York, 1990 (recently replaced by an updated version called *No More Teams*), says that most people equate effective collaboration with effective communications. He says that's wrong, and explains the difference:

> *Effective communication is only a precursor to meaningful collaboration. Most people in most organizations honestly believe that good communication is indistinguishable from good col-*

laboration. It's not. The difference is not unlike that between an acquaintance and a friend—one has polite conversation with an acquaintance; one really talks with a friend. The depth of experience, the shared bonds of interest, and the emotional commitment all guarantee that the quality of the interaction will be different.

Schrage also talked about the rules for collaboration. Of his 13 rules, I have paraphrased the 5 that are most important for group collaboration in organizations:

1. *A shared, understood goal.*   That goal is the purpose for which the collaboration exists, and which propels it forward.

2. *Mutual respect, tolerance, and trust.*   Collaborators respect each other and focus on each others' strengths. Trust is implicit in the relationship.

3. *Creation and manipulation of shared space.*   Shared spaces are the tools that make the collaboration work. This isn't just physical space, but also shared spaces such as discussion groups. All collaborators have equal access to this shared space, which is critical for making the collaboration yield more than the sum of its parts.

4. *Continuous, but not continual, communications.*   Collaborators communicate without interfering with each others' work.

5. *A physical presence is not necessary.*   Technology enables communication and collaboration without a physical presence being required.

Once the team members start bonding and cooperating, you'll see changes in the way they collaborate and work together. If you already have e-mail, they may use it for communicating, especially among a geographically dispersed team. This will help people start working together and create a foundation for groupware. Do everything you can to help the team work together and build cooperation, trust, and collaboration. The team can start by taking small steps toward working cooperatively and collaborating. When they start, they should take what my friend Shannon Lewis calls *baby steps*. When babies first start to walk, they take a tiny little step. With the confidence from that tiny little step, they take another tiny little step. As they build their confidence, they take just a little bit larger step, until they find themselves actually walking. It's like that with teams. With each tiny little step, members build the confidence to take a larger step, until they're not only walking, but running. Help the team start finding small ways to work together. These don't need to be big leaps, just tiny little baby steps.

You can have some team members get together to define and write up how they do their jobs—the steps and handoffs to each other—and how they can improve the coordination. This will involve them in figuring out how to solve their problems together, and will give them a jump start into the process of defining their groupware needs. You can even help the team start working on guidelines and norms that they will use to communicate appropriately with each other when they participate in discussion groups and forums.

Step 3: Start Changing the Rewards System

One thing that will cause groupware to fail is if people have disincentives for its use. In other words, if you encourage people to work in teams, but you reward only their individual achievements, you'll unconsciously sabotage the team process. If you reward people through their performance reviews for their contributions to teams, to helping others, and to sharing their knowledge, then you'll reinforce the importance of collaboration and groupware. If you don't intend to change your reward system, then you'll want to think through how much you expect from groupware. Research has shown this to be one of the biggest demotivators to the use of groupware.

Before you introduce groupware, you'll need to start changing the culture to encourage and reward contributions and collaboration. These rewards should be team-based, with everyone encouraged to contribute and use information. Employees have more motivation for sharing if that's a criteria on performance reviews and their raises depend upon sharing. Make sure that people get benefits commensurate with what they're contributing.

Step 4: Identify Your Groupware Needs

Once people are collaborating, you can start introducing the tools that can help them work together more effectively. They're probably ready to move on to figuring out what they need and selecting and using it.

Sell Them on Groupware

First, help them understand what groupware is and what it can do for them. This is the point where the *Three Times (3X) Rule* may apply. My colleagues and I in BPI at JCPenney used that term to describe a phenomenon we saw quite frequently. Whenever you introduce something new and abstract, it frequently goes right over people's heads, or they may get some part of it but not the whole concept. For people to really get it, they have to see it and hear it *three times.* Sometimes you can accomplish this in a single presentation by explaining it in your introduction, then fully explaining it in the body of your presentation, and then explaining it again in the summary. This works for something that doesn't shatter paradigms, but for something really different or abstract, it may take three distinct occasions. I don't mention this lightly— this is very important. I've seen it often enough to know that it's a nearly universal truth. We first picked up the idea from BPI colleagues at another company, and sure enough, we saw it happen consistently. Therefore, when you first start to describe collaborative tools, people will say "of course," but they may not really understand until you've shown them several times. Once they've internalized what it means to them, then they'll get it!

It's also important for techies to remember the one simple rule about communicating with nontechies—*it's more important to communicate a concept so your audience understands than it is to be technically correct.* Yes, that goes against our nature—we want to be technically correct. But if you say something that's technically correct and your audience doesn't understand, then you've wasted their time and yours, and have created an impediment to future communication. It's not enough simply to send a message—communication means that the recipient both received and understood your message. If you speak in French and your audience only understands English, they become very frustrated. The same thing happens when you speak in technical jargon—they don't understand, they become frustrated, and they'll tune you out—not just this time, but forever. That's not what you want to accomplish. The goal is a shared understanding.

Identify Their Groupware Needs

When the team understands what groupware is and what it can do for them, they'll want to identify problems and needs that groupware can solve. As I mentioned in Chapter 7, it's best to get the user team together in a room with a facilitator to talk about what they need. There should be lots of discussion and lots of creativity applied to finding solutions to problems. They should start by identifying a list of their problems and needs, and then distill that into a prioritized list of requirements. It may be necessary to select just one or two applications for a pilot and save the other needs and requirements for later. A lot depends on the tools that are available and how much *pain* the team can stand.

In choosing which applications are most important or appropriate for the groupware pilot, you should consider whether this is something most of the organization can use and how important it is to the business. It should be important, but not mission-critical. The application should be something of value, and it's even better if you can measure its results, but this shouldn't be a showstopper for a worthy application. It's helpful if the application is something that everyone can understand, relate to, and see the value of. This will make it much easier to sell to the organization. Workflow applications will be the most complex, and should probably wait until after other groupware applications have been successfully implemented.

Step 5: Do an Initial Pilot

The purpose of the pilot is to learn what works, and what doesn't work, in a limited environment without putting the entire organization at risk. You get a chance to identify all the problems in the technology and in the way employees work, and can resolve and document them for the benefit of the rest of the organization. The team will learn about how employees interact when they use groupware. They should share this information with the rest of the organization so others avoid the same problems.

Select Appropriate Groupware and Plan for Pilot

As I mentioned in Chapter 7, the team of users should choose the tools. Once the IT group evaluates the tools and selects those that qualify based on the user and IT criteria, they should then present them to the team. They should also provide the team with information about how each product measures up to the selection criteria, alerting them to any concerns they have about any products. They should discuss cost and implementation issues as well. The team may want to play with the tools and demos on their own before actually making a decision.

When the team reconvenes to make the decision, a facilitator can help focus the decision-making process and help the team and IT develop a pilot implementation plan. The pilot gives you a chance to determine, on a smaller scale, if there are meaningful measurements you can derive to generalize to the entire organization.

Get a Commitment

An important part of the planning process is the commitment from the team to meet certain requirements for the pilot. Members must agree to commit the time to making the project work and to using the application regularly and consistently. If all members don't use it, then it's an inconvenience to those who do, and you may not get valid results from your test.

If the team will use a conferencing tool, they may want to set up some guidelines in advance. They may want to set a maximum message size, as some Internet groups do. They may want large items, or certain types of items, to be placed in document databases rather than in discussion groups. The team may want to set some rules of *netiquette* for discussions. You should thoroughly test these guidelines to see if they should become the organization's guidelines.

Install Groupware

You should arrange for loading software on individual machines if required. If you must install software, you should do it almost simultaneously on all machines so the team can use it as soon as it's available. More and more, we'll see groupware as applications residing on servers with access from browsers. They may require little more than helping the team know how to access the application, and support should be minimal.

Train Team

How should you train the team to use groupware? With intranets, the operation of the browser is so easy that users need very little training, and that should be the case with most intranet groupware also. The vendor may have provided a tutorial that takes care of most of the operational training. Where users do need training is in how to most effectively use the tools, and finding that out is one of the goals of the initial pilot.

You should assess how much additional training you need, and either develop it or arrange for its delivery. Users should receive training when the groupware is ready for use. The trainer should be available to assist the team with questions about the application and how to use it. You will probably need more extensive training for workflow applications, but those will probably be among the last applications you implement.

Share Experiences and Identify Changes

The team should record their experiences, questions, and answers for future reference by new users. As they use the application, they should save and record their suggestions, guidelines, and hints on how to use it. When the team identifies things that should change, these should also be recorded. It's probably also a good idea to have some meetings to discuss these changes and gather suggestions for making the application easier and better.

Encourage Employees to Use Groupware

One of the greatest challenges is to help team members discover how best to use these new tools within the current culture. The group will be figuring all this out and at the same time trying to get their work done. Employees may find that the skills required in their work will change as they move from verbal to written communication. With written communication, you don't have all the nonverbal cues by which to judge the message, and this can sometimes make communications difficult. You'll need to keep encouraging the team to work through these things. Just remember, you're building your future groupware champions.

When Is the Pilot Finished?

When you start the implementation, you should define how you'll know when the pilot is complete. Ideally, the pilot should take anywhere from one to six months, depending on the complexity of the applications chosen. Most intranet groupware applications are fairly simple and straightforward and will require less time to pilot than an application as complex as Notes.

When the team finishes the pilot, groupware will be fully ingrained in their processes, and there shouldn't be any desire to go back to the old way of doing things. The team members become the champions and evangelists for the rest of the organization. They will share the lessons they have learned with others so they can have a smoother time implementing groupware.

Measure Results

Since companies haven't been bothering to determine ROIs for intranets, they probably won't bother for intranet groupware and workflow either. After all, the costs are simply incremental costs on top of an existing network and intranet, so it's very difficult to separate the costs of groupware from everything else. It's also almost impossible to put a dollar value on groupware benefits such as improved coordination, better decision making, and improved customer service. Even if you can, how can you know the improvements are solely from the impact of groupware? You can't. Therefore, I expect that companies will try to calculate ROIs for the BPI approach, but probably just won't bother with ROIs for the user-focused approach.

One thing you can do is to analyze and document the situation before and after to identify readily apparent results. The information and anecdotes you collect from this type of analysis will make it much easier to sell groupware to other groups throughout the organization.

At the beginning of the project, team members should record their activities and the time it takes to accomplish each. When the pilot is complete, team members should again review their lists and record the time it takes to do the same tasks using groupware. They should note any additional tasks and identify any eliminated tasks. They should also record not only quantitative improvements, but qualitative ones as well. This information, along with any anecdotes they supply, will be an important part of the success stories you'll share with others to help them understand the value of groupware.

Step 6: Start Other Pilots

With what you've learned from the initial pilot, you can proceed to start more pilots. Ideally, you can roll out groupware to the organization as a series of pilots or you can let it be pulled through the organization and spread like wildfire.

You can use any success stories from the first pilot to pitch the idea to other teams. You should go through the same kind of meetings with the new team to determine and prioritize their needs. In some cases, the same application is a perfect fit for the new team, and it's a fairly simple process to implement it and share lessons learned. This could be a good time for testing more difficult implementations to refine the process before moving to other groups. This could also be a time for working with more challenging teams than before, but make sure to start the process of collaboration before introducing the tools.

In other cases, you may find that you need different applications and may have to go through the same process all over again for the different application. It may be appropriate to have several pilots going simultaneously.

Step 7: Create Enthusiasm to Reach Critical Mass

Your initial and subsequent pilots should provide you with lots of success stories for selling the concept of groupware to other parts of the organization. Use as many of them as you can. You can do demos as you did for the Internet or intranet and turn it into a pull, rather than push, implementation. If the application is already available on the server, it may be a case of giving out a tip sheet to tell users how to access and start using the application. You can show them and talk them through it in demos. You can build tutorials and even keep the demo applications on the server so they can know how to use it. Make it very easy for users to get started by themselves.

Once you reach critical mass, peer pressure will drive it into the rest of the organization. As you start having success with the early groupware pilots, the people involved will tell their friends about it and they will want it, too. Just as with selling the intranet, cultivating groupware will change from selling the concept to people asking for it. If it's as successful as you want it to be, then it will start spreading by itself.

When groupware starts to become pervasive, people don't even notice that it's there. It's an everyday part of the way they work and is woven throughout the fabric of the organization. These tools will enable people to make better decisions and do a better job of serving customers.

Business Process Improvement Approach

The second approach to implementing groupware is the BPI approach, which usually produces workflow solutions. There are two basic types of workflow:

1. *Formal,* such as insurance claims processing. The process and the business are the same, and all work follows a defined process flow. It usually depends on document databases with a workflow engine and sophisticated rules. This type of workflow generally begins and ends with the external customer. We're not seeing this type of workflow on intranets yet.

2. *Informal,* such as office forms. Once a form is completed, either the form has smart routing and knows where to go next, or you specify and send it to its next

destination. Informal workflow usually relies on e-mail for its routing. This type of workflow supports internal customers in such processes as HR and accounting, and you may also use it for task management. This is the type of workflow we're seeing on intranets.

Workflow works only if you integrate it into your business processes to make the process efficient and effective.

We'll first look at what BPI is, and then at the steps of the BPI approach. Though TQM, BPI, and reengineering usually range from four to seven steps, we'll use a five-step process here:

1. Identify the problems with the process.
2. Define the current process and why the problems occur.
3. Create a future process that will solve the problems.
4. Develop an implementation plan for the future process.
5. Implement the new process.

The first four are the same as those used in the Benefits BPI Proposal for the traditional model for building intranets (Chapter 6 in *Intranet Business Strategies* or Chapter 8, Figure 8.1, in this book).

What Is Business Process Improvement (BPI)?

To understand BPI we'll first look at what a process is, talk about the different variations of process change ranging from TQM to reengineering, and then look at who's involved in a BPI project.

What's a Process?

A process is a series of steps that start and end with the customer and fulfill a customer need. Figure 10.1 illustrates the high-level steps of simple order-fulfillment process. It starts when a customer calls and places an order. The salesperson enters the order, and then it moves to the credit department. If the customer's credit is good, the order moves on to distribution to pick, pack, and ship the order. Distribution sends the packing list to the accounting department, who generates an invoice and sends it to the customer. Finally, the customer receives the product.

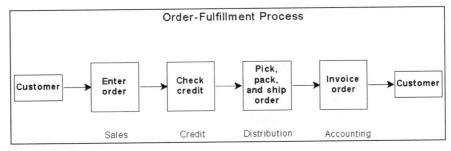

Figure 10.1 Order-fulfillment process.

As we saw, this process involved several different functional areas of the company, including Sales, Credit, Distribution, and Accounting. All of these functional areas participated in a single process, filling a customer order, which started and ended with the customer. As you can see, processes focus on the customer and cross over functional lines.

An important concept about processes is that you need only those steps that add value for the end customer—everything else is waste and you should remove it. That's what business process improvement is about.

Degrees of Process Change

Process improvement comes in lots of different varieties, which makes it very confusing to those who are not directly involved but who need to know what's happening. Let's look at just three variations.

- **Total Quality Improvement (TQM)** focuses on *small, continuous improvements* to highly focused processes. TQM is an ongoing process.

- **Business process improvement** focuses on *larger improvements,* and generally to enterprise-wide processes. Once you complete BPI, you should continue to improve the process by using TQM for gradual refinements.

- **Reengineering** focuses on *nuking business-critical processes and re-creating them from scratch.* Once implemented, you should continually improve the new process through TQM or BPI until it comes time to nuke it again and start over. Michael Hammer, the guru of reengineering, describes it as "the fundamental rethinking and radical redesign of business processes to achieve dramatic improvements in critical measures of performance, such as cost, quality, capital, service, and speed." (Michael Hammer, "Reengineering: The Implementation Perspective Seminar," Hammer and Company, March 1993).

As you can see, these three are really just variations of process improvement based upon their radicalness and degree of change. They fall on the continuum illustrated in Figure 10.2. TQM is the least radical; BPI is moderately radical; and reengineering is the most radical. Though some practitioners of each may argue with my distinctions, this is what I've seen most commonly. All three use similar tools and techniques. Since BPI is the middle-of-the-road approach, we'll use that for our discussion throughout the rest of this chapter, but the steps I'll talk about apply to any of these three. (For more information about TQM, BPI, and reengineering, refer to the sources listed in the appendix.)

Who's Involved in BPI?

Regardless of the approach, there are generally four types of people involved in BPI:

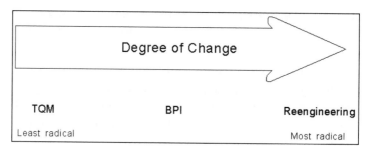

Figure 10.2   Process improvement continuum.

- *BPI team members.*   Team members come from all areas involved in the process. Since processes cross over many functional boundaries, the BPI team is usually highly cross-functional. It's also a good idea to include a technologist on the team, as well as an outsider to provide different perspectives (this may be someone from outside the process or even from outside the organization). Teams usually range from 6 to 12 members. Though full-time BPI teams are the ideal, it's sometimes hard to relieve team members from their day-to-day responsibilities, so there have been cases of successful part-time teams.

- *BPI facilitators.*   The team may have one or two facilitators to run and document the meetings. Facilitators must be neutral and balance team process with content.

- *Executive sponsor and/or process owner.*   The team usually has an executive sponsor at a high level who creates the vision and funds the team. As the team moves into later stages, sponsorship may transfer to a process owner who will own the final process.

- *Subject-matter experts.*   There are several types of subject-matter experts (SMEs). They may be process participants who help the team identify the steps and measures of the current process, and may suggest ways to change or improve it. SMEs may also include technologists brought in to help create the technology applications and infrastructure required for implementing the new process.

Step 1: Identify the Problems with the Process

This first step involves identifying the process problems you need to work on and launching the team to improve the process. BPI usually starts because there's already a noticeable problem with a process. Often, it's precipitated by customer complaints, such as not receiving the right order or orders taking too long. Sometimes competitor actions precipitate BPI projects, such as when a competitor continually gets new products to market faster. When a specific business problem reveals the need for BPI, that's when you create a compelling business case and charter a team to fix the process. The team receives the business case to provide documentation about the problems as well as stretch goals for the new process to meet.

The team will start out in the forming stage. This is the time for team building; and for BPI groups, I strongly recommend best-practice visits to other companies. By doing a search of the literature, you can turn up best practices and identify which companies are on the leading edge. Often, they're winners of the Malcolm Baldrige Award, and as part of the Baldrige requirements, will have programs to share what they've done with other companies. Many leading-edge companies are willing to share their experiences with others, especially those from other industries.

Step 2: Define the Current Process and Why the Problems Occur

The next step involves charting the process and identifying the causes of problems. The team studies the current process by interviewing and shadowing process participants. It draws process flowcharts for the current process, defines the problems found, and measures important process criteria, such as cycle time and quality.

Often, as you're determining the process flow, you'll find that there are numerous steps where a person or group hands off the process, and the product just sits and waits for processing. In many cases, the product may sit for hours, or even days, waiting for a few minutes' worth of value-adding work. These cases often call for workflow solutions to automate the performance of some tasks and keep the product moving. In some cases, better communication and coordination is needed, and groupware solutions are the right answer. Figure 10.3 shows a simple process flowchart to give you an idea of how to document the process. It shows the various steps and handoffs in an order process for a manufacturing company. With so many handoffs, this process is a good candidate for a workflow solution.

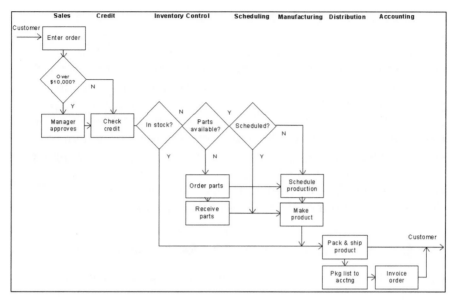

Figure 10.3   Order process flowchart.

Defining the current process is probably the hardest part of a BPI project. That's the time that the team will move from the forming phase into the storming phase and may openly disagree. Gradually they will move into the norming phase, where they'll start to feel comfortable with each other and with their task.

Step 3: Create a Future Process That Will Solve the Problems

In preparing to create a future process, the team creates a vision of what the new process should look like. It studies this process at other companies and identifies best practices. It also looks in depth at technologies that could provide process breakthroughs. By doing so, the team prepares to create the future process. It's only through knowing what's possible that a BPI team can create a truly breakthrough process. Since creating the new process involves selecting and specifying the appropriate technology for it, it might be worthwhile for the BPI team to utilize parts of the product selection process outlined in Chapter 7.

When the team designs the future process, it will need to be at its most creative. Because of the dynamics of today's marketplace, creating the new process requires dramatic changes, and in some cases, blowing up the process and starting over. At this stage, the team should be doing more creativity exercises and fun and games. They should be moving through norming and on to performing. The creativity exercises should help accelerate this process and may even move the team to a new plateau, where we characterize it as a high-performance team. A high-performance team is one in which members truly understand and care about each other. The products of a high-performing team are greater than the sum of the contributions of individual team members.

Step 4: Develop an Implementation Plan for the Future Process

Once the team has designed the new process, they develop the plans for implementing it and create a proposal similar to, but far more detailed than, the proposal we looked at in Chapter 8 (Chapter 6 in *Intranet Business Strategies*). This proposal contains details from every stage of the BPI project, including a description of the problems that caused us to investigate the process, a description of the process and its specific problems, a flowchart of the current process that identifies handoffs and measurements, a description and flowchart for the planned future process, and full implementation details, including costs, savings, benefits, and an implementation time line.

Change Management Plan

BPI projects usually develop change management plans as part of the implementation plan. They spell out who you need to communicate with and what message they should receive. If possible, you should use the things I suggested in the user-focused approach in your change management communication plan. For example, it's so important to get user, or stakeholder, buy-in. If you worked with process participants all along during the BPI process and got their input and ideas, then you should be aware of their needs. You might even consider sitting down with them

and reviewing the current process flowcharts, handoffs, and measurements as a sanity check. Then you could share with them the
new process design and get their reactions and suggestions. This
would provide them with the knowledge that you understand
their problems and are working to make things better for them.
This will help to gain their buy-in. You could also show them the
technology you've looked at and discuss why you selected particular products or technologies. You may want to share with them
the spreadsheets and documents that you used to evaluate and
select these products. What happens in the unlikely event that
you don't get their buy-in? You should reconsider your choices
based on any new information the process participants provided
you. After all, they're the ones who will have to use it and live
with it, so they need to be happy. It's best to do this before you put
together your proposal and request funding, because afterward
it'll be much harder to change.

Step 5: Implement the New Process

Once the proposal gets approval, you move forward to implement
the new process and acquire or build the necessary technology.
When companies recommend groupware or workflow as part of
the new process, how do they proceed to implement it? Typically,
the implementation plan for a large process calls for creating a
prototype or simulation of some kind, followed by a pilot. If the
pilot is successful, then you'll use the implementation plan as is,
or modify it to move into a full-scale rollout.

Prototype

A prototype is where you take the new process and simulate it,
either on paper or with software tools. This can be valuable for
working out possible glitches in workflow, but is less valuable for
general groupware solutions.

Pilot

Piloting is much like what you did in the user-focused approach.
If you have worked with the users and gotten their buy-in, then

piloting should be very similar to what we've already talked about. Fortunately, putting groupware and workflow on top of the intranet isn't an expensive proposition, so if the pilot isn't totally successful, you just back up and figure out what went wrong and approach it differently.

Rollout

If the pilot is successful, you can move on to a large-scale rollout following your implementation plan and making any necessary modifications. I really don't see any reason that a rollout couldn't consist simply of one pilot after another until everyone has it.

How Can a Consultant Help You Implement Groupware and Workflow?

You may wish to bring in a consultant to help you with your groupware or workflow implementation. Here are some of the things a consultant can do:

- Help you assess your culture and develop ways to customize your groupware implementation to work best within your culture
- Help you identify and deal with organizational issues such as reward systems and incentives and disincentives to sharing and collaboration
- Help you identify the organization's goals for groupware or workflow
- Help guide or facilitate the business process improvement team, including helping them develop process flows, bringing in best practices for them, and helping them identify new technologies for the process
- Help you identify the right team to work on groupware
- Help you with team building and bonding for the team
- Help the team develop collaboration skills

- Facilitate meetings to help the user team identify and prioritize their needs for groupware and workflow, and to decide and create the implementation plan for groupware
- Help you determine which products will meet both user needs and organizational needs
- Help you identify and set up needed infrastructure
- Help create product demos for showing products to the team
- Help develop workflow system procedures and rules
- Help promote groupware and workflow to groups throughout the organization
- Help work with suppliers and customers to integrate collaboration into your business partnerships
- Help you meet your groupware goals

Groupware Do's and Don'ts

Here are some lists of things I've discovered that do and don't work in creating collaboration and implementing groupware.

Groupware Do's

We know from successful groupware implementations what works well. Here are things you should definitely do:

1. Start by changing the culture, and balance that with technology.
2. Change the reward system and measure people on their teamwork and sharing of information.
3. Successful implementations are usually bottom-up, grassroots efforts. It's most effective if groups want groupware.
4. Give employees incentives so they will want to use groupware. Many companies have used groupware to

ease the burden on employees when filing expense reports. By making a chore easier to do, they gain instant participation. Also, groupware makes it easier for employees who need to travel or want to telecommute.

5. For expensive groupware implementations, such as Lotus Notes, having a champion is still critically important. With intranet groupware being much less expensive, a strong champion or executive sponsor is becoming less necessary, but can still help you get rid of obstacles and help employees see the vision of groupware. It's important that the champion or sponsor not get too involved in the pilot, because that can stifle the process of learning what will and what won't work. However, people will use the technology faster if an executive serves as a role model in the use of the technology.

6. Make sure your choice of software fits your processes, rather than making your processes fit your software.

7. Start collaboration with face-to-face meetings so people can relate to each other. After that, you can progress to using groupware.

8. Use role modeling to spread the concept of groupware. When someone they respect uses groupware and encourages them to do so, many employees will get on board. The initial pilot group will influence lots of others to start using groupware. If the team involved in the initial pilot is cross-functional, they will go back to their respective areas and encourage others to use it. As a result, it may spread rapidly. For example, in working with a BPI team that I facilitated, we shared new ideas and tools with them. As very influential members of many areas of the company, they shared those ideas and tools with others in their areas. They became more effective, and so did those who worked with them.

9. Use trainee programs for teaching and spreading collaboration skills and groupware use.

10. Some organizations have combined groupware with "*open-book management*" to enable true sharing of

knowledge. This requires that management trust its employees and treat them as adults, opening up the books for all to see.

Groupware Don'ts

From failed groupware implementations we've learned what not to do:

1. Don't start by choosing the technology and then trying to find a problem to fit it.
2. Don't expect to open the box and roll it out—it may require some customization to make it work for your organization.
3. Don't parachute it into your organization and let users sink or swim with no preparation, training, or understanding of what it's for and why they'll benefit from it. If you do it that way, you're throwing away your money because they won't use it the way you want.
4. Don't decree that people will use groupware. People resist things when they have no choice, but will fall in line when they see a benefit to them from using it.
5. Don't try to use workflow and groupware to reengineer your business processes. Develop the new process and then implement groupware as one of the components of the new process.
6. Don't try to use groupware to change the politics of your organization—change the politics first, then groupware can change the culture.

Checklist: Implementing Groupware

Figure 10.4 summarizes the steps involved in implementing groupware in your organization.

1. User-focused approach

- Step 1: Are you ready?

  - How's the company culture? (Most important of the three assessments)

    - A *yes* to any question is a red flag.

      - Is there an entrenched hierarchy?
      - Is it a highly command-and-control environment?
      - Do all decisions come from the top?
      - Does the organization consist of many highly competitive employees?
      - Are department heads protective of their turf?
      - Do some departments hide and protect their information?
      - Are meetings mostly one-way flows of information?
      - When something fails, does the person responsible get banished to *corporate Siberia?*
      - Does the company reward individual achievement and discourage collaboration?
      - Do policies and procedures forbid or discourage employees from trying something new?
      - Do some employees, especially managers, hoard information?

- ◆ Are managers constantly checking up on employees?

- ◆ Indicators that you're ready for groupware—*yes* answers indicate you're ready.

  - ◆ Is the culture open and participative?
  - ◆ Is the organization flexible and adaptable?
  - ◆ Does the organization encourage collaboration and sharing of knowledge?
  - ◆ Does the organization encourage and reward learning and trying new things?
  - ◆ Are there teams in place, and is there team-based compensation?
  - ◆ Is senior management willing to try new things—even to lead the charge?

- ◆ How's the business environment?

  - ◆ Are your competitors already using groupware?
  - ◆ Do you need tools to help manage large-scale projects?
  - ◆ Is your organization experiencing major business change?
  - ◆ Do you need to change your business processes to improve cycle time, cost, quality, or customer service?

- How's the technology environment?

    - Do you have a LAN in place?
    - Do you have your remote locations connected into a WAN?
    - Do you have an intranet?
    - Are your networks stable and well managed?

- Step 2: Select a group and have them start collaborating

    - How do you choose the right group?

        - Heavily involved in meeting the goals of the business
        - Already works together, or is just starting to do so
        - Cross-functional team, such as BPI or intranet team
        - Involved in core business processes
        - Multiple groups

    - Characteristics you should look for in individuals and teams

        - Cross-functional
        - Geographically dispersed
        - Represent a dominant functional area
        - Team size of 6 to 12
        - Individuals who can be freed up
        - Natural leaders
        - Flexible, adaptable, and persistent

- ◆ Individuals with the right computer equipment

- ◆ How do you create the team?

  - ◆ Four stages of teams

    - ◆ Forming
    - ◆ Storming
    - ◆ Norming
    - ◆ Performing

  - ◆ Team building and bonding

    - ◆ Myers-Briggs Type Indicator (MBTI) to identify communication and work styles
    - ◆ Skilled facilitator, or SSA
    - ◆ Team bonding—experiential programs, trips, and social events

- ◆ How do you start collaboration?

  - ◆ Get to know one another and like one another before starting
  - ◆ Face-to-face relationships
  - ◆ Schrage's rules for collaboration

    - ◆ A shared, understood goal
    - ◆ Mutual respect, tolerance, and trust
    - ◆ Creation and manipulation of shared space
    - ◆ Continuous, but not continual, communications

- A physical presence is not necessary

  ◆ Take *baby steps*

- Step 3: Start changing the rewards system

  - Reward collaboration and sharing of knowledge
  - Make sure people get benefits commensurate with what they're contributing

- Step 4: Identify your groupware needs

  - Sell them on groupware—help them understand what it is and what it can do for them
  - Identify their needs ·

    - Identify problems and needs that groupware can solve
    - Distill into prioritized list of requirements

      - Should be something of value, but not mission-critical
      - Helps if results are measurable
      - Workflow can wait

- Step 5: Do an initial pilot—learn what works

  - Select appropriate groupware and plan for pilot

    - Present tools to the team

- Provide information about how each product measures up to the set criteria
- Alert them to any concerns
- Discuss cost and implementation issues

- Facilitated decision-making session

  - Make decision
  - Develop a pilot implementation plan

- Get a commitment

  - Commit time to make project work
  - Agree to use application regularly and consistently
  - Set rules of netiquette for discussions

- Install groupware
- Train team when groupware is ready
- Share experiences and identify changes

  - Identify problems in the technology

- Learn how employees interact when they use groupware
- Record experiences, questions and answers, suggestions, guidelines, and hints
- Have meetings to discuss suggestions and experiences

- Share with the rest of the organization during rollout

- Encourage employees to use groupware
- Identify how you will know when the pilot is finished
- Measure results

  - Many companies aren't bothering with ROIs for intranets and may not bother for intranet groupware—it's only an incremental cost on top of the network
  - Almost impossible to value groupware benefits
  - Determine value by analyzing and documenting *before* and *after* tasks and times
  - Identify anecdotes and success stories

- Step 6: Start other pilots

  - Use success stories to pitch more pilots
  - Have meetings with the new team to determine and prioritize their needs
  - Try more difficult uses or more challenging teams
  - Could have several pilots simultaneously

- Step 7: Create enthusiasm to reach critical mass

  - Have demos and create a pull implementation
  - Talk them through it in demos
  - Make it easy for users to get started—if application is on server, give them tip sheets for accessing and using
  - Provide tutorials

2. Business process improvement (BPI) approach

- Usually for integrating workflow into business processes—two types of workflow:

  - Formal, such as insurance claims processing—not yet on intranets
  - Informal, such as office forms—common intranet application

- What is BPI?

  - What's a process?

    - Series of steps that start and end with the customer and fulfill a customer need
    - Involve different areas of the company—cross over functional lines
    - Requires only steps that add value for the customer—BPI removes everything else

  - Degrees of process change

    - Total Quality Management (TQM)—least radical
    - BPI—middle of the road
    - Reengineering—most radical

  - Who's involved in BPI?

    - BPI team members
    - Facilitators
    - Executive sponsor and/or process owner
    - Subject-matter experts

- ◆ Step 1: Identify problems with the process

  - ◆ Identify problem processes due to customer complaints or competitor actions
  - ◆ Create a compelling business case
  - ◆ Charter a team to fix the process
  - ◆ Provide the team with stretch goals for the new process
  - ◆ Do team building and best-practice visits

- ◆ Step 2: Define the current process and why the problems occur

  - ◆ Interview and shadow process participants
  - ◆ Draw process flowcharts
  - ◆ Define problems
  - ◆ Identify handoffs
  - ◆ Measure important process criteria, such as cycle time and quality

- ◆ Step 3: Create a future process that will solve the problems

  - ◆ Team does creativity exercises
  - ◆ Create vision for new process
  - ◆ Study process at other companies
  - ◆ Identify best practices
  - ◆ Look at technologies that could provide process breakthroughs
  - ◆ Design the future process

- ◆ Step 4: Develop an implementation plan for the future process

- ◆ Develop implementation plan
- ◆ Create proposal

  - ◆ Describes process and its specific problems
  - ◆ Flowcharts current process with hand-offs and measurements
  - ◆ Describes and flowcharts planned future process
  - ◆ Shows implementation plan with costs, savings, benefits, and time line

- ◆ Change management plan

  - ◆ Who to communicate with
  - ◆ Message they should receive
  - ◆ Review current process, new process design, and selected products with process participants
  - ◆ Reconsider your choices if you don't get buy-in

- ◆ Step 5: Implement the new process

  - ◆ Prototype—simulate new process on paper or with software tools
  - ◆ Pilot—work with users to see how the new process works and make modifications if necessary
  - ◆ Rollout—large-scale rollout or one pilot after another

3. How can a consultant help you implement groupware and workflow?

- ◆ Assess your culture and develop ways to customize your groupware implementation
- ◆ Identify and deal with organizational issues
- ◆ Identify the organization's goals for groupware or workflow
- ◆ Guide or facilitate the BPI team
- ◆ Identify the right team to work on groupware
- ◆ Help with team building and bonding and help the team develop collaboration skills
- ◆ Facilitate meetings to help the users identify and prioritize their needs, decide on groupware products, create the implementation plan, and discuss experiences and suggestions
- ◆ Determine which products will meet needs
- ◆ Identify and set up infrastructure
- ◆ Create product demos
- ◆ Develop workflow system procedures and rules
- ◆ Promote groupware and workflow throughout the organization
- ◆ Work with suppliers and customers to integrate collaboration into business partnerships
- ◆ Help meet groupware goals

4. Groupware do's and don'ts

  - ◆ Do's

    - ◆ Start by changing the culture, and balance that with technology
    - ◆ Change the reward system and measure people on their teamwork and sharing of information
    - ◆ Encourage bottom-up, grassroots efforts

- ◆ Give employees incentives so they'll want to use groupware
- ◆ For expensive implementations, have a champion
- ◆ Champion or sponsor shouldn't get too involved in the pilot
- ◆ Make sure the software fits your processes
- ◆ Start collaboration with face-to-face meetings
- ◆ Use role modeling for spreading groupware
- ◆ Use trainee programs for teaching and spreading collaboration skills and groupware use
- ◆ Combine groupware with *open-book management*

- ◆ Don'ts

  - ◆ Don't start by choosing the technology and then trying to find a problem to fit it
  - ◆ Don't expect to open the box and roll it out
  - ◆ Don't parachute it into your organization and let users sink or swim
  - ◆ Don't decree that people will use groupware
  - ◆ Don't try to use workflow and groupware to reengineer your business processes
  - ◆ Don't try to use groupware to change the politics of your organization

Figure 10.4   Implementing groupware checklist.

chapter eleven

The Impact of Groupware and Workflow

How Will Groupware Change Organizations?

Groupware and workflow will cause the following changes to organizations:

- Improve group productivity. Empowered teams and collaboration allow you to create a product that's greater than the sum of its parts.
- Make geographic boundaries and time zones irrelevant.
- Help create a sense of community and shared vision.
- Facilitate communication that changes the structure and hierarchy of power.
- Change the culture to be more open and honest.
- Help build trust.
- Help people become more willing to share their knowledge with others.
- Handle routine tasks so individuals can become more creative and innovative.
- Allow employees to see things from the perspective of others.
- Tear down functional walls.
- Help create a flexible and adaptable organization.
- Give employees access to the information they need.

- ◆ Empower employees to make decisions and serve customers.
- ◆ Support a high-performance learning community. George Pór, founder of Community Intelligence Labs in Santa Cruz, California, talks about high-performance learning communities. (Corporate Knowledge Networks: People probing, generating and sharing Knowledge and experience via Technology, for increasing Value, at http://www.co-i-l.com/know_garden/intranets/.) He says:

> What differentiates a high-performing learning community from any corporate community is that the former has "knowledge ecology": a dynamic and living web of computer-linked people with their experience, ideas, and expertise, that interact, feed, and grow upon each other.
>
> In nature, minerals, plants, animals and the weather continually interact in a delicate balance. Births, deaths, high pressures and low pressures, growing and shrinking gene pools are all part of that balance. The higher is the diversity of an ecosystem, the stronger its chance to survive. The same applies to the knowledge ecology.
>
> It's a cyber-ecosystem that provides a context and infrastructure for continuous learning.

How Will Groupware Change Business Processes?

Groupware and workflow will cause the following changes to business processes:

- ◆ Reduce cycle time and cost of business processes
- ◆ Support virtual offices so salespeople can spend more time with customers, which should increase sales
- ◆ Let customers collaborate with you to develop products that meet their needs

- Allow you to produce products faster and more cheaply to satisfy customer needs
- Enable more telecommuting, which can remove costs from processes
- Allow simultaneous development of products by having multiple shifts around the world, which will speed up development
- Allow you to incorporate reengineering best-practices and process-management tools into your processes
- Allow you to eliminate unnecessary layers of management

The Future of Intranet Groupware and Workflow

We're just beginning to use technology to support people and business processes. There are so many ways for us to use groupware that it will take considerable time to tap into all these possibilities. As groupware gets more sophisticated, we'll see it reach the point where employees can't function without it, much as with telephones today. We'll see more and more collaboration across the Internet with customers and suppliers, and our organizations may truly become virtual. No one will need to know who is or is not an employee. Virtual organizations will be fluid and flexible, and will enable us to meet the demands of the marketplace.

As we have more and more information available to us, we'll start to suffer from information overload. We'll see more tools, such as agents, to relieve us from this. I believe that groupware and workflow will become ever more tightly woven into our business processes so that they become integral to the processes' functioning. The tools will become more sophisticated, and we'll use them within all our processes. Workflow applications may soon be able to handle most processing and approvals automatically, which will not only remove time and cost from our processes, but will relieve much manual drudgery as well.

Summary

Intranet groupware and workflow are just getting started. It's much too early for us to have learned many lessons, but I do have some observations. Intranet groupware is relatively cheap, so just try something—anything—to see how it works. You can always change it later. This is the time to experiment, maybe even have multiple projects, so you can get a feel for what works best in your organization. From there, you can choose the products that work and start piloting in various areas. Again, be more concerned about getting people to collaborate first, and then adding the tools to help them. The tools are secondary to the people and how they wish to work together.

We've experienced a radical shift as a result of publishing on intranets, but this will pale in contrast to the impact on our businesses of intranet and Internet collaboration. Without them, you'll be unable to speed up your processes and shave costs from your products in order to compete. Because of the effect of the learning curve, those who lag behind in adopting intranet groupware and workflow may never catch up. Now's the time to start. Good luck!

Appendix

Groupware and Intranet Resources

Companies That Contributed to This Book—Introduction

- Amgen Incorporated at http://www.bio.com/companies/amgen.html.
- AT&T Corp. at http://www.att.com.
- Bell Atlantic Corporation at http://www.bel-atl.com.
- Booz Allen & Hamilton Inc. at http://www.bah.com.
- EDS at http://www.eds.com.
- JCPenney Company, Inc. at http://www.jcpenney.com.
- Rockwell International Corporation at http://www.rockwell.com.
- SAS Institute Inc. at http://www.sas.com.
- Silicon Graphics, Inc. at http://www.sgi.com.
- Texas Instruments Incorporated at http://www.ti.com.
- Turner Broadcasting System, Inc. at http://www.turner.com.
- United Parcel Service of America, Inc. at http://www.ups.com.

Netiquette—Chapter 1

- *The Net: User Guidelines and Netiquette* at http://www.fau.edu/rinaldi/net/index.htm.

What Is Happening in Business Today—Chapter 2

◆ Gary Hamel and C. K. Prahalad, *Competing for the Future,* Harvard Business School Press, 1994.

◆ Don Peppers and Martha Rogers, *The One to One Future—Building Relationships One Customer at a Time,* Currency/Doubleday, August 1993.

◆ Don Tapscott, *The Digital Economy: Promise and Peril in the Age of Networked Intelligence,* McGraw-Hill, 1996.

Learning Organizations—Chapter 4

◆ Peter M. Senge, *The Fifth Discipline: The Art and Practice of the Learning Organization,* Doubleday/Currency, 1990.

Uses of Intranets—Chapter 5

◆ Yahoo's list of intranet articles and resources is at http://www.yahoo.com/Computers-and-Internet/Communications-and-Networking/Intranet/.

◆ *How Sun saves money, improves service using Internet technologies* at http://www.Sun.com:80/960101/feature1/index.html/.

Intranet Groupware Products—Chapter 6

◆ IBM/Lotus Notes at http://www.lotus.com.

◆ IBM Internet Connection for FlowMark at http://www.software.ibm.com/ad/flowmark/exmn0b21.htm.

◆ Netscape/Collabra at http://www.netscape.com/.

◆ Microsoft at http://www.microsoft.com/.

◆ Novell GroupWise 5 at http://groupwise.novell.com.

◆ Open Text Livelink Intranet at http://www.opentext.com. Demo is at http://www.opentext.com/livelink/ll_cavea.html.

◆ Action Technologies Metro 1.1 at http://www.actiontech.com.

◆ Allaire Forums and Cold Fusion at http://www.allaire.com/.

◆ Amicus Networks Community Builder at http://www.amicus.com/product.htm.

◆ Attachmate Open Mind 3.0 at http://www.attachmate.com/.

◆ Cap Gemini Innovation WebFlow at http://webflow.cginn.cgs.fr:4747/.

◆ Connectix VideoPhone 1.1 for Windows at http://www.connectix.com/.

◆ DataBeam neT.120 Conference Server at http://www.databeam.com/.

◆ Digital AltaVista Forum 2.0 at http://www.altavista.software.digital.com/. The AltaVista Roundtable is at http://www.altavista.software.digital.com/roundtable/nfintro.htm.

◆ ForeFront RoundTable at http://www.ffg.com/.

◆ FTP/Campbell Services OnTime Web Edition 4.0 at http://www.ontime.com/.

◆ Galacticomm Worldgroup Internet Server and Worldgroup Manager at http://www.gcomm.com/home.html.

◆ JetForm at http://www.jetform.com/.

◆ Lundeen Web Crossing at http://webx.lundeen.com/.

◆ McCall, Szerdy & Associates C.A. Facilitator for the Web at http://www.facilitate.com/.

◆ Motet at http://www.sonic.net/~foggy/motet/.

◆ NetManage at http://www.netmanage.com/.

◆ Now Software Now Up-to-Date at http://www.nowsoft.com.

◆ Oracle InterOffice at http://www.oracle.com/.

- O'Reilly WebBoard at http://webboard.ora.com/.
- Paradigm Software WorkWise-Enterprise at http://www .workwise.com/.
- Proxima Podium 2.01 at http://www.proxima.com/.
- Quarterdeck/Future Labs TALKShow at http://web .futurelabs.com/welcome/.
- RadNet WebShare at http://www.radnet.com/.
- Screen Porch Caucus 3.0 at http://screenporch.com/.
- Searchlight Software Spinnaker at http://www .searchlight.com/home.htm.
- Spyglass/OS TECHnologies WebNotes at http:// webnotes.ostech.com/.
- Symantec/Delrina FormFlow 2.0 at http://www .symantec.com/formflow/.
- Thuridion CREW at http://www.thuridion.com/.
- UES Track-It at http://www.columbus.ues.com/.
- Ultimus WebFlow at http://www.ultimus1.com/.
- Ulysses Telemedia Networks/Intraprise Technologies Odyssey at http://www.ulysses.net/.
- WebCal at http://www.webcal.com/.
- WebFlow SamePage at http://webflow.com/.
- White Pine Enhanced CU-SeeMe at http://www .wpine.com/.

Building Your Intranet—Chapter 8

Security

- Eugene Spafford's computer security hot list at http:// www.cs.purdue.edu/homes/spaf/hotlists/csec.html. This list doubles as the official WWW hot list of the Computer Operations, Audit, and Security Technology (COAST) Laboratory at Purdue. This is a great starting point in your quest to learn about firewalls and Internet security.

- Marcus J. Ranum's Internet Firewalls FAQ at http://
www.v-one.com/pubs/fw-faq/faq.htm.
- World Wide Web Security FAQ at http://www.genome
.wi.mit.edu/WWW/faqs/www-security-faq.html.
- Encryption technology from RSA Data Security, at
http://www.rsa.com.
- Yahoo's list of companies that specialize in computer
security at http://www.yahoo.com/Business_and_
Economy/Companies/Computers/Security/Consulting/.
- Newsgroups:

  - comp.security.announce—announcements about
  security (moderated)
  - comp.security.firewalls—anything pertaining to network firewall security
  - comp.security.misc—security issues of computers
  and networks
  - comp.security.unix—discussion of UNIX security

Selecting an Internet Service Provider

- *Selecting an Internet Provider* in UUNET Technologies'
Internet Business Applications Guide at http://www.
uu.net/busguide.htm.
- The List at http://thelist.com. This resource provides a
variety of searches to help you locate ISPs. It gives you
information such as the names, area codes served, phone
and fax numbers and e-mail addresses, their URL, and
services they provide and the fees for them.
- Commerce Net's Internet Service Provider Directory at
http://www.commerce.net/directories/products/isp/isp.
html/.
- Newsgroups about Internet access providers:

  - alt.internet.services
  - alt.internet.access.wanted

Acquiring an Internet Domain

◆ InterNIC Registration Services at http://rs.internic.net/
   rs-internic.html/. This site provides instructions for registering U.S. domain names. They are temporarily registering Canadian domain names, also.

◆ Yahoo's list of various domain registration authorities
   throughout the world is at http://www.yahoo.com/
   Computers_and_Internet/Domain_Registration/.

Selecting Hardware and Software—Servers, Browsers, Authoring Tools, and Other

◆ Intranet Soundings at http://www.brill.com/intranet/ijx/
   is a moderated message exchange dedicated to intranets.

◆ Intranet Exchange at http://www.innergy.com/ix/ is
   another moderated message exchange about intranets.

◆ Web Compare at http://www.webcompare.com/ lists
   servers and browsers and includes comparisons and
   charts of features.

◆ Stroud's CWSApps List at
   http://cws.wilmington.net/cwsa.html.

◆ World Wide Web FAQ at http://www.boutell.com/faq/
   for researching web servers and browsers, authoring web
   pages, images, scripts, and other Web resources.

◆ The Complete Intranet Resource at
   http://control.cga.sc.edu/intranet.htm.

◆ Network World Fusion at http://www.nwfusion.com/.

◆ WebMaster Magazine's Technology Notes at http://www
   .cio.com/WebMaster/wm_tech_notes.html.

◆ PC Magazine at http://www.pcmag.com/ has:

   ◆ Intranet Tools Directory at http://www.pcmag.com/
      IU/intranet/reviews/ir-dir.htm

   ◆ Product Index at http://www.pcmag.com/IU/
      index.htm

- HyperText Markup Language (HTML) at NCSA at http://union.ncsa.uiuc.edu/HyperNews/get/www/html.html. This is a good resource for current information on tools and authoring.
- Newsgroups about:

  - Servers:

    - comp.infosystems.www.servers.mac—Web servers for the Macintosh platform
    - comp.infosystems.www.servers.misc—Web servers for other platforms
    - comp.infosystems.www.servers.ms-windows—Web servers for MS Windows and NT
    - comp.infosystems.www.servers.unix—Web servers for UNIX platforms

  - Browsers:

    - comp.infosystems.www.browsers.mac—Web browsers for the Macintosh platform
    - comp.infosystems.www.browsers.misc—Web browsers for other platforms
    - comp.infosystems.www.browsers.ms-windows—Web browsers for MS Windows
    - comp.infosystems.www.browsers.x—Web browsers for the X-Window system
    - Providing Web access:

      - comp.infosystems.www.providers—discussion of Web server software, including general server design, setup questions, server bug reports, security issues, HTML page design, and other concerns of information providers

- For specific products, check out vendor sites such as:

    - Netscape at http://www.netscape.com
    - Microsoft at http://www.microsoft.com
    - SGI at http://www.sgi.com

Designing and Authoring Documents

- Guides to Writing Style for HTML Documents (NCSA) at http://union.ncsa.uiuc.edu/HyperNews/get/www/html/guides.html.
- William Horton, Lee Taylor, Arthur Ignacio, Nancy L. Hoft, *The Web Page Design Cookbook: All the Ingredients You Need to Create 5-Star Web Pages,* John Wiley & Sons, 1996.
- Jim Sterne, *World Wide Web Marketing: Integrating the Internet into Your Marketing Strategy,* John Wiley & Sons, 1995. Jim is an internationally known WWW marketing guru. In this book, he focuses on what to do and not do. Many of the things he says apply equally well to intranets, where not all users have high-speed links. Jim also talks at length about navigation within a Web site. You may find lots of guidance in his book.
- Newsgroups about authoring:

    - comp.infosystems.www.authoring.cgi—writing CGI scripts for the Web
    - comp.infosystems.www.authoring.html—writing HTML for the Web
    - comp.infosystems.www.authoring.images—using images and imagemaps on the Web
    - comp.infosystems.www.authoring.misc—miscellaneous Web authoring issues

Usability Testing

◆ Darrell Sano and Jakob Nielsen, *SunWeb: User Interface Design for Sun Microsystem's Internal Web,* at http://www.sun.com/sun-on-net/uidesign/sunweb/. This very interesting report is about how they created and tested the user interface for SunWeb.

People Issues and Change Management—Chapter 9

◆ David Coleman, "March '96 Hot Tip: Groupware Tools for De-Engineering" at http://www.collaborate.com/tip0396.html.
◆ Tom Davenport, "Software as Socialware," *CIO,* March 1, 1996, pp. 24–26.

Implementing Groupware—Chapter 10

Groupware and Workflow

◆ David Coleman, *Groupware: Collaborative Strategies for Corporate LANs and the Intranet,* Prentice-Hall, 1996.
◆ Layna Fisher, *New Tools for New Times: The Workflow Paradigm,* second edition, Future Strategies, Inc., 1995.
◆ Susanna Opper and Henry Fersko-Weiss, *Technology for Teams: Enhancing Productivity in Networked Organizations,* Van Nostrand Reinhold, 1992.
◆ Internet groupware newsgroups:

  ◆ comp.groupware: Discussion of groupware software and hardware in general.
  ◆ comp.groupware.groupwise: Discussion of Novell's Groupwise product.

- comp.groupware.lotus-notes.admin: Discussion of Lotus Notes system administration.
- comp.groupware.lotus-notes.apps: Discussion of application software for Lotus Notes.
- comp.groupware.lotus-notes.misc: Discussion of miscellaneous topics related to Lotus Notes.
- comp.groupware.lotus-notes.programmer: Discussion of programming for Lotus Notes.

- Groupware Central at http://www.cba.uga.edu/groupware/groupware.html.
- The Groupware Yellow Pages at http://www.consensus.com/groupware/.
- The Workflow and Reengineering International Association (WARIA) at http://www.waria.com/waria/.
- Workflow on the Web at http://www.gold.net/users/ef48/.
- Voice on the Net at http://www.von.com/ is a good resource about Internet telephony and videoconferencing on the Net.

Teams

- Jon R. Katzenbach and Douglas K. Smith, *The Wisdom of Teams: Creating the High-Performance Organization,* Harvard Business School Press, 1993.
- Michael Schrage, *No More Teams! Mastering the Dynamics of Creative Collaboration,* Currency/Doubleday, 1995.
- C. W. Metcalf, *Lighten Up: The Amazing Power of Grace Under Pressure,* Nightingale Conant Corporation. An audiotape about humor.
- Michael J. Gelb, *Mind Mapping,* Nightingale Conant Corporation. An audiotape about mind mapping.

- Carolyn Nilson, *Games That Drive Change,* McGraw-Hill, Inc., 1995. This book has a chapter dedicated to games for communication. This is just one of a number of books about games for teams and trainers.
- Locate facilitators through misc.business.facilitators newsgroup.
- Myers-Briggs Type Indicator (MBTI)

   - Association for Psychological Type at http://www.aptcentral.org/
   - Center for Applications of Psychological Type at http://www.capt.org/

Business Process Improvement and Reengineering

- H. James Harrington, *Business Process Improvement: The Breakthrough Strategy for Total Quality, Productivity, and Competitiveness,* McGraw-Hill, 1991.
- Thomas Davenport, *Process Innovation: Reengineering Work Through Information Technology,* Harvard Business School Press, 1993.
- Michael Hammer and James Champy, *Reengineering the Corporation: A Manifesto for Business Revolution,* HarperCollins, 1993.
- Dorine C. Andrews and Susan K. Stalick, *Business Reengineering: The Survival Guide,* Prentice-Hall, 1994.
- Michael Hammer and Steven A. Stanton, *The Reengineering Revolution: A Handbook,* HarperCollins, 1995.
- James Champy, *Reengineering Management: The Mandate for New Leadership,* HarperCollins, 1995.
- Michael Hammer, *Beyond Reengineering,* HarperCollins, 1996.
- A Business Researcher's Interests, at http://www.pitt.edu/~malhotra/interest.html, has a huge collection of

resources about BPR, process innovation, change management, knowledge management, and emergent organizations.

♦ The Library at the Electronic College of Process Innovation (http://www.dtic.dla.mil/c3i/bprcd/mlibtop.html) contains a vast collection of resources about benchmarking and best practices, BPR, change management, creative and innovative thinking, cross-functional teams, customer analysis, data and knowledge management, implementation, information management, information technologies, leadership and management, organizational design, performance measurement, process modeling and analysis, project management and methodologies, strategic and business planning, strategic alliances and partnering, total quality management, and training and learning.

Index

AboutPeople, 103, 138
AboutTime, 103, 138
accounting and financial
    processes, 79–80
Action Technologies Metro,
    121, 124–26
Action Workflow System,
    121, 124–26
ActionItem, 124
ActiveX Controls, 111, 113,
    115, 207
ADSL (asymmetrical digital
    subscriber line)
    modem, 199
Allaire Forums and Cold
    Fusion, 126–27
AltaVista Forum, 132–33
Amicus Networks Commu-
    nity Builder, 127
Andreessen, Marc, 5, 11,
    161–62
asymmetrical digital sub-
    scriber line (ADSL)
    modem, 199
AT&T, 19–20, 35, 38, 291
Attachmate Open Mind,
    128–29
authoring tools, 204–5, 211,
    297–98. *See also* under
    specific products

bandwidth, 27, 62, 76, 227
Bell Atlantic Corporation,
    35, 291
Benefits BPI Sample Pro-
    posal, 8, 186–94
benefits process improve-
    ment (BPI) approach.
    See BPI approach

Berners-Lee, Tim, 5
Booz Allen & Hamilton Inc.,
    36, 89, 291
Bozo Filter, 136
BPI approach
    creating a future process,
        267–68
    defining the process,
        266–67
    degrees of process
        change, 263–64
    developing an implemen-
        tation plan, 268–69
    identifying problems,
        265–66
    implementing the new
        process, 269–70
    process, defined,
        262–63
    web resource addresses,
        301–2
    who's involved in BPI,
        264–65
    See also user-focused
        approach
brainstorming, 14, 212–13
Break Room, 84
browser
    applications of, 40, 211
    cost per user, 23
    enhancement tools, 12
    function of, 11
    use as front ends, 81–82
    web resource addresses,
        297–98
    See also under specific
        products
bureacratic model,
    229–30

C.A. Facilitator for the Web,
    136
caching tool, 211
calendaring and scheduling
    tools, 49, 60–61, 155.
    See also under specific
    products
Campbell, Ian, 7, 46–47
Campbell Service OnTime,
    135
Cap Gemini Innovation
    WebFlow, 129–30
CardFile, 143
Carlson, Todd, 21
Caucus, 141
Caucus Markup Langage
    (CML), 141
CERN (European Laboratory
    for Particle Physics), 5
Chameleon, 137
Chaos, Five Laws of, 237
chat
    description of, 14,
        74–75
    tools, 50, 65–66
    uses of, 61, 74–75, 81
    what to look for when
        choosing products, 156
    See also under specific
        products
Checklists
    Choosing Intranet Group-
        ware, 168–78
    Implementing Group-
        ware, 273–85
client. *See* browser
CML (Caucus Markup
    Language), 141
Cold Fusion, 126–27

Coleman, David, 235, 237–38, 299
collaboration, 37–39, 52–53, 252–54
collaborative computing. *See* groupware
Collabra. *See* Netscape
Collabra Share, 106–7
communication, 28, 37–38. *See also* e-mail; news-groups
communications processes, 72–76
CommunityACT, 127
Community Builder, 127
concurrent development, 18. *See also* collaboration
conferencing. *See* news-groups
Connectix VideoPhone, 130
consultants, 196–98, 270–71
conversion tools, 205. *See also* under specific products
CoolTalk, 104–5, 111
CREW, 142–43
CU-SeeMe, 62, 146–47
customer support processes, 92–93

data conferencing tools, 64–65, 156. *See also* under specific products
database query tools, 205. *See also* under specific products
DataBeam neT.120 Conference Server, 131–32
Davenport, Tom, 246–37, 299, 301
DBS (direct broadcast satellite), 199
dedicated leased lines, 199
Delrina FormFlow, 142
demo building, 210–14
demo, presenting the, 214–16
DeNiro, Allan, 217
design engineering, 86–87
development, concurrent and shared, 18–19

Digital AltaVista Forum, 132–33
direct broadcast satellite (DBS), 199
discussion forums, 133
discussion tools, 51
document conversion tools, 205. *See also* under specific products
document database tools, 205. *See also* under specific products
domain name, 201–2, 296
Domino, 67–68, 99–100
dump session, 150
Dun & Bradstreet Software SmartStream, 147

EDI (Electronic Data Interchange), 24, 29, 89
EDS
  Global Communicators Network, 75
  infoAlert, 90
  installation kits, 23, 208
  intranet uses, 36, 81–82, 88
  knowledge repositories, 84–85
  PointCast I-Server, 35
  process management tool, 84
  web address, 291
electronic data interchange (EDI), 24, 29, 89
electronic meeting system (EMS), 50, 63–64, 156
e-mail
  function of, 9–11, 51, 67
  protocols, 67
  security, 31
  uses of, 24, 67, 110, 133
  what to look for when choosing products, 156–57
  See also under specific products
EMS (electronic meeting system), 50, 63–64, 156
encryption, 105, 200, 203
ESFJ (Extravert Sensing Feeling Judging), 250–51
Ethernet, 9

European Laboratory for Particle Physics (CERN), 5
Explorer, 110–12
extravert, 166, 250
Extravert Sensing Feeling Judging (ESFJ), 250–51

facilitator, 164, 221, 265
FAQ (Frequently Asked Questions) list, 80
Fiber Distributed Data Interface (FDDI), 9
firewall, 26, 200, 294–95
Fitzgerald, Laurie, 237
Five Laws of Chaos, 237
FlowMark, 101
ForeFront RoundTable, 135
FormFlow, 142
forming, 249
Forum (AltaVista), 132–33
Forums (Allaire), 126–27
four stages of teams, 249
Frequently Asked Questions (FAQ) list, 80
FTP (file transfer protocol), 15
FTP/Campbell Services OnTime, 135

Galacticomm Worldgroup Internet Server, 135
Global Customer Contracts, 90
gopher, 15
graphical user interface (GUI), 5, 24, 40
graphics tools, 211. *See also* under specific products
Graves, Michael, 88
groupware
  advantages and benefits of, 164–66
  changes caused by, 287–89
  conferencing, 67–68, 166
  cost of, 161–62, 164
  definition of, 45
  disadvantages of, 166–68
  document management, 165–66
  do's and don'ts, 271–73
  electronic meeting system (EMS), 50, 63–64

evaluating features,
153–59
future of, 289
growth of market, 46–47
how to choose, 149–64
how to use, 71–93
identifying user needs
for, 150–51
information overload, 167
integrated or specialized,
159–60
knowledge, 53–55, 165
making its implementa-
tion successful, 239–40
managing change, 235–38
need for, 52–55
pilot, 256–60
platforms, 152
product demos, 163–64
product openness,
152–53
product web addresses,
292–93
resistance to, 232–33
stages of change, 234–35
training and support,
160–61
vendor support, 163
videoconferencing,
49–50, 62–63
voice conferencing,
61–62
web resource addresses,
291–302
what it does, 47–52
why you need, 52–55
why you should consider
intranet, 55–57
See also BPI approach;
knowledge repository;
newsgroups; tools;
user-focused approach;
workflow
group writing tools, 52,
69–70, 158–59. See
also under specific
products
GUI (graphical user interface), 5, 24, 40

Hahn, Eric, 104, 106, 108–9,
152–53
Hammer, Michael, 264
home page, 5, 69, 131, 133,
222, 224

hot buttons, 213
hot list, 141
HTML (Hypertext Markup
Language), 22–23, 99,
204–5, 226, 297
human resources processes,
77–79
Hypertext Markup Lan-
guage. See HTML

IDC (International Data Corporation), 7, 46–47
IMAP4 (Internet Mail
Access Protocol 4), 51,
67, 105–6, 154
information overload, 167
information systems pro-
cesses, 80–84
information technology,
changing role of, 39–40
InfoWorld, 17
initiation forms, 124
Integrated Services Digital
Network (ISDN)
modem, 199
internal web, 10–12,
223–24. See also
intranet
International Data Corporation (IDC), 7, 46–47
Internet domain, 201–2,
296
Internet Explorer, 110–12
Internet, history of, 4–5
Internet Mail Access Protocol 4 (IMAP4), 51, 67,
106, 154
Internet model
building your intranet,
198–205
consultants, 196–98
creating your audience,
205–9
determining need, 195
determining readiness,
195
domain name, 201–2
how to proceed, 195–98
Internet policies, 224–26
Internet service
providers, 200–1
intranet team, 217–26
lessons learned, 228–29
making it pervasive,
226–28

promoting your intranet,
216–17
security, 200
success factors, 228
Internet phone, 61, 104, 147
Internet Relay Chat (IRC).
See chat
Internet service provider
(ISP), 200–1, 295
InterNotes Web Publisher,
99–100
InterOffice, 138–39
interpersonal and group
communications,
74–76
intranet
advantages and benefits
of, 20–29
advantages over
client/server, 29–30
building your, 183–230
components of, 8
cost to implement, 23
definition of, 3–4
determining need for, 32
disadvantages of, 30–32
future of, 15–16
growth of, 6–7
history of, 5–6
intangible benefits of,
27–29
reasons to create, 17–21
results of implementa-
tion, 33–41
standards of, 25
tangible benefits of,
21–27
uses of, 7–8, 292
See also groupware;
intranet team; security;
internal web
intranet team
building and bonding,
249–52
collaboration, 252–54
composition of, 219–21
creating enthusiasm,
260–61
creating the, 248–49
development of internal
web, 223–24
facilitator, 221
four stages of, 249
Internet policies, 224–26
meetings, 221–22

intranet team *(Continued)*
objectives, 222–23
training, 226
why you need one,
218–19
IntraNet Forum Server, 137
IRC (Internet Relay Chat).
See chat
ISDN (Integrated Services
Digital Network)
modem, 199
ISP (Internet service
provider), 200–1, 295

Java, 104–5, 108–9, 115,
131, 207
JCPenney, 37, 82–83, 219,
291
JetForm, 135–36
journal, 114
jWeb, 214, 219, 222–23

keypads, 63–64
knowledge, 53–55, 165
Knowledge On Line, 89
knowledge repository
tools, 51, 84
use in Office 97, 113
uses of a, 73, 92, 133
what to look for when
choosing products,
158
See also under specific
products

Lambert, Tim, 81
LAN (local area network), 9,
111, 184–85
Learning Organization, 55
Listserv, 12
Livelink Intranet, 114–21
Live/Media, 102
local area network (LAN), 9,
111, 184–85
locker, 143
Lotus
choosing Notes or group-
ware, 154–55
Domino, 99–100
InterNotes Web Pub-
lisher, 99
Notes Release 4.5,
97–100
other software exten-
sions, 100–1

Team Room, 101
Vendor Independent
Messaging, 51, 67
Lundeen Web Crossing, 136

Mail Application Program-
ming Interface (MAPI),
51, 67, 106
mail lists, 12
Majordomo, 12
manufacturing, 89
MAPI (Mail Application
Programming Inter-
face), 51, 67, 106
marketing, 90
marketing and sales pro-
cesses, 90–92
MBTI (Myers-Briggs Type
Indicator), 166, 301
McCall, Szerdy & Associ-
ates, 136
Metro, 121, 124-26
Microsoft, 109–120
Internet Explorer, 110–12
Office 97, 112–14
Mills, Cathy, 37, 219
MIME (Multipurpose Inter-
net Mail Exchange),
25, 67, 102, 105
Mosaic, 5, 11
Motet, 136
multimedia, 26–27, 110
Multipurpose Internet Mail
Exchange (MIME), 25,
67, 102, 105
Myers-Briggs Type Indicator
(MBTI), 166, 301

National Science Founda-
tion (NSF), 4–5
Navigator
Collabra Share, 106–7
CoolTalk, 62, 104–5
Galileo, 105
Gold, 105
3.0, 102–5
workflow applications,
108–9, 121
See also Netscape
Net.App solutions, 100
neT.120 Conference Server,
131
netiquette, 14, 257, 291
NetManage, 136–37
NetMeeting, 111–12

Netscape, 11
cost of, 161–62, 207–8
open standards, 152–53
purchase of Collabra, 101
Secured Sockets Layer,
154, 167
See also Navigator
network, 9
Network News Transfer Protocol (NNTP), 51, 68
newsgroups
benefits of, 12–14
conferencing, 51, 67–68,
157
Exchange, 110
external and internal, 74
Navigator, 102
web resource addresses,
295–297
what to look for when
choosing products, 157
See also netiquette;
Usenet
NNTP (Network News
Transfer Protocol), 51,
68
norming, 249
Notes. *See* Lotus
Novell GroupWise, 114
Now Software Now Up-to-
Date, 138
NSF (National Science
Foundation), 4–5

Odyssey, 144
Office 97, 112–114
OnTime, 135
Open Mind, 128–29
open standards, 152–53
Open Text Livelink
Intranet, 114–21
operational processes,
87–89
Oracle InterOffice, 138–39
O'Reilly WebBoard, 139
organizational communica-
tions, 72–73
Outlook, 113–14

Paradigm Software Work-
Wise-Enterprise, 139
performing, 249
personal productivity tools,
48
pilot, 256–60, 270

platforms, 152
plug-ins, 102–4, 167–68
Podium, 139
PointCast I-Server, 35
polling, 133
POP3 (Post Office Protocol 3), 51, 67, 106
presenting the demo, 214–16
process management processes, 84
processes, 71–93
product development processes, 84–87
product openness, 152–53
professional services development, 89
Proxima Podium, 139
purchasing, 88–89

Quarterdeck/Future Labs TALKShow, 140

RadNet WebShare, 141
Realtime Transport Protocol (RTP), 104, 111
research and development, 84–86
return on investment (ROI), 56, 193–94, 259
ROI (return on investment), 56, 193–94, 259
rollout, 270
RoundTable, 135
RTP (Realtime Transport Protocol), 104, 111

sales, 90
SamePage, 144–46
SAS Institute Inc., 34
Schrage, Michael, 252–53
Screen Porch Caucus, 141
search tools, 204. *See also* under specific products
Searchlight Software Spinnaker, 142
Secured Sockets Layer (SSL), 154, 167
security
    determining needs, 200
    encryption, 105, 200, 203
    intranet access, 26
    risks, 31
    Secured Sockets Layer, 154, 167

servers, 203–4
    web resource addresses, 294–95
Senge, Peter, 55
servers
    capabilities of, 107–8
    function of, 11
    implementing, 23, 25–26, 202
    security, 203–4
    types of, 202–4
    web resource addresses, 297
    See also under specific products
SGI (Silicon Graphics Inc.), 36, 88, 291
shared development, 18–19
shared document editing tools, 52, 69–70. *See also* under specific products
Silicon Graphics Inc. (SGI), 36, 88, 291
Silicon Junction, 36
Simple Mail Transfer Protocol (SMTP), 51, 67, 106
SmartStream, 147
SME (subject matter expert), 265
SMTP (Simple Mail Transfer Protocol), 51, 67, 106
Social Systems Analysts (SSA), 236
Spinnaker, 142
Spyglass/OS Technologies WebNotes, 142
SSA (Social Systems Analysts), 236
SSL (Secured Sockets Layer), 154, 167
standards, 223–24
status and interaction forms, 124
storming, 249
Stricklin, Jimi, 217
subject matter expert (SME), 265
Sun Microsystems, 73, 80
SunWeb, 299
support processes, 76–84
Symantec/Delrina Form-Flow, 142

Take Action!, 145
TALKShow, 140
TCP/IP (Transmission Control Protocol/Internet Protocol), 9, 25, 185, 199, 208
Team Room, 101
teams, 217–26, 248–54, 300–1
Telnet, 15
TESN (Turner Employee Services Network), 216–17
Texas Instruments
    intranet use, 36, 38, 163
    newsgroups, 74, 86
    web address, 291
Three Times (3X) Rule, 255
Thuridion CREW, 142–43
TI. *See* Texas Instruments
Token Ring, 9
tools
    authoring, 204–5, 211, 297–98
    availability of, 207–8
    browser enhancement, 12
    caching, 211
    calendaring and scheduling, 49, 60–61, 155
    chat, 50, 65–66, 156
    choosing, 206–7
    conversion, 205
    data conferencing, 64–65, 156
    database query, 205
    discussion, 51
    distinction between groupware and workgroup, 45
    document database, 205
    graphics, 211
    group writing, 52, 69–70, 158
    search, 204
    videoconferencing, 62–63, 76, 156
    voice conferencing, 49, 61–62, 156
    web resource addresses, 296–98
    what to look for when choosing products, 153–59
    whiteboarding, 64–65, 156

tools *(Continued)*
  workflow, 52, 70–71, 159
  See also electronic meeting system, knowledge respository; newsgroups; under specific products
Total Quality Improvement (TQM), 263–64
TQM (Total Quality Improvement), 263–64
Track-It, 143
traditional model
  Benefits BPI Sample Proposal, 186–94
  determining need, 184
  determining readiness, 184–85
  implementing the project, 194
  measuring results, 194
training, 208–9
Transmission Control Protocol/Internet Protocol (TCP/IP), 9, 25, 185, 199, 208
Turner Broadcasting System, Inc., 216–17, 291
Turner Employee Services Network (TESN), 216–17

UES Track-It, 143
Ultimus WebFlow, 143
Ulysses Telemedia Networks/Intraprise Technologies Odyssey, 144
U.S. Patent Information Services, 85
Usenet, 13, 74, 82. *See also* newsgroups

user-focused approach
  creating enthusiasm, 260–61
  determining readiness, 242–44
  identifying groupware needs, 255–56
  pilots, 256–60, 270
  rewards system, 254–55
  selecting a group, 244–48
  teams, 248–54
  See also BPI approach
UUNET Technologies, 200

Vendor Independent Messaging (VIM), 51, 67
videoconferencing, 62–63, 76, 156
VideoPhone, 130
VIM (Vendor Independent Messaging), 51, 67
Virtual Private Network (VPN), 200
Virtual Reality Modeling Language (VRML), 104, 207
voice conferencing, 61–62, 156
VPN (Virtual Private Network), 200
VRML (Virtual Reality Modeling Language), 104, 207

web resource addresses, 291–302
WebBoard, 139
WebCal, 144
Web Crossing, 136
Web Fair, 216
WebFlow (Cap Gemini), 129–30

WebFlow (Ultimus), 143
WebFlow SamePage, 144–46
Webmaster, 220
WebNotes, 142
WebShare, 141
Weinberger, David, 165–66
White Pine Enhanced CU-SeeMe, 62, 146–47
whiteboards
  NetMeeting, 111
  shared, 104
  tools, 64–65, 156
  uses of, 72, 88
  varieties of, 64–65
  voice conferencing, 61
  what to look for when choosing products, 156
  See also under specific products
WorkBox list forms, 124
workflow
  Electronic Data Interchange, 89
  function of, 46
  future of, 289
  tools, 52, 70–71, 159
  two types of, 261–62
  web resource addresses, 299–300
  what to look for when choosing products, 159
  See also under specific products
WorkWise-Enterprise, 139
Worldgroup Internet Server, 135
World Wide Web (WWW), 5–7. *See also* internal web; security